FREEING TERESA

A True Story

about
My Sister
and Me

ADVANCE PRAISE FOR *FREEING TERESA*

"With characteristic courage and determination, Franke James took on the health care system and her own family to free her sister Teresa from a nursing home. By turns gut-wrenching and awe-inspiring, *Freeing Teresa* shows how the disability rights ideal of 'nothing about us without us' is the only way to make decisions about frail or aging family members. This story will break your heart and then fill it up again."

CATHERINE McKERCHER, author of *Shut Away: When Down Syndrome Was a Life Sentence*

"This is a gripping story about courage, love, and an unshakeable belief in human potential—about people who possess a rare combination of optimism with savviness about power, law, and human nature. Inspirational."

MARTY SELDMAN Ph.D.,
WSJ Bestselling author of *Survival of the Savvy*

"Full of insight, heartbreak and inspiration, *Freeing Teresa* offers a compelling glimpse into the experience of people with disabilities. This no-holds-barred story is a must-read for decision-makers, advocates, family members, and anyone who cares about disability rights."

KARLA VERSCHOOR, Executive Director, Inclusion BC

"We chart the prevalence of injustice in numbers, but it's stories like this that lead us to a deeper understanding of the magnitude of its impact on human lives."

GABRIELLE PETERS, disabled writer, community activist

"Franke James has written a courageous, personal account of fighting the system—and her family—to free her sister, Teresa, from forced care. It is a study in family dynamics and how individual perspectives, regardless of how 'well-meaning' they may be, can place our loved ones' human rights at risk. *Freeing Teresa* reflects in microcosm society's struggles to maintain appropriate supports for seniors and people with disabilities who need care, in the face of those who resent expenditures on the 'unproductive' amongst us."

> ALANNA HENDREN, Executive Director,
> Developmental Disabilities Association

"The battle to have Teresa be the best she can be—and to spend her life in a loving environment—is the heart of this book. A truly amazing story about an inspiring person and those who made it happen. A must-read for anyone who cares about human dignity and equal rights."

> GEORGE MELNYK, Professor Emeritus
> Communication, Media and Film, University of Calgary

"*Freeing Teresa* is authentic, raw and riveting. It was an emotional roller-coaster—one that will be very real for many disabled people. At its core, it's about hope for a better life and resilience."

> ISABEL MAVRIDES-CALDERON,
> @Powerfullyissa, disability advocate

FREEING TERESA

A True Story

about My Sister and Me

Franke James

with Teresa Heartchild and Billiam James

Freeing Teresa, Book One

The James Gang, Iconoclasts Inc.

02024001029

Freeing Teresa is a work of nonfiction.
Some names and identifying details have been changed.

Publisher: The James Gang, Iconoclasts Inc.

Book and cover design by Franke James and Billiam James.

Colour Edition ISBN: 978-1-9994061-6-5
Hardcover ISBN: 978-1-9994061-3-4
Trade Paperback ISBN: 978-1-9994061-0-3
E-book ISBN: 978-1-9994061-2-7
Audiobook ISBN: 978-1-9994061-1-0

frankejames.com
teresaheartchild.com
freeingteresa.com

FOR THOSE WHO ARE DIFFERENT

Those Monsters, illustration by Teresa Heartchild

THOSE MONSTERS

A SELF-TALK POEM BY TERESA HEARTCHILD[1]

You're not afraid of those monsters.

Tell them I have power of attorney.

Please be nice to my daughter.

We don't want to hurt their feelings.

Protect my daughter.

Let me speak. Let me speak.

You have the power of attorney.

Contents

Cast of Characters

Franke: The Activist
Sister (Married to Bill)

Siobhan: The Planner
Sister (Married to Jared)

Teresa: The Self-Talk Poet
Youngest Sister (Single)

Phoebe: The Harmonizer
Sister (Married to Spencer)

Dad: The Retired Lawyer
Father (Widowed)

Conrad: The Guardian
Brother (Married to Candi)

Bill: The Campaigner
In-Law (Married to Franke)

Deirdre: The Boss
Sister (Married to Chuck)

Police: The Righteous Cop
The System

NOTE: With the exception of Teresa, my siblings do not wish to be identified with this story. I have used pseudonyms for them. The silhouettes above are symbolic representations echoing their absence in my life. My father was a strong supporter of Teresa's inclusion, however, I have blurred his face in most photos where he appears.

"Who are you going to be?" is a tricky Question because NOBODY really KNOWS what Life will throw at THEM.

And how they will change as a result!

Author's Note

THIS IS A TRUE STORY which has taken ten years to write. What took me so long? Well, first I had to live it—and what a rollercoaster journey it's been! To help Teresa assert her rights, I needed to draw on everything I'd learned as an environmental activist. But what I didn't know at the start was that Teresa was just the tip of the iceberg.

I hope that by sharing our story—including the activist tools I have used—that change will happen. And the tenth anniversary of freeing Teresa is a joyful and important reason to publish this book. Joyful because Teresa has flourished, despite her naysayers' dire predictions. Important, because forced care is happening to people with disabilities around the world. Most people don't escape. And the world shrugs.

It is shocking to realize that ableism almost held Teresa back from fulfilling her true potential. Now in 2023, Teresa is an artist, author and self-advocate. She has won arts grants, published two books, and thanks to the Canada Council, travelled to exhibit her artwork internationally. In 2019, she was recognized as a "Champion for Change" by the BC Human Rights Commissioner. None of this would have happened if things had gone according to plan. But extricating Teresa from it all was the biggest challenge of my life.

Back in 2013, life was good. Teresa was happy living with our father. I was writing my third book, *Banned on the Hill*, which you'll hear more about, but family was my safe spot. My refuge. No matter what winds were buffeting me professionally, I felt I could always count on my family.

I had no idea of the hurricane just around the corner and how it would upend our lives. It all started with the question: "Where will Teresa live?" (Sadly, Teresa herself wasn't involved in the planning). Our family couldn't agree on what was best if Teresa couldn't live with Dad anymore. At first, I thought it was just a difference of opinion but, before I knew it, this had spiralled into a public issue involving the police and government care agencies. That's when I realized this wasn't just about our family. It was about the difficulties that many people with disabilities face in exercising a basic human right: the right to choose where you live.

Freeing Teresa is a product of the digital age when our lives can easily be tracked. When the events began, I was in disbelief: Surely this can't really be happening? Am I misinterpreting things? So, I set out to create an accurate record of the life-changing action swirling around me. Being able to prove the facts—what was said and done—is critically important, especially in this age of misinformation. To be believed, we need to "bring receipts." This book is based on extensive digital records: emails, photographs, videos, audio recordings, police records, health records, court records including sworn affidavits, and my journals. For each chapter, I've noted the sources that I relied on. Please see the Endnotes for details. Most of the dialogue has been condensed and edited from recorded discussions and emails. Italicized dialogue represents paraphrased email correspondence from third parties. At all times I have endeavoured to retain the context and meaning of the original dialogue.

Stories are how we share our experience with others and future generations. I know that many in my family do not want to be associated with this book. So, we have not included the family surname in the text and my sister Teresa is using the pen name "Teresa Heartchild." Where the family name appeared in images, we've blacked it out. I have used pseudonyms for most family members and removed their images from photos. (See the Afternote and List of Photos for details.) For my late parents—who were always Teresa's champions—I have blurred their faces in most cases so they are not recognizable.

I also appreciate that each person involved will have their own explanations for their actions and their own point of view on what occurred. Will the intervening time—ten years now—have changed their minds or softened their hearts?

A NOTE ON LANGUAGE: This story takes place from 1960 to the present. When we were growing up, the R-word and the term "mentally handicapped" were commonly used in medical reports, by government agencies, by support groups, in schools, and in my own family. Since then, the R-word has become an insult. So in most cases in the quoted text, I have replaced the R-word with "mentally handicapped," which has not taken on such a negative meaning. Because my book talks about institutionalization and social prejudices, I have used this older language within that context, rather than the more respectful terms we use today. You may also notice language and ableist concepts that I was once comfortable with; however, this story is also about a growing awareness of my own ableist beliefs and my efforts to be free of them.

A TRIGGER WARNING: This story includes extensive description and discussion of discriminatory attitudes and actions toward people based on their disabilities and/or age.

FREEING TERESA

CHAPTER ONE

The Silver Recorder

November 30, 2013, 8:00 p.m.

THE COPS DIDN'T BUZZ UP. THEY ARRIVED ON THE FOURTH floor, unannounced. Outside my dad's front door, the police assembled their witnesses and waited for the paramedics.

Inside, we were having fun making videos. I was pointing the camera at my younger sister Teresa.[1] She was clearing the table after our pizza dinner and I asked her, "So, how does it feel to be back home?"

"Awesome," she said. "We've got everything here." And she flashed a V for victory. Teresa is short—tiny, as she describes herself—she has a ready smile, a peaches and cream complexion, and straight shoulder-length brown hair. She had lived with Dad all her life, and before these troubling events, she had no idea that her life was about to change.

I turned towards the kitchen where Dad was washing coffee mugs. He looked me in the eyes and said fondly, "My goodness, you guys are real pushers." All my life, Dad had praised my drive to get things done. On that day, he was ecstatic because we had helped him rescue Teresa. As I moved in closer, he asked, "What are you doing?"

"I'm shooting a video of you," I said.

"Of me?"

"Yeah, right now," I said, holding up my iPad.

He smiled as he neatly hung the dish towel on the rack.

Teresa sat down at the small dining table beside my husband, Bill. He's good-looking with short greying hair and is very fit, still running marathons in his fifties. Teresa was showing him her trophies. Bill said, "Hey Franke, get this on video: Teresa showing us her calendar and favourite things."

Teresa and Bill were slowly flipping through Teresa's calendar, chatting about events, when we heard the knock at the door. As Bill went to answer it, I kept the camera on Teresa. She was smiling happily, picking up her calendar and trophies and carrying them back to her room as Bill went to open the front door.

And there they were—two big cops, two paramedics with a stretcher, and others behind them. I caught a glimpse of my older sister, Deirdre, wearing a bulky maroon coat.

The first cop stepped in. He was bigger than Bill and looked beefy, especially with his bulletproof vest and the gun on his hip.

"Who are you?" he barked.

I heard Deirdre's voice coming from the hallway, "That's Bill."

The cop immediately asked Bill to leave.

Bill backed away from the door, asking, "Can I see some documentation?"

The cop ignored him and took another step in. "Come on out," he ordered. Then he spotted me—blonde hair, slim, in a long black cardigan with a red scarf—and I was holding my iPad. It was pointed right at him. He waved me towards the front door, saying, "Come on out."

I was shocked and shook my head, no. I was not leaving. I was afraid the cops were here to take Teresa back.

Just then Teresa came out of her room, curious to see what was going on. She was born with Down syndrome and had lived with my dad all her life.

Bill turned back and, seeing her, he called, "Teresa!"

I dropped the iPad on the table and grabbed Teresa, pulling her away from the door.

Hearing strange voices, my dad came back to the dining room. He stood straight and tall beside me, wearing a collared T-shirt, a dark sweater and dark pants. Although surprised to see the police, he was quiet and composed. This was a skill developed from his years of being a lawyer.

The two cops strode in. The others followed, crowding into Dad's tiny kitchen. Deirdre and my other sister, Siobhan, marched in with their husbands, followed by two paramedics. They lined up behind the cops and stared at us grimly.

I was hoping that the Toronto police would listen to both sides of the story. But I was worried. We had been through a lot in the past few days. Everything I thought I knew was being thrown into question. My hand was in my pocket, holding my small audio recorder. I took it out and pressed *start*.

Then the first cop spoke, "We want to make sure that you're okay."

His words were probably meant to reassure, but they still sounded threatening.

Teresa answered, "We're okay. We're fine."

The cop started to speak, "There's an allegation that..."

But my attention was riveted on Deirdre. She raised her arm, pointing at me.

"We're being recorded!" She stabbed her finger at me. "Franke! She's got a tape recorder."

I stepped forward. "Yes, I've got a recorder." And I held up my small, silver recorder for everyone to see. "Is that okay?"

THIS IS A STORY about the battle for my sister's freedom and, unexpectedly, my own. None of us lives in a vacuum. Each one of us plays a role in society and in history. Every generation is inextricably part of the tug-of-war for civil rights. One generation fights and surges forward, grasping the trophy of new ground gained and new resolutions. But then the next forgets what all the fuss was about and relaxes their grip. Then the hard-won gains slip away. The war is never won. The struggle for equality is never done. But sometimes by standing up for what's right, you can make a difference.

I wasn't looking for a fight with my family. I already had my hands full fighting the government's censorship of my climate change art. Ironically, that "learning experience" turned out to be essential training. But let's start this story at the beginning, at another stand-off in this very same hallway during a happier time nine months earlier.

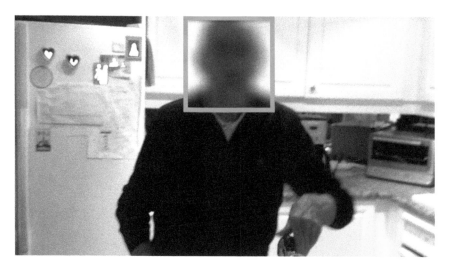

Dad, washing the dishes: "My goodness, you guys are real pushers"

NOTE: I come from a family with seven children: Conrad, Deirdre, Lynne, Phoebe, Siobhan, me, and Teresa. Apart from Teresa, none of my siblings support the telling of this story. So, my dad's face has been blurred in most cases, and the images of many family members have been redacted in white. I'm also using pseudonyms for most of my family.

Bill and Teresa with her calendar and trophies

The cops arrive. Note: The officers' faces have been redacted

Franke with her camera earlier that day at Aiker Place

CHAPTER TWO

Eyes Fly Open

February 23, 2013

"I'M NOT GOING. I WANT TO STAY HERE WITH DAD." Teresa was facing us with her arms crossed.

I took a deep breath. "But Teresa, we're hoping to take you to a play," I said. "And we already bought three tickets."[1]

We had just arrived, and Teresa was grumpy. We were standing in the small front hall of Dad's apartment. Teresa was still dressed in cozy blue sweatpants and didn't look like she was going anywhere. I realized that we might have a challenge. Teresa has a mind of her own and we certainly needed her cooperation if we were to go on this outing.

Dad was delighted that we had invited her to a cultural event. He greeted us with a warm hug, and I gave him a quick kiss on the cheek. Dad was wearing a butter-yellow cashmere sweater and beige slacks. He had always loved golf, and he continued to sport the wardrobe. With his shoulders back and his chest forward, he looked remarkably vigorous for a man of ninety. He said to Teresa, "Come on, sweetie, Franke and Bill are here to take you to a show."

Teresa just shook her head. "No." While she knew we'd invited her out somewhere "fun," this was a change from her daily routine. She was resistant. But I was excited about seeing the show *Rare*, a creative collaboration by playwright Judith Thompson and nine actors with Down syndrome. I really wanted her to see the play. A friend of mine, an actor who also has a sibling with an intellectual disability, had recommended it. She said I would be blown away. I was hyped. But the challenge was to inspire Teresa.

"Come on, Teresa, you'll love it," I said. "It's a play performed by actors with Down syndrome."

Teresa was not impressed. And neither was Dad. He said to me in a hushed voice, "Teresa doesn't know she has Down syndrome." My eyes opened wide, and I glanced quizzically at Bill. Why was Dad saying this? Of course Teresa knew she had Down syndrome, but in truth I'd never asked her. We all knew that she had it. Teresa was born with an extra chromosome, a genetic variation that affects one in seven hundred people. Down syndrome is associated with a range of intellectual disabilities from mild to severe, and distinctive physical characteristics. Teresa is accomplished in many ways, for example she reads and writes, but due to her protective upbringing, she is not very independent. Mom and Dad took care of everything, from lining up her daily schedules to managing her finances.

If you met Teresa, you would recognize that she is different. I was pretty sure she knew it too, but I didn't want to correct my father, which is ironic considering I had no problem telling the Prime Minister he was wrong. I just kept my mouth shut and focused on getting her out the door. I knew we couldn't push too hard or she'd dig in even more, so we continued to use encouragement. And that was Dad's approach too.

"Oh, Teresa, you lucky girl! You're going to the theatre!" His voice had a cheery lilt to it. "Isn't this wonderful?"

Bill encouraged her too, waving towards the front door. "Let's go, Teresa. It's going to be lots of fun."

Gradually, with all three of us pleading and telling her how very exciting it would be, she softened. "Alright, I'll go to the theatre with you." She went to her bedroom to get her things.

That winter's day in 2013, we were at Dad's two-bedroom apartment, just blocks away from where we all grew up. (After my mother died in 1999, my father sold the four-bedroom family home, and he and Teresa moved into the condominium.)

Dad offered us a seat, but I declined. I wanted to keep up the momentum, so we stood waiting by the door. The walls were covered with photos, black-and-white and sepia-toned. There was a photo of Dad as a handsome young law graduate around 1949. Beside it was a photo of him as a child in short pants and a tie, standing with his arms resting gently on his younger brother's shoulders. We never knew Dad's brother, as his plane was shot down in World War Two. After that, Dad was keen to help the war effort and joined the Air Force's radar division.

Finally, Teresa returned in a down parka, a hat and boots. She was dressed just right for the cold weather. "You three are so good together," Dad said warmly. Then he looked at me. "Honey, you should really think about having Teresa live with you when I'm gone."

I dodged the suggestion as tactfully as I could. "Thanks, Dad," I answered, "but Conrad has already promised to let Teresa live in his basement apartment. And with all I have on my plate, we just couldn't."

As her sister, I wanted to help Teresa fulfill her potential, but I couldn't imagine her living with me and Bill. We had so many things on the go, and I was busy writing my next book.

Dad smiled and said, "Well, you just never know what you'll do for love."

"Oh Dad, we love Teresa," I laughed. "And we'll be sure to do lots of fun things with her whatever happens." And with that breezy reply and a peck on his cheek, we headed out to take the subway downtown.

At the subway, Teresa sticks out her tongue and Franke laughs

Outside, it was a cold, cloudy winter day, but we were in high spirits setting out on an adventure. As we walked to the subway, Bill encouraged Teresa to play the balance-beam game. Teresa hopped up on the low flagstone wall that bordered the sidewalk. She smiled gleefully as she walked with her arms outstretched like airplane wings. She was proud of herself, and we cheered her on.

Although it had been hard to get Teresa out the door, it was obvious she was enjoying herself. The subway was just a couple of blocks away, and I had my 35mm digital camera with me to record the day's events.

Click: Teresa rode down the steep escalator at Yonge-Lawrence station, bundled snugly in her dark-brown parka and off-white wool toque.

Click: Bill took a picture of Teresa and me sitting on a bench waiting for the subway train. I was wearing a black down parka and a furry blue scarf. I was laughing and smiling, and Teresa was sticking out her tongue!

Bill makes a funny face as he sits with Teresa outside the theatre

Click: Carrying a small, patterned handbag, Teresa walked confidently in the historic Distillery District, where the theatre was located.

Things were going fabulously until we arrived at the theatre. Suddenly, Teresa refused to go in.

I sputtered, "What? Why? We have tickets. We have to go in."

But that logic didn't work with Teresa. "No, I don't want to."

I spotted a concrete bench, and we sat together in the cold, trying to convince her. I explained to Teresa that we were going to see this play just for her. No luck. I told her that the tickets cost a lot of money. No luck. I told her that the play was about to start, and they wouldn't let us in if we were late. No luck.

I was getting impatient. Nothing I said seemed to make any difference. She was still refusing to bend.

Click: Teresa was sitting beside Bill, who was making a funny, sour face. Teresa looked down with a small smile.

Then Bill said, "How about we go for coffee and a cookie after the play?"

Voilà! Teresa agreed, "Now you're talking!" She has always been a good negotiator.

We hurried into the theatre and took our seats, two rows from the front and right in the middle. Perfect, I thought. But Teresa's grumpiness had returned. She sat there, scowling, her brown coat zipped up, her toque pulled down. I could see that she resented being dragged to this play. I leaned over and feeling like a cheerleader said, "Teresa, this is going to be fun! This play is performed by actors with Down syndrome!"

Then Teresa squeezed her eyes shut.

What? I looked at Bill with my jaw dropped open, and we both shook our heads. We bought good seats so she could enjoy the play and now she shut her eyes. And there was nothing we could do about it. I studied the playbill, looking for the actors' names.[2]

The lights dimmed. The curtain rose. The actors came out wearing masks, and I marvelled at the effect. With masks, it was hard to tell whether they had Down syndrome. What clever staging, I thought. They look normal! And I felt a prick at my conscience. I glanced at Teresa, but her eyes were still closed tight. Then one of the actors spoke.

Teresa's eyes flew open.

I had never thought about the sound of a person's voice as an identifying characteristic of Down syndrome. But I could tell, and so could Teresa. And from that moment on, she was transfixed, totally focused on what the actors were saying.

There were nine performers, now unmasked. As they introduced themselves, I found myself nodding. Nick was twenty-eight and was "looking for a serious boyfriend." Krystal was twenty-three and said, "nobody owns me." Andreas said he was thirty-seven and "I am not broken." Each actor challenged my preconceptions of Down syndrome.

They were all unique personalities, exuding energy, desire and independence on stage.

It was part revelation, part reminder. People with Down syndrome *are* just like any of us. They feel love. They feel hurt. They have dreams of having jobs, and apartments of their own, and finding someone to love, and raising children someday.

Their stories made me think of how Teresa feels. Dylan said he doesn't like people bossing him around. Suzanne said she gets upset when her roommate steals her belongings. Mike said he feels hurt when people tease him. Others chimed in that they too had been bullied. When Dylan said he hated having Down syndrome, the other actors gasped with shock. Dylan said it was because the kids at school teased him. He asked his mother if his Down syndrome condition would disappear. But she said no, it was something he would have to learn to live with. I felt sad hearing that Dylan wanted to change himself into something else so that he could belong. It reminded me of being teased in high school, and how I tried (and failed) to fit in.

I was particularly moved when the actors talked about their parents. They feared death—not their own, but the death of their parents or caregiver. They were afraid of being left alone in the world, and it made my heart ache. Krystal talked about losing her "superhero" dad, and I thought about Teresa losing her father. It would be a big blow when that time came. I looked over at Bill, and he was teary-eyed too.

Then the actors talked about potential parents' reactions to the news that their unborn baby would have Down syndrome. Nick said it made him angry that most parents abort them. When he was born the nurse told his mom, "You know, you don't have to keep him."

Krystal said one of her relatives advised her mother to put her in an institution, but her mother said no, she was going to keep her new daughter.

In the final scene, Krystal read a letter to all the pregnant mothers in the audience. With her punky burgundy hair, she exuded sassiness and confidence. She said her parents were scared when they first heard the news, but they decided to go ahead anyway. Now they are so happy they did because she's turned out to be a wonderful daughter. Krystal ended her letter by telling the expectant mothers, "Never give up, and always keep on going because people who have Down syndrome are very talented and they would love to be raised by you. Be brave."[3]

The honesty and directness of her words hung in the air. It was a loaded political message. Choosing to abort babies with Down syndrome was common in many countries around the world, an attitude that threatened her very right to exist. In Nazi Germany, more than 200,000 people with mental and physical disabilities were deemed to be "unworthy of life" and were murdered between 1940 and 1945.[4] Today, in Iceland, prenatal screening followed by abortion has almost eliminated the birth of babies with Down syndrome.[5]

Krystal's message was powerful, one that my own mother would have loved; she fully embraced Teresa and the challenge of nurturing her talents. Just as my friend had promised, I was inspired by *Rare*. But it also made me feel like we should be doing more to help Teresa lead a full life. I nudged Bill and said, "What do you think it would take to get Teresa up on stage?"

"A lot of coaching," he whispered, "but maybe, someday."

By the end of the show, Teresa was beaming. "It was awesome!" Seeing actors with Down syndrome on stage had made a big impression.

We went into the foyer, and some of the cast members were still there. Actors Sarah, Dylan, James, and Krystal all shook Teresa's hand and posed for pictures. Dylan was sweet and gave Teresa a hug. Even though Teresa was twenty years older than most of them, she still looked young.

After the play, Rare *actor Dylan Livaja with Teresa*

Teresa obviously admired them, and she glowed with pride as she told me, "I have Down syndrome too!"

I gave her a big hug and chuckled at how surprised Dad would be when she told him.

As soon as I got home, I wrote in my journal, "Teresa needs to work on ways to express herself, through dance, art, storytelling. All of them would help Teresa to express her thoughts and feelings and help her bond with others."

Then, excitedly, I called my older sister Phoebe to tell her about the play. She wasn't home, so I left a message. "*Rare* is great! You've got to see it. It will totally change your ideas about what Teresa can do in life!"

CHAPTER THREE

The Blacklisting Party

September 14, 2011

I UNZIPPED MY NEW BLACK DRESS AND CAREFULLY PULLED IT on over my head. It was unlike anything I'd worn before. It had a tight-fitting silk bodice, and its short skirt was made of layers of scalloped ruffles that gave the dress a sculptural presence. It felt wonderful on my body, like fashionable armour.

Nobody knows what life is going to throw at them. And how they will change as a result. I twirled around watching the skirt flutter. It made me laugh to think this is what a blacklisted artist looks like. I had a battle on my hands: defending myself against the Canadian government's secret censorship of my climate change art. I had no idea that this free-speech battle was just a warm-up, training for a much bigger fight that would transform my life—the battle with my family to save Teresa's freedom.

I cinched my waist with a rhinestone belt, applied red lipstick, put on a ruby necklace and strappy red high heels. I ran my fingers through my short, wavy blonde hair. I was ready.

I went downstairs to see if Bill agreed. "What do you think?" I raised my arms and spun around. He smiled and pulled me close, our lips and hips touching. I guess I looked okay.

Franke stands by her poster, "Dear Prime Minister, Please Stop Blacklisting"

The blacklisting party was at 6:30 that night.[1] Word had been spreading ever since the *Toronto Star* published its story six weeks earlier, "Artist sees red over government 'blacklisting'."[2]

The blacklisting saga began when the Canadian Government approved—then cancelled— an educational grant to support my art show which was travelling to twenty cities in Europe.

Apparently, some higher-ups in Foreign Affairs were disturbed when they learned that the artist being sponsored was me. Word was that a senior official exploded and said, "Who was the idiot who approved an art show by that woman, Franke James?"[3]

At the time I shrugged off the word "idiot." A government official had insulted me, and soon I would flip it back. But now, a few years later, I cringe at this awful slur. I am embarrassed to say I didn't know about its

The unnamed official reacts to the news of Franke's art show

ugly history in the institutionalization of people with intellectual disabilities. I didn't realize that the word "idiot" was so harmful

However, insults aside, I was blacklisted—and I was determined to show the Canadian government that they'd picked on the wrong person.

Which is why I was having a blacklisting party! As the guests arrived, they congratulated me on my new notoriety. I knew that none of them would have wanted to change places with me, but they could see I was useful. I was a tangible symbol they could support in the fight for our right to speak up.

While I appeared fearless, I was in fact afraid. Afraid of many things. Afraid I would get sued. Afraid that people wouldn't believe me. Afraid that I would not be able to stop the government's bad-mouthing of me. Despite my fears, I had decided to run towards the controversy.

If we don't tax polluters who will pay to clean up the mess?

I was following the unconventional advice of a seasoned activist. When he suggested it, my first thought was, Yikes! Do I really have to? But his rationale made sense. He said when people in power do stupid things like this, the controversy almost always becomes a bigger story than it otherwise would have been. As a result, it causes even more havoc for those at the heart of the problem.

Over one hundred guests showed up to the party. The mood was upbeat but serious. In Canada in 2011, Prime Minister Harper was exercising harsh message control. Our government was silencing scientists, spying on citizens, and even dictating what to talk about.

A grassroots political activist, Doug Smith, told me I should be thanking Stephen Harper. He explained: "In his laughable stab at censorship, the Prime Minister is honouring a comic tradition in which dour autocrats promote provocative art *pro bono* by trying—in vain—to suppress it."[4]

We had a full house by the time we started the speeches. Toby Heaps, the editor-in-chief at *Corporate Knights* magazine, had agreed to come and say a few words. He had boyish good looks and was casually dressed head to toe in tasteful beige. Only a black T-shirt under his V-neck sweater hinted at his inner rebel.

In fact, Toby was one of the first people I had called. He reached out to his circle of influencers and soon I had public support from activists at 350.org, ForestEthics, and Greenpeace. This showed me how—and why—it's so important to build a network of supporters if you want to turn lemons into lemonade.

Toby climbed on top of a table so everyone could see him. There was a wireless microphone clipped to his sweater, and he held some notes as he started to speak.

"The Government of Canada's apparent censoring of Franke James's work is a high mark of praise," he said. "It indicates the power of Franke's message and the government's relative insecurity, stemming from their increasingly tenuous, anti-science positions."[5]

This blacklisting party was the brainwave of my friend Jim Harris. As the former leader of Canada's Green Party, he was very comfortable fundraising. Jim, who is outgoing and quick-witted, knew how to give a rousing speech that had the crowd laughing and clapping and opening their wallets. Just what we needed to take my art to Ottawa.

And then it was time for my speech. We didn't have a podium. Bill held my hand as I stepped up onto a box. It was a marvellous sight to see so many people in our home, filling every corner, couch and chair, and spilling out onto our back deck.

Among the missing guests were my dad and Teresa. I knew that Dad was a fan of Harper, so I didn't press him to attend. Teresa could have come. Since she lived with Dad I didn't press her either.

Siobhan, Jared, and two guests join the party

NOTE: In photos throughout the book, the images of many family members have been blanked-out echoing their absence in my life.

My sister Lynne also expressed her regrets as she was fighting her own battle and had a series of medical appointments that week. My older sister Deirdre and only brother, Conrad, couldn't make it either. I wasn't surprised as they often dismissed my climate change art and activism. They didn't get it. However, I was delighted that my older sisters, Phoebe and Siobhan, came with their husbands (Spencer and Jared, respectively).

I looked out to the crowd and said, "Making Harper's blacklist is something I never dreamed of! Who would have thought I could get into so much trouble by writing a letter to my dear Prime Minister? In a true democracy, multiple points of view are allowed." I lifted my arms and spread them wide. "I want to send a big, loud message to the Prime Minister: stop blacklisting artists and scientists!"

The audience cheered and got on their feet, clapping. Who knew Canadians could get so excited about free speech? I felt energized. We were going to do this, and it was going to be great.

Another bright spot was hearing one of my siblings stick up for me. "The Canadian government needs to be held accountable," my sister Siobhan said, "and I'm so proud of Franke for taking them to task!"

Joining us virtually that night was Colin Mutchler, a San Francisco–based activist who ran a media crowdfunding company. Loudsauce's mission was to help people raise money to put their messages on outdoor advertising spaces, like billboards and bus shelters. Mischievously, Colin suggested putting the art where the Prime Minister would have to look at it, in Ottawa. I laughed out loud at the idea and now we were making it happen.

Everyone who donated was helping me pay for outdoor billboards so we could put my art up on the streets of Ottawa—and the Prime Minister couldn't stop us. I was both thrilled and anxious.

Some people were afraid to help. Some people just didn't want to help. And some people wanted to remain anonymous, saying "As cowardly as it sounds, I'm a tad reluctant to add my two cents, at least not before my Canadian citizenship comes through."

I might have been reluctant too if my citizenship was at risk. I took it for granted that I had the right to speak out. Talking about stuff (that others want hushed up) has often stirred up trouble for me. However, the Blacklisting Party was like a coming-out event. I was turning the efforts to silence me into something that people wanted to talk about. But I never imagined I would need to use these skills to protect my sister.

CHAPTER FOUR

Exploding the Myth

1977-1979

THE TV CAMERA ZOOMS IN ON A YOUNG TEENAGER'S FACE AS she focuses intently, writing in her notebook. She looks pretty and is wearing large glasses; her long brown hair is neatly pulled back with barrettes. A deep baritone voice says: "This is Teresa Heartchild."[1]

Teresa and I are mesmerized watching this. It's a 1979 documentary that has taken on mythic importance in my family, but which we have not seen in over forty years. I concentrate again on the video. The host, Warner Troyer, looks so much of the 70s, dressed in an orange turtleneck and a tweed jacket. He is introducing Teresa in order to explode myths about people with developmental disabilities. Each scene starts with a myth, printed out in black.

"Myth: The mentally handicapped should be segregated in institutions. It's best for them." (Teresa lived at home.)

"Myth: Mentally handicapped children should not mix with normal children." (Teresa went to a girls' school with "normal" kids.)

"Myth: Mentally handicapped people are strictly limited in what they can do." (Teresa was breaking barriers and starring as a role model for social inclusion.)

Close up from Exploding the Myth *with thirteen-year-old Teresa*

Teresa was proof that all these myths were false. Teresa was just thirteen years old. The documentary first aired nationally in 1979. It was called *Exploding the Myth*.[2]

"That's me!" Teresa says, pointing to the screen. I find it magical to see Teresa as a young teen. She's nicely dressed in a white cable-knit cardigan and black pants. We see her sitting on our living-room carpet doing gym exercises with a red rubber ball. She rolls the eight-inch ball down her outstretched legs to her toes. Then, using her stockinged feet, she kicks it up, catches it and smiles, clearly delighted with herself.

As Teresa bounces the ball, we hear my father's voice—a time capsule from the past: "When Teresa was born, we had quite a number of questions..." The camera shifts to my parents, seated together. "And we didn't like the answers."

My parents look very establishment, a well-off couple in their mid-fifties seated on the cream brocade couch in our living room with two of

Teresa is featured in an ad for Exploding the Myth.[3] *Note: redacted family name*

their teenage kids. (Teresa is not in the room, which was too bad since the conversation was all about her.) Conrad, in jeans and running shoes, is beside Mom; Siobhan, in a floral jumper and Birkenstocks, is perched on an antique seat beside the couch. My dad is wearing a caramel-coloured sweater with dark pants. He looks self-assured and relaxed with his arm outstretched on the couch behind my mother's shoulder. Dad looks over at my mom and says, "When we took Teresa back from the hospital, Patricia said that as far as she was concerned, Teresa would learn to read and write, and that she would develop good physical coordination."

However, my mom, dressed in a knitted blazer and skirt, seems tense. She was not used to being filmed. I watch her swallow as she speaks and I can tell that she is nervous. She chooses her words carefully. "Teresa is valued the same as our other children. We've given her the same advantages, and she has thrived." At that time, this was a radical approach.

Siobhan, Dad, Mom, and Conrad during the Exploding the Myth *interview*

I was away at university during the filming, but the story Troyer told was one that I'd heard many times. When Teresa was born with Down syndrome in 1964, the doctors told my parents she was "severely handi-capped" and would need lifelong care. They advised my parents to put her into an institution so she could get the care she needed. At that time, the medical authorities framed disability as a "complex phenomenon that required expert intervention and management by trained professionals."[4]

Many parents would have taken the doctors' word as gospel and put their child "away" but my parents were already raising six kids. They ignored the experts and brought their baby home. Troyer said, "They decided they would make the effort to give Teresa every possible chance. It was a tough decision, but obviously it has paid off."

Teresa had become a symbol for possibility and hope.

Despite their outwardly staid appearance, my parents were true activists. After thirteen years of raising Teresa at home, they were going public. They were proving the experts wrong. I find it thrilling to hear them speaking out. Seeing their activism come to life gives me shivers, and it helps me make sense out of all that's happened.

WHEN TERESA WAS BORN, I was eight years old. I remember the moment Mom first told me about Teresa. I had sensed something was wrong, but I didn't know what. My bedroom was dark. Mom was wrapped in a housecoat, sitting on the edge of my bed saying prayers. She fingered her rosary beads as she told me that my baby sister was sick and that we should pray for her. Her face was in the shadows, but I could hear her deep voice clearly. Mom said that Teresa was born with a hole in her heart that might require surgery.

I was terrified. The idea that my new sister might die was frightening. Tears streamed down my face. Then Mom broke the news that Teresa also had a genetic condition and wouldn't be like the rest of us. She said Teresa was "mentally handicapped" and would need extra help to do all the things that we took for granted.

To console me, my mother told me that God gives you challenges in life. She believed that everything happened for a reason. She said Teresa's birth was a test and that Teresa would be raised at home and receive the same love as the rest of us.

Teresa never required heart surgery, and she came home to live with us. She was a beautiful blonde-haired baby, and she quickly became a central part of all our lives. Mom was true to her word. She flourished.

I would often see my mother on the phone trying to convince people that Teresa should be allowed to participate in things. Mom would be sitting on our carpeted hall stairs, her dark hair tightly pulled into a sleek bun, legs casually crossed, with the black rotary dial landline beside her. She'd have a cup of black coffee in one hand and the phone handset in the other, while we'd be racing around and playing at her feet. Mom was intent on carrying on her conversation despite all the commotion. Her voice was unwavering: "Teresa deserves to be treated like everyone else." As I watched her speak, I knew I wouldn't want to tangle with my mother! She was a ball of fire.

When Teresa was just an infant, Mom hired a personal fitness trainer to help Teresa develop her muscle strength and coordination. I tagged along and remember standing outside the room as Teresa screamed. The trainer, Mrs. Kehlmann, was manually rotating Teresa's infant arms and legs. I worried that she was being hurt, but Mom assured me it was good for her. Over the next few years, I watched with awe as Teresa got better and better—doing sit-ups, climbing ropes, and jumping on a trampoline. Mom would be snapping photos to document Teresa's progress. This one-on-one coaching was revolutionary in the mid-sixties, especially for a child with Down syndrome.

I took it for granted at the time, but Teresa went to the same private girls' school as I did. She wore the same uniform as me—a navy tunic with the school's circular crest, a white blouse, navy knee socks, and brown oxford shoes. I was proud of her and protective too.

Looking back, I watched how my parents cajoled, lobbied, and campaigned for Teresa's inclusion in all aspects of life. Their advocacy seemed so natural and right.

INDEED TERESA WAS ONE of the lucky ones to be raised at home. In 1960, four years before Teresa's birth, news stories revealing the awful truth about the institutions were beginning to leak out—they were hellholes. Intriguingly, my parents knew Betty and Jerry Anglin, who helped to draw attention to the dire conditions. I heard their names frequently as a child. My parents may have invited the Anglin's over to our house to visit, perhaps to play cards or bridge. But I don't know if they were good friends or just acquaintances, because their solutions to the awful state of institutions were so completely different.

In 1959, Jerry took newspaper reporter Pierre Berton on a tour of the Ontario Hospital School. The name was a euphemism because it was neither a school nor a hospital. It was an institution. When it was founded in 1876, it was called the Orillia Asylum for Idiots and the name later changed to the Ontario Hospital School, and then the Huronia Regional Centre.[5]

Concerned that the staff would not be forthright, Berton enlisted Jerry Anglin's help to go on a tour since Jerry's twelve-year-old son resided there. They drove up together from Toronto to Orillia to return Mark to the institution. "While Berton and Anglin were chatting in the front seat of the car, Mark became sick and vomited in the back seat. This was his reaction to returning to the institution. Upon their arrival, Berton was shown around and given a tour of some of the oldest and worst buildings."[6]

Six days later, on January 6, 1960, Pierre Berton's article, "What's Wrong at Orillia: Out of Sight, Out of Mind" was published in the *Toronto Daily Star*.[7] Berton described the deplorable conditions and treatment of the 2,800 people there, saying it was "overcrowded and understaffed" and that "prisoners in reformatories have better facilities." He ended with a call to action. "Remember this: After Hitler fell and the horrors of the slave camps were exposed, many Germans excused themselves because they said they did not know what went on behind those walls; no one had told them. Well, you have been told about Orillia."

The blinders had been torn off. Berton's story riveted the public's attention and a firestorm erupted around the Ontario government's policy of "relying on huge, out-of-date and overcrowded institutions."[8] Couldn't the money be more humanely spent on providing facilities in the community? The seed of the deinstitutionalization movement had been planted.

My mother and father were part of the wave of parent activists who rejected institutionalization. No doubt they felt the sting of social disapproval, but they had an unshakeable commitment to fairness, an abundance of love, and wills of steel. They were successfully raising six children, and their seventh would be showered with the same attention as the rest.

However, for many families and for those who were wards of the Children's Aid Society, institutionalization remained a solution. Four thousand names were on the waiting list in 1960. In the book *Make Them Go Away*, disability rights author Mary Johnson offers this explanation:

> Although the move to deinstitutionalization had begun in the 1960s in the wake of findings of abuse and horrid conditions in the large warehouses—people tied to beds, lying in their own feces; people covered with bruises and abrasions from beatings; people with sores infested with maggots—those who should have been most horrified at the conditions, the parents of those who were kept there, often fought to keep them open.
>
> Critics charged that the parents simply wanted them open so they would not have to deal with offspring they saw only as burdens, that this was why they had put them there in the first place. It was a fact that those wanting to keep the warehouses open were invariably the families of the people who were housed in them.[9]

The Berton exposé in 1960 was pivotal in alerting the public. However, closing institutions would require decades of dogged persistence. The

Ontario Association for the Mentally Retarded (OAMR), a non-profit organization which eventually became Community Living Ontario, was one of the leaders in this long campaign.

"Not only should we knock institutions, we should blow them up," Jim Montgomerie, OAMR vice-president, said. "They're no good for any-body."[10] His comments reflected a larger communications strategy. The OAMR had worked with the Ontario Ministry of Community and Social Services to produce the TV documentary *Exploding the Myth*.

THE GOAL OF THE DOCUMENTARY was to debunk the myths hampering the lives of people with intellectual disabilities and preventing them from living in the community. Troyer explained: "The herd instinct. The fear of the unknown and the different ... These are the causes of a distorted mythology that is developed around mentally handicapped people the world over. It is the intent of this film to change those primitive attitudes once and for all and shatter this vicious mythology."

The show was advertised coast to coast, with Teresa's picture often featured in TV guides. "*Exploding the Myth* represents television at its best," the *Ottawa Citizen* wrote in its review. "It is difficult not to be affected by this program ... It forces the viewer to re-examine his own attitudes concerning the mentally handicapped, and I hope in the end we will be willing to grant them their simple request for, at the very least, a chance."[11]

The documentary features interviews with former residents. One man, who was institutionalized for twenty-seven years, tells how he was beaten and had no freedom at all: every minute of every day was dictated. If the residents disobeyed orders, they were punished and made to feel like criminals. A young woman with dark, curly hair and glasses pleads for respect: "We're just like every other person. I've never committed a serious crime—to be put away for so many years of my life. Neither killed nor harmed anybody else!"

But it's not just institutions that were at fault, it was social prejudice and judgemental attitudes that were effectively closing the door. The documentary covers a heated debate at a zoning meeting where a group of angry citizens opposed the approval of a group home in their neighbourhood. Opposition from property owners blocked many group homes and forced them to out-of-the-way areas to avoid aggravating too many neighbours. This was like a stepped-down version of institutionalization: they can live somewhere in the community, just not in my backyard.

The NIMBY attitude continues to this day. In 2014, the current premier of Ontario, Doug Ford, then a city councillor, drew criticism for saying that a group home in his district had "ruined" the community.[12]

Troyer said society's belief that people with intellectual disabilities were "strictly limited in what they can do" was unfairly restricting their opportunities. To show how far beyond these artificial limits people can go, they visited Las Vegas, where the Famous People's Players (the brainchild of Diane Dupuy, author of *Daring to Dream*) were performing on stage. It was a shining example of how people with intellectual disabilities could become exceptional achievers and stars.

MY MOTHER IMAGINED Teresa's future: "We've had expectations and ambitions for all of our children. And very fortunately, each and every one of them has been able to achieve and to fulfill their ambitions. Now, we expect that Teresa, too, has ambitions and expectations. She has definite things that she wants to do. As you all know, she's very capable in the kitchen. She helps prepare dinner every night. She tidies up, she vacuums, she irons, you name it around the house. And we are of course, hoping

Teresa pours coffee and irons a shirt

that in the future, when she's about eighteen or so, she will be able to move into a group home where she will have a very successful adult span of life."

This moment in the film is striking for me because it's at odds with what actually happened. In the 1970s, group homes were seen as a good solution. But by the time Teresa was in her twenties, the idea had been shelved. Many people started to think that group homes were just mini-institutions and that it is healthier for people to stay with their families. That is certainly what Dad thought. Teresa continued to live with Dad as her primary caregiver. Dad was doing double-duty since Mom, previously a dynamic go-getter, had suffered a debilitating stroke in 1983. Dad rejected any suggestion that Mom should go to a nursing home, or that Teresa should move to a group home. He was happy to take care of both of them.

For me, Teresa's role in *Exploding the Myth* was the linchpin of the documentary. She was living proof that inclusion worked.

Troyer praised my parents' approach, saying, "It takes great patience and courage to raise a handicapped child at home." Then he addressed the fundamental problem: prejudice and discrimination. "So, when we consign all mentally handicapped people to one group with low potential, there is only one word to describe our attitude: prejudice. Unhappily, prejudice leads to discrimination. And when you talk about discrimination against mentally handicapped people, you're talking about civil rights."

That was the critical point that the documentary had been building to—the myth that only "normal" people should have full human rights. Troyer asked, "Do the mentally handicapped have the same civil rights as the rest of us?"

Globally there had been some progress. In 1971, the United Nations signed an international declaration stating that people with intellectual disabilities have the same rights as all human beings. Then four years after that, they adopted the *Declaration on the Rights of Disabled Persons.*[13]

But Canada was a laggard. In 1979, Canadians with disabilities did not have civil rights protecting them from discrimination based on their disabilities. *Exploding the Myth*, and the media coverage and conversations it stirred up, helped to shift the public's attitude. Three years later, in 1982, the Canadian Charter of Rights and Freedoms was passed. For the first time in Canada, it was explicitly stated that every individual is equal, "without discrimination based on race, national or ethnic origin, colour, religion, sex, age or mental or physical disability."[14]

Today, Teresa watches the documentary with rapt attention. Emotions flicker across her face, as she sees the video of our parents from so long ago. The show ends with a song, "Give us a chance." Her bottom lip quivers as though she's about to cry, but then she holds up her hands and makes the heart symbol. "That was beautiful. That was awesome."

Bill, Teresa and Franke in 1979

I feel the same way. It brings tears to my eyes and fills me with hope. When it first aired in 1979, we were all buzzing. But by 2013, the show had been buried in the film archives for decades. Nevertheless, the stories about it had become part of our family myth, reinforcing my belief that our family would always support Teresa to be the best she could be.

CHAPTER FIVE

The Dinner Party

July 6, 2013

"**D**AD WON'T LIVE FOREVER."

In just seven days, Dad would be celebrating his ninety-first birthday. The family chatter was realistic: "We need to make plans for the inevitable." And then it went to the biggest worry: "Where will Teresa live?" But Dad and Teresa themselves were not concerned. They loved living together. "We support each other," Dad would always say. "We're a team."[1]

That summer evening was a breather for me in my ongoing book campaign. We were having two of my older sisters, Phoebe and Siobhan, to dinner with their husbands. I thought all these concerns would be on the table, particularly the last one.

Teresa herself didn't want to talk about living anywhere else. She just wanted to stay with Dad. I expected that when the time came, Teresa would consider the options and decide for herself. But my siblings' style was more paternalistic. Certainly, as far as Dad was concerned, there was no question. He had made his plan. Dad wanted Teresa to live with one of us kids after he passed away. After Mom died, my brother Conrad stepped up and said he'd do it. It was settled. But personally, I wondered if Conrad would back out. Maybe Dad had doubts too, which is why he had asked me to reconsider having Teresa live with Bill and me.

The question about what happens to people with disabilities after their caregiver parents die is a dilemma. Do they want to live with other family members? Will they move into a group home? Can the disabled person live on their own?

Siobhan had been worrying about all this for years. Recently she had been trying to get the family to plan for their future. She emphasized that Dad did not want to go to a nursing home. His major investment was his condo and that's where both Dad and Teresa wanted to continue to live—with each other. This sounded good to me.

The week before, I had taken Dad to the doctor. It was the first time I had done this, and I enjoyed the outing. Siobhan had warned me he wouldn't know which way was up or why he was there, but everything went well. I was thrilled that Dad had passed the eye-test with flying colours. The doctor said he was "perfect" for a man of ninety.

Feeling good that I was managing to balance family and work, I got ready for our dinner guests. Things had been hopping since my book, *Banned on the Hill*, came out three months earlier.

I was looking forward to showing Phoebe and Siobhan my new poster, "Do Not Talk About Climate Change." I'd launched my new book with an outdoor poster campaign which had been up on the streets of Ottawa. *The Guardian* wrote, "Artist finds inspiration in Canadian government's attempt to silence her."[2] And on CTV's *Power Play*, Don Martin quipped, "It's not nice to fool with Franke James."[3]

That same "Do Not Talk" poster was now hanging prominently on our dining room wall. I loved having it where I could see it, but I knew it would give some of my family indigestion. We were a mixed bag politically. After Bill and I sold our only car to reduce our carbon footprint, my brother-in-law Hank (Lynne's husband) told me what he thought. At

The "Do Not Talk About Climate Change" poster in Ottawa

a family party, he boomed, "You're not going to have any car? You guys are granola-crunching, tree-hugging whack jobs!"[4]

I didn't have a snappy comeback. But I used his comment in my next story, "My SUV and Me Say Goodbye." It nicely illustrated the flack I got from my family for "going green." Later, Hank showed up at my book launch wearing dark sunglasses and a smirk. It made me think of advice from the late screenwriter Nora Ephron on dealing with the dramas of life: "Everything is copy." It was a mantra I would repeat over and over in dealing with my siblings: Conrad, Deirdre, Lynne, Phoebe, Siobhan, and Teresa, the youngest.

My parents were practicing Catholics who believed in the rhythm method, so our large family was not a surprising result. I remember photos of us where we looked, as my mother would often say, "like peas in a pod."

As a kid, I fantasized that I was adopted. As an adult I know this isn't true, but it would explain how different I am from my other siblings. I have always carved my own path. In high school, I was fortunate to go to an alternative school rather than the traditional schools my siblings attended. This allowed me to be self-directed and study with a professional painter. Then I left the shelter of my family to study fine arts at distant universities, first on the east coast, and then on the west. My siblings all stayed in Toronto.

But my yearning to be part of backyard BBQs and family gatherings pulled me back. So, after finishing my master's degree in Victoria, we returned to Toronto. We were lucky to find a deal on a house in our old neighbourhood, where my husband and I started our own family. Our two kids—son Trevor and daughter Darcy—grew up surrounded by many cousins. It was a happy life with lots of birthdays, playmates, and family time.

Tragically, my sister Lynne died in 2012. She was a member of Mensa and aside from being brilliant, she had a strong sense of fairness. I'd looked up to her since I was little. Sadly, her life was cut short. Then we were six.

I was closest to Phoebe. She felt like a second mother to me. When I was young, she would often babysit me. I remember her bringing me hot chocolate and snacks while I watched TV, cozy in a warm blanket. If I was "very good," we'd go to the corner store the next day to buy something. I often chose paper dolls as I dreamed of becoming a fashion designer.

Fast forward a few decades, and Phoebe was still the nurturer, bringing homemade bread and jam to Dad and Teresa. By then, her many children were young adults. Her husband, Spencer, was a teacher. She worked in the finance industry.

It was quite an evolution. In her university days, she looked like a flower child. I saw them as long-haired hippies destined for a commune.

Yellow roses, blue thistle, and sprigs of berries for the summer dinner party

But Spencer's long locks didn't sit well with my grandmother; family legend has it that she showed up at their wedding with scissors in her handbag. Ha! I never saw the clippers. Now, his hair was neat and trimmed short, while Phoebe's hair was as long as ever.

Bill was out gathering food and wine for that night's celebration. I looked down at the flowers and greenery, mulling options to create a centerpiece for our dinner party. Yellow roses, blue thistle, and milk-white berries were all arrayed on the seafoam-coloured glass that topped our kitchen island. It would have to be low. I knew from experience that if it blocked anyone's view, Bill would whisk it away.

I chose a low glass vase, snipped six inches off the yellow roses, and quickly created a circular spray. I mixed in the sea holly thistle and some sprigs of berries, and voilà! When Bill and I married in our early twenties, I didn't know anything about flowers. His mother, the daughter of a florist, had a great eye for floral design. I learned from watching her. I placed the arrangement on a small tray on our dining room table. With our colourful place mats, tall candlesticks, crystal wine glasses, and crisp white-linen serviettes rolled into silver napkin rings, all the scratches and dings on our worn table disappeared. It looked fabulous. We were ready for our dinner party.

AT 7:30, OUR GUESTS arrived at the front door. We welcomed them with enthusiastic hugs. The two couples arrived together, bringing white wine and sweet treats. A flurry of compliments followed: Thanks for inviting us over. Your place looks beautiful! What you've done to it is amazing!

The transformation began with a simple vision: to make the house into a cottage in the city. Built in the 1930s, the house had been through many iterations, some more successful than others. We bought it fourteen years earlier, in part for its commercial zoning, so we could turn it into a live/work art studio. The house itself was a fixer-upper. Over the years, we slowly remade it, inside and out.

Delicious aromas wafted through the air as Bill cooked tenderloin steak and fresh salmon with rosemary and lemon. We gathered around the kitchen island for the latest family news. All my siblings had married (except for Teresa) and there were over twenty nieces and nephews, so there was always news.

My sisters walked into the living room and saw my poster. "It's so big!"

"It's the same one that was on the street in Ottawa," Bill responded. "We were there for a writers' conference, so the timing was great."

Then I picked up my new *Banned on the Hill* book. I pointed to the cover with a giant bug climbing the Parliament building's Peace Tower. "The cockroach was inspired by our friend Richard Littlemore, who wrote the introduction."

Phoebe smiles beside Spencer as he reads Banned on the Hill

"He called Franke a cockroach," Bill said. "But in a good way!"

"Yes," I said, "the compliments are pouring in. Richard compared me to the kind of cockroach that, after you hit them with your shoe, they stand up, shake themselves off, and walk away as if nothing happened."

Siobhan and Phoebe knew the story, but this was my first chance to show them the book. I flipped to the chapter showing the tally of government records I'd received. I looked at my sisters and said, "They thought they had all the power. When they blew me off, I realized I needed proof. And I got it. Over 2,000 documents."

"Franke's secret weapon is the truth!" Bill said.

We all laughed. My sisters joked they wouldn't want to get in a duel with me. And we all chuckled at the thought that I would ever cross swords with my own family.

Siobhan and Jared relax on the couch amidst Franke's collection of art books

I knew, though, that they didn't come to hear about my activism. They wanted to know how I was going to help solve the Dad-and-Teresa question. From my siblings' point of view, I was the family slacker. I found this irritating since we had Dad and Teresa to dinner regularly, and we took Teresa to cultural events and on fitness walks. But since I didn't handle the medical or financial affairs, my contributions were seen as less valuable. And I didn't get any gold stars for taking Dad to the doctor because we took a taxi. (The implication being: "If you drove a car like the rest of us, we wouldn't have to waste Dad's money on a taxi fare! Harrumph.")

Siobhan and Jared sat on the opposite sofa. Jared was intelligent with a dry sense of humour. Although not as fit as Spencer or Bill, who were both long-distance runners, he was nice-looking, slightly balding and wearing a soft-yellow golf shirt. Siobhan's dark-brown hair was short and

Bill lights the candles for dinner with Jared, Phoebe, Siobhan, and Spencer

---

there was something about her posture that made me think of someone regal. She was casually dressed in a patterned sweater with light-brown cropped pants. Jared smiled for the camera, but Siobhan looked away, frowning. Whatever she was worrying about, I figured we would hear over dinner.

When supper was ready, we carried our brightly patterned plates to the table, Bill at one end, me at the other. The couples mixed it up, sitting across from each other. While Bill lit candles, I snapped a few more photos. Spencer and Siobhan smiled, the greenery of our backyard visible through the windows behind them. On the other side, Jared and Phoebe sat in front of my big poster. Then Bill waved at me. "No more photos! Let's say thanks and eat while the food is hot!" He was right, of course. We all laughed. The wine flowed freely.

As expected, the conversation circled to: "What will we do about Dad and Teresa? If he moves to a retirement home, where will Teresa go?"

"But isn't Teresa going to live at Conrad's home?" I asked, thinking of my brother's long-standing promise. "That is Dad's plan."

Dad was very protective of Teresa, and he only trusted our family to provide a loving home for her. Conrad had promised years ago that he would let Teresa live with him. I was fuzzy on the terms of their agreement, but Dad told me he was going to leave some money to Conrad for Teresa's support, and to expand their house. It sounded reasonable. When Dad had made the same offer to us, I brushed his suggestion aside. We were happy with the freedom we had.

Phoebe was quiet. She looked at me, her blue eyes widening, her eyebrows arching, and her lips turning up to form a small, close-lipped smile. When she looked at me that way, I knew she wanted to say something, but she was holding her tongue. Siobhan, on the other hand, just gave me a withering look. It might be that she couldn't believe that I was that naïve. She may have been thinking: "Franke, do you really believe that? Wake up! Conrad is definitely not going to take Teresa."

I responded to their looks: "I know Conrad has reasons, lots of reasons." I paused. "But, if he is going to back out of his promise, he should let everyone know, especially Dad. We need to make alternate plans. It's not fair to Dad or Teresa." And then I planted a seed, "Maybe we should write a letter to Conrad, to make it official? We really need to get the issue on the table."

I sensed that Phoebe and Siobhan were supportive, but it was left up in the air.

A WEEK PASSED before Conrad hosted a birthday party for Dad at his lakeside cottage. Everyone drove up, except for us. I knew there'd be

Franke's waterlogged studio after the flood

blowback for not going along with the crowd, but I was swamped, literally and figuratively. Two days after the dinner party, my basement studio was flooded by the biggest summer storm to ever hit Toronto.[5]

I wanted to clean up the mess. I was overwhelmed with work too. Deadlines were looming and it was all just too much. So, I begged off going to my brother's cottage.

Of course, Conrad's party at the lake was a grand success. I heard from Phoebe, who managed to politely corner Conrad about his promise. She told Siobhan and me that we would not have to write a letter because he had finally acknowledged, as we suspected, that he and his wife, Candi, couldn't handle Teresa.

It was a step forward. At least we had clarity. We could start talking about options for Teresa's future that she'd be happy with. Then Phoebe added a caveat: *Conrad hasn't told Dad, and who knows when he will?*

CHAPTER SIX

What's Wrong with Teresa?

August 13–18, 2013

TERESA WAS READY TO GO. DEIRDRE WAS ANNOYED.
Once again, the responsibility of taking Teresa to her doctor's appointments had fallen on my older sister Deirdre's shoulders.[1] Teresa was insisting that Deirdre take her to Sick Kids Hospital. She was even wearing her Sick Kids hat. This was frustrating for Deirdre as her mission that day was to take Teresa to get her hearing checked, and she did not want to waste time going to Sick Kids.

Deirdre was a born organizer and as such was often bossy. When my sister Lynne died, I wondered who would fill her shoes. Lynne was a leader and her sense of what was fair and good guided our family. Who would now take the leadership crown amongst the siblings? Any one of us could have stepped up—all of us were adults—but for whatever reason, Deirdre assumed the unofficial "head" role. Since she worked as Dad's legal secretary for many years (and Dad had been widowed for over a dozen years), it was a fluid transition. She became a chief organizer of Dad's and Teresa's lives, from finances to health.

Maybe if Deirdre had turned up the car radio the trip would have been a lot of fun? Teresa loves music and they could have been happily singing tunes. My own fond memory of Deirdre is when she'd moved out on her own. We were zipping along Avenue Road in her sporty VW Karmann Ghia. Pop tunes were blaring; we were chatting about boy-friends, jobs, and dreams. We had our lives ahead of us.

I thought Deirdre was very sophisticated. Dad said she was beautiful. He once remarked that she resembled a young Elizabeth Taylor. (We had a family photo of Deirdre as a teenager leaning against a tree. With her long dark-brown hair, creamy-white complexion, and shapely figure, the movie star resemblance was apt.) Fast forward a few decades, and she was married to Chuck, managing four kids, and still looking a little bit Liz Taylor; her dark hair was cut in a short bob and streaked with silver.

However, as a teenager I was most impressed that Deirdre had made the leap to independence. That's what I wanted. As it turned out, my path was very different from the rest of my sibs, who all chose to stay in Toronto.

The important thing to know about Deirdre was that Dad trusted her completely. Whenever I had a question for Dad about something, he'd say, "Just ask Deirdre. She takes care of everything."

On this particular day, Candi, Conrad's wife, had agreed to take Teresa, but something had come up. So Deirdre stepped in, saying she'd do it: *I don't expect anyone else to volunteer because, everyone assumes I have nothing better to do!*

My sister Phoebe, who was always eager to smooth things over, answered the request for help by saying: *Deirdre has already suffered enough.* This seemed melodramatic. Teresa was just being herself. At any rate, Phoebe offered to pay for taxis and support staff so that Deirdre could get a break. But Deirdre rejected the offer: *I need to meet with the doctor myself, because Teresa's hearing loss might be related to her vision loss, and it all could be neurological.*

This seemed far-fetched to me. My hunch was that Deirdre was irritated because she had accompanied Teresa to the dentist the day before, and it took longer than expected. From Deirdre's telling, the extra time was because of Teresa's behaviour. When they finally got Teresa into the dentist's chair, she just sat there with her arms crossed and her jaw clenched tight. When she finally opened her mouth, she demanded a new doctor and a Tim Horton's iced coffee. Teresa's refusal to "follow doctor's orders" could be challenging, but really, she has always been clever about getting what she wants.

Teresa just wanted to go to Sick Kids. She had been their number one fan for years. No one knows why, exactly, but Bill and I recognized that it was a strong motivator. One of our longest walks with Teresa was from our home in North Toronto all the way downtown to Sick Kids—ten kilometres. We celebrated by buying Teresa a Sick Kids hat (the same one she wanted to wear that day) and Sick Kids books on healthy eating. Teresa was in heaven.

Of course, Teresa was an adult, not a child, so her doctor's appointments were not at Sick Kids. Deirdre was blunt about this, telling Teresa that they were definitely not going to Sick Kids Hospital. As an incentive, Deirdre promised to take her for a reward after.

Teresa had visited the ear doctor before. When they arrived at a big intersection by the hospital, she instructed Deirdre to go right. Deirdre turned, thinking that Teresa knew which way to go. However, that was not the case. They ended up at the hospital's emergency department surrounded by ambulances and paramedics. Teresa must have been thrilled, but undoubtedly, Deirdre was unhappy with their accidental detour. But Teresa can be an assertive back-seat driver. She often tells cab drivers and bus drivers which way to go. Deirdre may have felt foolish, but to me it shows how convincing Teresa can be, even if her sense of direction is a little mixed up.

Luckily for Teresa and Deirdre, they found their way to Dr. Mueller's office and a packed waiting room. When it was finally Teresa's turn, she refused to go in because this was not Sick Kids. Dr. Mueller kindly came out to the waiting room, but when Teresa saw him, she crossed her arms, effectively sending the message, "Don't touch me!"

This was classic Teresa. She often says this when a doctor, or nurse, or dentist comes a little too close too quickly for her comfort. Fortunately, Dr. Mueller had a sense of humour, and with a little back-and-forth bantering, Teresa eventually allowed him to look at her ears.

Deirdre alerted the doctor that there might be something neurologically wrong with Teresa because she'd been informed (by whom she didn't say) that Teresa was deaf in one ear and blind in one eye. The doctor was probably alarmed by Deirdre's worries as well because he sent Teresa upstairs to the hearing lab for testing.

When they got there, Teresa refused to allow the staff to put anything near her ears. Fortunately, Deirdre was able to persuade her to cooperate. Teresa was asked to listen and repeat words. Easy. But to make sure that Teresa was not reading her lips, the tech covered her mouth. That's when Teresa refused to play along.

So, they did the beep test. They hooked Teresa up with headphones and asked her to raise her hand whenever she heard the beeping sound. The tech started by pushing the buttons to make the sounds. At first, Teresa didn't respond; then she started saying "mmm" when it beeped and raising her hand when it didn't. They kept at it, and before too long, Teresa was saying "mmm," raising her hands and snapping her fingers whenever the tech tapped on the buttons. It might have sounded very musical, but the results were open to interpretation.

The tech tried the repeat-a-word test again. This time, Teresa repeated some of the words, saying "hot dog" but refusing to say others. She responded to "airplane" by saying "taxi." For "spaghetti" she said "popcorn." (Which sounded funny and creative to me.) But then Teresa started mimicking the tech, covering her own mouth while she was speaking. Somehow, they got enough responses so that when Dr. Mueller looked at the results, he was able to give Teresa the thumbs up on her hearing.

When Teresa heard the good results—the "diagnosis" as she would call it—she immediately asked the doctor to send her to Sick Kids. And Dr. Mueller, who understood what Teresa was really asking for, suggested that they go to Tim Hortons at Sick Kids. Teresa was delighted.

But of course, Deirdre refused to drive Teresa all the way downtown for a coffee. She said that made Teresa furious. Finally, Deirdre managed to satisfy Teresa with an iced coffee from a nearby McDonald's. At this point, it was hard to know who was happier: Teresa, because she'd earned herself a coffee, or Deirdre, because the four-hour excursion was finally over.

The doctor's trip sounded challenging but par for the course with Teresa. I wondered what she thought and so did Bill. So, a few days later, when they were out for their Sunday walk, he asked her, "What was your trip to the doctor like?"

Teresa didn't mention anything about getting angry with Deirdre, or the mixed-up driving directions. She just said, "Dr. Mueller was very good."

"How are your ears?"

"Much better!" Teresa said. "Except Dr. Mueller called me a P-E-S-T. Which hurt my feelings."

Bill cheers Teresa's progress as they walk along a leafy trail

"He called you a P-E-S-T? Aww, that's too bad," Bill said. Then he asked, "What did you think of that hospital?"

"Not so good," Teresa said with two thumbs down.

"Did you see any paramedics or ambulances?"

"Yes!" with a big mischievous smile.

"What do you think of Sick Kids Hospital?"

"Awesome!" She gave two thumbs up. Way up!!

CHAPTER SEVEN

The Elephant and the Whiteboard

August 18-26, 2013

CANDI WAS ALL FIRED UP. DESPITE HEARING THE GOOD NEWS about Teresa's ears (and that there were no neurological worries),[1] my sister-in-law was demanding a family meeting. *Now!* Candi has a cruise-ship style and a booming voice. Married to my brother, Conrad, she cheekily called herself an out-law. With pearls, polka dots, and short streaked hair, she'd welcome you with a smile, a hug, and a piece of her mind. That was what she was doing today but without the cheery grin. She was sounding the alarm: *It's time for the family to talk about the elephant in the room—Dad's and Teresa's care.*

Candi insisted that Conrad and the girls (Deirdre, Phoebe, Siobhan, and me) take charge of the situation and create a new plan. To make sure we didn't miss her point, she listed a slew of potential threats: *What would happen if Dad allowed a stranger into the condo? Or gave all his money away? Or just forgot where he lives? Who would be accountable for the losses and the mess?*

In contrast, I thought that Dad was doing well.

But my sister-in-law wanted the family to do something immediately: *Before we get complaints. Before it gets nasty.* Candi pointed to Dad's habit of "talking" to our late Mom as evidence of how bad things were. His "telepathic powers" might seem strange; however, as Catholics, we were taught to pray for those up in heaven and to the angels watching over us. I never questioned his belief in God, saints, angels, and departed loved ones, which included my late mother. Dad was heartbroken when she died after fifty years of marriage. He believed that he could still communicate with his soulmate, and that was fine by me. It was a beautiful love story.

However, Candi was determined that we wake up. She was giving us the tough news: *Dad and Teresa need much more support than we could ever provide.*

Of course, if Teresa was as difficult as Candi was saying, then it was no wonder that she and Conrad had backed out.

At any rate, it struck me as ironic that she did not want to invite the two elephants. Making plans for them without their knowledge or participation seemed unfair. Everyone else shrugged.

Siobhan, who had been worrying about this for years, came back matter-of-factly with her list of next steps: *Teresa needs a psychiatric assessment and an assessment for early-onset Alzheimer's.*

What the hell? I felt queasy about her to-do list. Maybe a psychiatric assessment could help Teresa identify skills to improve, but why test for Alzheimer's? Siobhan must have known that people with Down syndrome are statistically more likely to get diagnosed with the disease,[2] but I didn't see any indication that Teresa had any type of dementia. She had a memory like an elephant. If you promised her something, she would never let you forget. She kept asking for it, over and over again.

Then my brother-in-law, Hank, jumped into our conversation. As a former top cop at the local station, he commanded attention, and he was used to getting it. The first thing Hank did was dismiss our discussions: *You are all just spinning your wheels. This family had never had a plan to deal with the reality of Dad's aging and inevitable decline. So, it's a useless waste of time until you face the facts.* Then he called up the memory of my sister Lynne, saying that if she were still around, things would have been long since settled.

Balderdash. Years ago, I drew Lynne's attention (and everyone else's) to the fact that Dad would be unhappy that his kids were orchestrating things behind his back. Lynne agreed. But Hank didn't worry about that now. He said: *We should decide what's best—for both of them.*

Ever the sunny cheerleader, Phoebe smoothed over this rough spot: *We all love Dad and Teresa dearly. Keep going, we're all moving in the same direction.*

No, we weren't. But the group wasn't listening to me.

SIX DAYS LATER, Hank's recommendations still hung in the air. I opened my laptop and saw a new message from my sister Deirdre, the self-appointed head of our clan. It was a one-sentence email with the subject line "Teresa's whiteboard and walls." She attached six photos but offered no explanation.

I studied Deirdre's photos trying to understand why she sent them. I could see part of Teresa's head in one photo. The writing on the erasable whiteboard was a source of pride for Teresa. The board was big, five feet wide by four feet high, and it was filled with magic marker notes about people she had met, songs she loved, phone numbers to remember, and her schedule. It seemed like a joyful and healthy activity to me. And her cursive writing was far neater than mine.

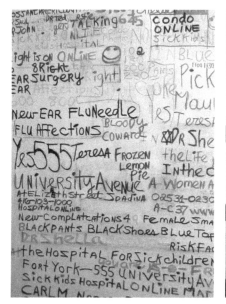

The writing on the wall by Teresa's whiteboard and nightstand

I flashed back to memories of Teresa's childhood bedroom when she had decorated her walls with magic markers. Mom had a relaxed approach, so much so that it inspired me to give a speech in grade school. I stood in front of the class, wearing a fresh white blouse, navy tunic, knee socks, and ugly brown lace-up shoes. As I told the class about Teresa's murals on her bedroom walls, everyone laughed. I held up one of her drawings to show her creativity. I still remember the applause from my classmates and teachers, who loved hearing about Teresa and her art. I was glowing with pride.

Why was Deirdre sending photos of Teresa's whiteboard? I didn't know but I found it disturbing. I tried to defend Teresa by emphasizing the positive. "Thanks for taking the pictures. Teresa is AMAZING! This is great. It clearly shows that she is using writing as an outlet for free expression."

Bill replied too, right after me. "Now we know why Teresa has such a fantastic memory. She writes things down!"

Candi was incredulous. *Are you joking?*

"No, we're not joking," Bill answered.

Candi described Teresa's writing as fanatical: *Teresa is obsessed with doctors, illness, and the Sick Kids Hospital. It is certainly not "free expression." Instead, it just makes things more difficult, especially for Teresa's caregivers!*

Bill snapped back: "Some people like the Maple Leafs (a hockey team). Some people like the Blue Jays (a baseball team). Teresa likes Sick Kids (a health care team). What's wrong with that?"

Teresa is just too stubborn, Candi answered.

Yes, Teresa could be stubborn. But so was everyone else in our family—maybe it was a genetic trait? The only exception was Phoebe, who could change directions faster than the wind; perhaps because she valued harmony above all else. But Teresa didn't like people ordering her around. And Teresa was not a kid. She was an adult who wanted to make her own decisions.

I looked again at the photos. Candi had said there were no happy experiences on Teresa's whiteboard. Thankfully, she was mistaken. Teresa had written about her favourite song, "Lean On Me"; her favourite food, lemon pie; the names of doctors and friends she had met on her Sunday walks; and the theatre performance, *Rare*, which we'd seen together. That cheered me.

Candi's view was different: *The writing on Teresa's whiteboard is very sad. It should be discouraged.*

This was a crystallizing moment for me. I felt like Teresa was being suffocated, unable to express her true feelings and thoughts without disapproval. I felt afraid and knew I had to do something to help her.

CHAPTER EIGHT

Teresa and Terry

September 16, 2012

DAD KISSED TERESA GOODBYE. THEN HE TURNED AND GAVE me a kiss, saying, "Thank you, sweetie." He looked at Bill and gave him a firm handshake. We were ready to go.[1]

The big day was here. And I was recording it all. We had stopped by the condo to pick up Teresa, and Dad had come downstairs to see us off. But first we took photos. Dad was wearing a black golf shirt and pants. Teresa smiled into the bright sunshine.

We arrived early at Upper Canada College to sign up for the annual Terry Fox Run and to get our race T-shirts. The college is in the centre of the city, near Toronto's Forest Hill neighbourhood. The grounds are expansive and expensive, including a football field, a red running track and a hockey rink. (It had been a dream of ours to send our son Trevor to UCC. With effort we managed it; he entered at grade seven and graduated to study computer science at university.)

The buzz of the gathering crowd was exhilarating. People of all shapes, sizes, ages, and abilities were milling around. Kids were playing on the inflatable slide. Volunteers were taking donations behind tables

Teresa with Franke and Bill on the Terry Fox Run

stacked high with T-shirts, books, and memorabilia. The official event began with a group warm-up. The leader, a young guy wearing a Terry Fox ball cap, picked up a microphone and called out exercises. The group followed *en masse*, reaching up to the sky, spinning around, and doing jumping jacks. Teresa joined in, bending side to side, touching her toes, and doing the downward dog. All limbered up, the crowd was ready to go. At the crack of the pistol, we were off. Teresa was pumping her arms, power walking as fast as she could. And beaming with joy. Fleet-footed runners passed us, but that was okay. Speed didn't matter. Everyone was welcome, whether on foot or using strollers, wheelchairs, or bikes.

I wasn't sure how far we'd walk. Every kilometre was marked with a Terry Fox sign standing on an orange pylon. At each kilometre, Teresa would smile and flash a V for another victory. She was outgoing and posed for photos with a traffic cop wearing an orange vest. Then we spotted St. John's Ambulance workers. Teresa stood in the middle of the trio. The tallest guy was laughing, hovering his hand over her head to show how much smaller she was.

We continued, winding through the leafy trails, enjoying the sunshine and camaraderie; Teresa walked briskly and often raised her hands to high-five the student volunteers who were handing out glasses of water.

At the six-kilometre marker we met our good friend Joel, who was doing the walk in honour of his wife Suzanne, who had died of breast cancer. Teresa was doing it for our late sister, Lynne, and for Dad, who had prostate cancer. I was surprised to read this news—in Teresa's hand-writing—on the dedication board at the race start. She knew more about this than I did!

At the eight-kilometre mark, we were back at the college. Teresa raised both arms in celebration, and power walked across the finish-line. Bill and I ran beside her snapping photos. She'd done it. Our fourth annual Terry Fox Run. Her longest Terry Fox ever.

"High five!" Bill said. "A new world record!"

"You did it," I said. "Eight kilometres. Congratulations!"

"Awesome!" she said. "Now that was a workout!"

I gave her a hug and savoured the moment. Teresa was thrilled with herself and had energy to spare. "I'm a speedster!" A few minutes later, she was dancing on the school's grassy fields while the band—guitarists, a bass player, and a drummer—filled the air with music. She twirled around wearing her official race T-shirt, swinging to the beat, and holding up her souvenir—a new Terry Fox book. I loved seeing her happiness.

TERRY FOX INSPIRED Teresa, Bill, and me. We admired his determin-ation and imagination that had turned adversity into positivity. We first heard of him when Bill and I were students at the University of Victoria. We watched him on the news, a solitary runner in a T-shirt and grey shorts running with a hopping gait and a big dream. We heard that he was a young athlete (about our age) who had lost his right leg to cancer. His

Teresa dancing at the Terry Fox Run

illness was tragic, but his response was brilliant activism. His experience in the cancer wards motivated him to demand change. Terry Fox said, "I could not leave knowing these faces and feelings would still exist, even though I would be set free from mine. I was determined to take myself to the limit for this cause."[2]

He began the Marathon of Hope in April 1980, by dipping his artificial leg into the Atlantic Ocean off Canada's east coast in Newfoundland. Then he turned and started his long run towards his home in British Columbia on the other side of the continent. He was determined to run every day and inspire everyone in the country to give. "When I started this run, I said that if we all gave one dollar, we'd have $22 million for cancer research," Terry said. "And I don't care, man, there's no reason that isn't possible. No reason!"[3]

Teresa raises her hands at the Terry Fox Run

He believed in the impossible. And he would not give up. Despite the difficulties, the pain, and his bleeding stump, he kept going, running the equivalent of a marathon a day along the Trans-Canada Highway. "The pain was there, but the pain didn't matter," he said. "I got satisfaction out of doing things that were difficult. It was an incredible feeling."[4]

He continued, unstoppable, for 143 days, running more than halfway across Canada: 3,339 miles from Newfoundland to Thunder Bay, Ontario. Then tragedy struck again. The bone cancer, which they had tried to stop by amputating his leg, had spread. He had two lumps in his lungs; one was the size of a lemon. His run ended on Labour Day, 1980. People across the country were devastated. There was an outpouring of support that brings tears to my eyes even today. People saw what he was trying to do and rushed forward to help. Donations poured in, finally totalling $23 million for cancer research.

When asked what kept him motivated Terry said, "I can't pinpoint one thing, because there's been so many things—things like the telethon, you know.... Every day I got all kinds of mail. And the kinds of things that people say to encourage me and support me really helped me out psychologically, because I know there's so many people pulling for me. And that just makes it easier to go from day to day."[5]

Terry won the Canadian Athlete of the Year, the Lou Marsh Award— an honour he treasured because it recognized that his achievement was an unparallelled athletic feat. He was named to the Order of Canada and listed as Canada's newsmaker of the year for two years in a row. When Terry died on June 28, 1981, the country wept. The government ordered flags to be flown at half-mast. Prime Minister Pierre Trudeau said, "It occurs very rarely in the life of a nation that the courageous spirit of one person unites all people in the celebration of his life and in the mourning of his death.... We do not think of him as one who was defeated by misfortune but as one who inspired us with the example of the triumph of the human spirit over adversity."[6]

Decades later, Terry's legacy lives on. He said, "Every one of us is important. Just look at what one person can do."[7] Over sixty countries participate in the annual event.[8] Like so many others, I have been inspired by his courage, his selflessness, and his activism. Teresa was motivated by Terry to get into better shape.

To celebrate, we went for brunch, where Teresa devoured a handmade waffle, maple syrup and coffee. That evening both Dad and Teresa came to our house for a Terry Fox dinner party to show off the day's photos and videos.

That was one year before all our family troubles began. If someone had told me back then that within the next year, three of my siblings would be working hard to put Teresa into a nursing home, I never would have believed it.

Teresa enjoys brunch with Bill and Franke

CHAPTER NINE

Arm-Twisted in Perpetuity

August 29, 2013

S IOBHAN WAS WORRYING ABOUT TERESA'S FUTURE. SHE explained: *Teresa will never get a spot in a group home. The biggest challenge will be getting her into the care system because the neediest people are always chosen first. The care agencies will see our large family and demand that one of us take her. Even if a crisis arises, we will be arm-twisted into taking Teresa in perpetuity.*[1]

So she came up with a new plan: *We should put Teresa into a nursing home.* Siobhan followed this with elaborate gyrations and justifications as to why this was necessary. She said: *We're not failing Dad. We're fulfilling our duties by providing the care that they actually need. Just imagine where Teresa will be in ten years if we don't do this.*

I thought Siobhan's proposal was a ridiculous and dismissed it immediately. Teresa was healthy and active. She was forty-nine, not seventy-nine.

But my other siblings thought it was a great idea. Five of them—my brother, Conrad; my sisters Deirdre and Phoebe; and their husbands, Chuck and Spencer—jumped in their cars and drove up to Wheiry Lodge, a nursing home in the northern part of the city for a family tour. Teresa was not invited, and neither was Dad. I refused to go.

Wheiry Lodge sits on four and a half acres of green space overlooking a wooded ravine. Its size and scale, with 391 residents, echoes the old institutions built a hundred years ago. But Wheiry Lodge was built in the 1970s, with a two-tone stucco exterior and rows of white-framed windows on every floor. If you were lucky, you might get a room that faced onto the park on the southern end, but most looked out over grey asphalt and cars in the parking lots that surrounded the building.

By happenstance, Siobhan couldn't make the tour that day, so Conrad took on the role of evaluating the facility and reporting back. As the only boy in a family with six girls, Conrad always held special status. My mother would say it was because he was going to carry on the family name. Whatever the reason was, Dad named him as an attorney for his property if needed, and as a future executor of his estate when the time came.

Conrad went to an all-boys school to counteract all the estrogen at home. For the same reason, he took judo lessons. I watched enviously from the sidelines as he and his class learned how to do flips. I wanted to take judo too, but money was tight. I was given art lessons instead. When I was sixteen or so, I made a photo-realist portrait of Conrad.

He was a cute teenager with dark hair and bangs, wearing a plaid jacket and a serious expression; not surprising since we'd just had a major fire and there was extensive water damage from the firemen rushing in with huge hoses. Sitting on our back porch along with the charred remains and trash, he was surrounded by disaster. Looking back, it's interesting that I chose to do a painting about the fire crisis. It upended our lives, and I stayed with neighbours for a while.

By the time Conrad was full grown, he towered over me. I thought he might go into a professional occupation, but he became an entrepreneur with his own construction business. Just like my dad, he enjoyed working with his hands. He did excellent work and was able to satisfy even the fussiest customers. I thought of this as I read his review of Wheiry Lodge. I can imagine my sisters and him, stepping out of their cars and looking around like curious tourists.

Conrad described their reaction: *We liked what we saw. We were all very pleased with the premises, the locale and the employees.* Hearing this, you'd think it was a high-end resort with lush lawns, premium beds, and white-gloved waiters. But in reality, it was a city-run nursing home, most of which are woefully underfunded.[2] And while these facilities may feature some nice landscaping, you're more likely to see plastic-covered mattresses and disposable examination gloves.

My siblings toured the wards and saw many double rooms. This led Phoebe to suggest: *Teresa should have a private room. Otherwise, it would be quite a step down from what Teresa had at the condo.* Perhaps anticipating that the others might worry about the extra costs, she offered: *We could all chip in for an upgrade.*

But fiscally minded Siobhan brushed that offer aside: *The government will pay for Teresa at Wheiry Lodge. But if we give Teresa extra money, she could lose all her government funding, and then Teresa would become a financial burden to the family.*

I'd heard variations on this concern many times. I saw it as a rationale to justify why Teresa should get less. At any rate, Siobhan emphasized the upside of a double room: *If Teresa had a roommate, she wouldn't be lonely.*

Of course, she wouldn't be lonely if she stayed with Dad. It reminded me of Charles de Gaulle, who had a daughter with Down syndrome in 1928. He refused to send Anne to an institution to live with "strangers," and she lived at her family's home all her life. "We must take responsibility for her wherever she is and whatever she will be,"[3] de Gaulle said.

Conrad after the fire

His advocacy was remarkable because, at that same time, the Nazis were killing people with disabilities for being "useless eaters" and a burden.[4]

As my siblings continued their tour, they must have noticed what Phoebe told me later, that the residents were much older and frailer than Teresa. *While we were happy with the facilities,* Conrad noted, *some of us were concerned that there would be no activities to keep Teresa's mind occupied.*

I was glad that he was worried that Teresa would be bored, but Siobhan had an answer: *Teresa could still attend her day programs.* (These were subsidized community-run programs. Teresa went twice a week and participated in a variety of group activities.)

This clinched the deal for Conrad: *If Teresa could continue with her day programs, then Wheiry Lodge could work as her home base.* He explained why this was so urgent: *We are in crisis mode. Dad is getting worse every day and he won't be able to care for Teresa much longer.*

This seemed like an exaggeration to me.

Conrad asked everyone (particularly me) who had not seen Wheiry Lodge to arrange a visit. Again, I refused to go. We should have been looking for a way for Teresa to stay in the condo or live in the neighbourhood.

Then Conrad explained his change of heart—his reasons for not taking Teresa into his home: *In retrospect, my promise to take care of Teresa was made too quickly. I would never ask my own children to do such a thing. Taking Teresa would be unfair to both Candi and me. And even to Teresa herself! She deserves to live out the rest of her life with some degree of supervised independence.*

I guffawed, hearing that. There might be slick, glossy brochures that describe nursing homes as "supervised independence" but to me that was like putting lipstick on a pig. Many exert control by locking residents on secure floors, using chemical restraints (psychotropic drugs) and physical restraints, too.[5] If Conrad didn't want to take Teresa, that was his choice. But it wasn't fair to put her in an institution now—she had been spared that at birth by Mom and Dad.

Nevertheless, Siobhan insisted this was the best option: *Although we would all like to take Teresa, she is too much to handle and we are too old. I know that we don't want to disappoint Dad, but he has put us into an untenable spot.*

CHAPTER TEN

Dad's Power

August 31–September 6, 2013

W OULD DAD TURN ON THE OVEN AND FORGET? WOULD
*Teresa leave a pot on the stove to catch fire? Would the whole
place go up in a blaze?*

My sister Siobhan was stressing out about safety at the condo.[1] She
had a knack for predicting epic disasters—she could have done well selling
insurance. But on this day, she was sharing her worst fears with the Community Care Access Centre, which everyone referred to as the "CCAC." It
was the government agency that managed Teresa's support and funding.
And now, they had been called in to manage Dad's support too.

The CCAC staffers responded with a solution: take the fuses out
of the stove. The fact that Dad wouldn't be able to cook anything, and
would be frustrated that the oven wasn't working, was shrugged off. Dad
had Meals-on-Wheels and, if he needed to cook anything, he could use
the microwave.

I wouldn't want to be fooled that way. All his life, Dad was a handy-
man, doing everything from installing chandeliers to putting innovative
"step-in" bindings on skis to building radios. At the age of forty-nine
(coincidentally the same age as Teresa was now), he was featured in the

National Post newspaper about the rise of do-it-yourselfers building everything from planes to radios.[2] Bespectacled Dad, in a business shirt and tie, was photographed with my eleven-year-old brother, Conrad, at his side. They were intently examining the innards of a Heathkit A-15 radio which they had built at home together. Dad said, "Making that stereo wasn't nearly as tough as I expected. The whole project, which took thirty hours, turned out to be very relaxing."

But those days were gone. The CCAC agreed to provide immediate crisis support to watch Dad cook. This could have been good if it meant that my siblings would let Dad and Teresa stay at the condo. But, even before the experiment was allowed to run its course, Siobhan cut my optimism short: *This is a short-term fix. Both Dad and Teresa are declining, physically and mentally.*

I was sure that Dad would never agree to Siobhan's plan for Teresa. He hadn't even put Mom in one after her stroke. At the time the doctors had suggested they withdraw life support, but Dad refused. As soon as he could, Dad brought Mom back home. Together they worked on her recovery. He helped her learn to walk again by holding Mom up, with his arms under her armpits as she practised taking baby steps across the kitchen, over and over again. It was remarkable to watch how Dad transformed himself into a full-time caregiver. He and Mom cherished each day of their changed lives, often telling me about their latest small victory. Mom lived at the house with Dad and Teresa for another sixteen years. And she died at home, just as she wished.

Then Phoebe shared her opinion: *We should help Dad stay in the condo. In comparison to the residents at Wheiry Lodge, Dad is a ninety-one-year-old rock star.*

I had a glimmer of hope reading this. Deirdre seemed to be having second thoughts too. After the Wheiry Lodge visit, Deirdre had searched

Dad and Teresa dressed in matching powder blue on Labour Day

online for alternative housing options. She connected with the mother of a young woman with Down syndrome, who suggested that our family explore HomeShare and a program called LIGHTS. Either option would allow Teresa to continue living in the community.

I was relieved. If Deirdre was getting cold feet, she could steer the group towards something better.

THE FOLLOWING WEEKEND, Dad and Teresa came over for a Labour Day dinner. Teresa helped Dad carry in a striped gift bag with red wine, ice cream, and their favourite chocolates, After Eight mints. I snapped a few photos and caught Dad sneaking a bite before we lit the candles. Teresa was in fine form. As always, Dad expressed his appreciation for everything—the home-cooked roast chicken, the fresh white roses, and the warm pecan pie. Sipping a drink after dinner, he said, "This sure beats Meals-on-Wheels! When you get to my age, you'll be happy to know that you can still enjoy fine food and drink. Oh my, this is good!"

I gently asked Dad about their plans for the future, and he made it clear that he wanted to stay in the condo with Teresa. As far as he was concerned, they still had a long runway ahead of them.

THE NEXT WEEK, my sister-in-law Candi restarted her *Elephant in the Room* campaign for a meeting about Dad and Teresa without inviting either of them.

I felt uneasy about the group organizing their lives behind the scenes, so I said, "Please go ahead and have the meeting without me. My vote is that Dad and Teresa should stay together in the condo as long as possible—ideally until Dad dies. Teresa needs a transition strategy to move into a group home."

At the time, I thought group homes were okay, but now, I'm not so sure. I wouldn't want it for myself, as you lose your autonomy. Another mark against group homes is the pandemic. People with developmental disabilities who live in group homes are much more likely to get Covid and die from it.[3]

Still feeling the afterglow of our dinner party, I added a note to remind everyone how well they both were doing.

Candi replied: *It's unfortunate that you can't spare one hour of your time for a family meeting. And I'm eager to hear what kind of magic you would use to help the family find a group home when as far as I know, there are no spots anywhere. Have you been paying attention?*

She signed off, wishing me success with my art tour and adding: *While you are away, I will be working with your siblings who are devoting their time to plan for the well-being of your father and your sister.*

Phoebe caught the dig and tried to smooth things over: *Both Franke and Bill want the best for Teresa—just like everyone else.*

But Siobhan piped up again with her worries: *Teresa's safety should be our number one priority. Dad was frantic when Teresa went AWOL for almost two hours.*

Absent without leave? It seemed like she couldn't imagine Teresa as an independent adult, even for just a few minutes. All my life, the assumption was that Teresa couldn't go anywhere on her own. It was not that she was unable; it was that she was "not allowed." I wished Siobhan had seen *Rare.* Maybe seeing the play would have helped her realize that Teresa has a lot of smarts and could learn to navigate safely.

Siobhan gave us hints of the plan she had been working on with the care agency. The CCAC had interviewed Teresa and now they wanted to speak with Dad. As far as the CCAC was concerned, Dad, who was the named power of attorney, would have the final approval on any plans for Teresa.

Thank heaven! Dad still had power.

But Siobhan warned: *This could present us with a sticky situation. The CCAC wants Dad brought into the loop about the real plans for Teresa's future care, especially after his death.*

And with that, Siobhan turned her focus to Conrad: *Please meet with Dad as soon as possible and tell him the truth—that you will not be taking Teresa.*

CHAPTER ELEVEN

My Troublesome Conscience

September 12-13, 2013

"MEET THE ONE WOMAN WHOM THE GOVERNMENT CAN'T shut up."

The audience took the bait, laughing and applauding.[1] I was at Dalhousie University in Halifax, on stage with Steve Mannell, Director of the College of Sustainability, who introduced me with that quote from *The Guardian*.[2]

Each year the college hosts a public lecture series on the environment. Often, they hire actors to portray historical (that is dead) activists like Rachel Carson, the author of *Silent Spring*, or others from the past. This year, they had me. Mannell joked about this, saying, "We don't need an actor to play her part because she's right here."

I must have looked like an unlikely figure to stand up to a big bully. I was small, female, and old (at least to the students). But I didn't look too boring. I was wearing all black, a sleeveless dress with a leather bodice, and a silver-studded belt. And behind me, larger than life, was my artwork. I was there to tell them about my battle for free expression with the Prime Minister of Canada, Stephen Harper.

"The Troublesome Artist" in Halifax

"Making it onto Harper's blacklist was something I never dreamed of?" I said. "Up to that point, I was just going along on my blissful way, speaking my mind without fear."

By the time I landed in Halifax, I had been fighting the blacklisting for two years. Rather than silence me, the government had provided me with a platform that was making international news. The big bully had slapped me down and I was defending myself with a paintbrush, a little humour and some chutzpah.

"Getting in trouble for this was a black swan moment for me—an unpredictable event which in hindsight appears to have been inevitable." I showed the crowd my family portrait with the seven kids—Deirdre, Conrad, Siobhan, Phoebe, Lynne, Franke, and Teresa—counted out on the fingers of my two hands and said: "Growing up in a family of seven kids, I was always taught to speak up."

Franke's drawing of her family from her essay, Banned on the Hill

As I looked out at the sea of faces, it brought back warm memories of my time as a university student hearing visiting artists talk. Seeing their ordinariness in the flesh as they clicked through their slides, telling us about their winding career paths, made me feel that I could do it too. Now it was my turn to inspire, or at least try. And so I told them my story about finding my voice and using my art to fight back and shine an even brighter light on the whole mess. I ended by asking the audience to join me. "We need to stand up and tell them that blacklisting and censoring does not work. Especially if we are wielding paintbrushes."

After my talk, a student came up to and told me what she thought: "You are somewhat of a badass." (I laughed. That's something my siblings would certainly agree with.) Steve Mannell described me, saying: "She has become a troublesome artist for asking the tough questions."[3] Even Phoebe told me what she thought: *You look like a warrior princess!*

Was she implying that I was dressed like a comic book character? I didn't probe, but at least she was being supportive. Of course, neither of us knew about the upcoming battle or that she would land on the other side.

WHEN I GOT BACK to our hotel room, I checked my email and all my worries about Dad and Teresa came flooding back. Deirdre had announced that she had just shredded eighty boxes of Dad's legal files. (Thank goodness she wasn't working for the federal government, because I would never have gotten the thousands of freedom-of-information documents.) Dad's legal practice was in real estate, wills, and estates, so he had amassed a lot of paper. And since Deirdre had worked for him for many years, she would have known the rules. But I felt uneasy. Had he double-checked? And why was she emptying out his condo? What was the hurry?

I remembered Bill's story about helping the family move some of Dad's files last summer. When Bill arrived, Deirdre was directing traffic while her husband, her son and a few others were busy stacking file boxes onto dollies and wheeling them out. Dad was plunked down in the middle of his living room, watching, somewhat perplexed and definitely unhappy. Everyone ignored him until he stood up and said, "The next thing you'll be taking out of here in a box…is me!"

Bill said they all looked at Dad, laughed, shrugged, and carried on.

THE NEXT MORNING, I was in a Halifax studio with the veteran journalist, Silver Donald Cameron. "Your presentation at Dalhousie University last night got a standing ovation from a packed house," he said. "That must have felt pretty good."

"It was fun," I said. "It was great to see the age range, from university-age students right up to the silver-haired crowd."

Silver Donald Cameron introducing Franke

We both laughed. Silver Don had a warm, relaxed manner. His deep voice had a musical lilt to it, a swinging cadence. We were recording ou conversation for *The Green Interview,*[4] his latest media project. It was a series of interviews with environmental voices like David Suzuki, The Yes Men, and Elizabeth May. I was honoured to be included.

He began with his introduction: "Whoever said, 'you can't fight city hall,' didn't know Franke James.

"Franke is an artist and a writer who wanted to do something about climate change, so she got rid of her bulky, gas-guzzling SUV. Without a car, she didn't need a parking spot at her home, so she wanted to plant a garden in what had previously been her driveway. That got her into trouble with City Hall. She fought and fought and won.

"Then she wrote a visual letter to Prime Minister Stephen Harper, asking a few very simple questions like, 'If we aren't going to get rid of fossil fuels, who is? If we aren't going to do it now, when are we going to do it?' The Prime Minister didn't reply, but he wasn't happy. When

Franke was offered a chance to do a European tour with her art, Canadian embassies first opened their arms and then slammed their doors. They say, 'You can't fight Parliament Hill,' but Franke did. She discovered that her tour had indeed been quashed for political reasons. She struck back with another book: *Banned on the Hill*, and with posters plastered all over Ottawa, and later all over Washington.

"Poor Stephen Harper. Did he even know what hit him?" Silver Don chuckled.

We were sitting around a pine table. Silver Don was casually dressed, wearing jeans, a dark shirt and a red vest. He tapped on the cover of my book, *Bothered by My Green Conscience*, and said, "Here's a picture of Franke James, but it doesn't look like you at all. Tell me about that."

Yes, the whimsical portrait did not look like me. I have blonde hair, but I don't have a tree trunk for a neck, I would never wear a pinafore, and I can't hold a SUV in my arms. At that moment in the studio, I was wearing a sleeveless knit dress with a jazzy op-art pattern. I looked at Silver Don and said, "The Alice in Wonderland image represents my inner self. It's my 'What is happening in the world? This is really upside-down!' self."

I told Silver Don about my battle with City Hall when I first had this feeling. I had asked the city about replacing our brick driveway with a permeable green driveway, but the city inspector said, "No! It is illegal to get rid of your driveway in North York. And it has to be made of concrete, asphalt or interlock. And you cannot plant more than one tree."

I shook my head and said, "The morning after I woke up and thought, What? That just doesn't make any sense! This is like I am living in an *Alice in Wonderland* world! And so I put this image of Alice into my story, "Paradise Unpaved." I've had a lot of fun using the Alice character in my stories. There is a certain innocence to her. The world is upside down, and this isn't the way it should be."

Silver Don pointed the book cover again. "Conscience is not a word we hear a great deal anymore. What does it mean to you?"

"I was raised in a Catholic family, and my mother often talked about listening to your conscience. Back then, such talk just went in and out my ears. But as an adult, I found that my conscience was telling me certain things. The inspiration for my story, 'My SUV and Me Say Goodbye,' was my conscience telling me: 'Okay, you're driving around in a big SUV and you're saying that you're concerned about global warming. This doesn't make sense. I had this quiet dissatisfaction about where I was going: It doesn't feel right, maybe we should sell the car? The story is about resolving that inner battle."

"Your conscience draws out the actions that will make you less discontented with yourself," Silver Don said. "That's really the essence of what the implicit challenge to others is: Look inside. See what you need to do outside. And that brings us back to the SUV and to your injunction to do the hardest thing first. Why?"

"I think we are faced with a monumental challenge—climate change. Society is telling us that we should change our light bulbs, but that doesn't make you feel very powerful. People are not going to brag about that. The idea of 'doing the hardest thing first' gives people that sense of power."

"The hardest stuff first means getting the biggest hit first."

"Yes, do something ambitious," I said.

Silver Don asked about my battle with the federal government.

"I was never supposed to find out what was going on. This was all behind-the-scenes censorship. I needed to dig for evidence, because no one was going to believe me unless I had written proof. We received 2,172 pages of freedom-of-information documents, from four different government departments, all related to me."

Franke is animated as she tells her story

"Were you shocked?"

"Yes!" I laughed. "You would think that the bureaucrats have more important things to do than meddle in an artist's show in Europe. But I guess they were very concerned with message control. They were afraid that my message would show how dirty and polluting the tar sands oil is."

"They were rightly fearful."

"The interesting thing is that my initial show didn't have anything about the tar sands in it."

"Did it not?"

"No. The initial show was about personal action and responsibility. It was about doing the hardest thing first."

"Big Brother was watching, in the most literal sense, biding his time until there comes a moment when you can be swatted. It's the most insidious censorship, all behind closed doors. But you've caught them telling flat-out lies, too."

She did this a lot and it kind of irked me. It probably came from years of her working as Dad's legal secretary. Phoebe had already reacted with a mix of worry about Dad's health and gratitude towards Deirdre for her efforts, but then said: *It's all very upsetting.*

I opened it and stated searching anxiously. Deirdre's attachment was a lengthy Word document, which she told us with some vigorous finger-wagging had taken a great deal of her time to compose: *one hour and seven minutes.* This made me think she was either punching a time clock or wanted us to be suitably grateful for the many hours she was spending taking Dad and Teresa to medical appointments.

There were gobs of details. Deirdre was giving us another blow-by-blow report on the appointments. At first, I laughed. Apparently, Teresa had greeted the doctor like an old friend, casually saying, "Hi, Cushmen." The doctor was amused, but Deirdre wasn't. Dr. Cushmen had given Teresa a quick physical, and he filled out some forms for Teresa. Deirdre didn't explain what the paperwork was for.

The second trip was also about paperwork, but this time for Dad. Deirdre had set it up so that Dr. Cushmen could assess Dad and, if necessary, complete the forms so that he could be admitted to a nursing home. But that was not why Dad thought he was going. He was concerned about the side effects of a blood-thinning drug he had been prescribed. He had even brought notes, which Deirdre called a cheat sheet, describing his symptoms that included insomnia and bleeding fingers. Deirdre, on the other hand, brought along Dad's unused pills to prove he wasn't taking his meds. She also wanted to share her concerns about Dad's poor marks on some recent memory tests.

Dr. Cushmen started the appointment by asking Dad if he knew why he was there. Dad said he wanted to talk about his blood-thinning medication. But the doctor explained that this appointment was for an assessment of whether to move into a nursing home.

Dad objected. He didn't want to go into a nursing home. He wanted to stay at his condo to care for Teresa. This gave his life purpose and meaning. That sounded just like Dad. He would often say, "Teresa and I are a team. We help each other."

Nevertheless, Dr. Cushmen completed the forms for Dad's placement. The doctor duly noted Dad's objections by ticking a box on the form, but nothing further was done.

Deirdre seemed to be relieved. She had the signed form she wanted. But for me, it was distressing because they weren't listening to Dad. And Deirdre's tone seemed unnecessarily negative. She repeatedly described Dad as forgetful, confused and failing. This didn't sound like Dad. The best she could say was that after the appointment, Dad was appreciative and docile. This made him sound uncharacteristically sheep-like.

On their way back to the condo, Deirdre drove Dad by Conrad's house and our old family home, which were on the same street. When they got there, Deirdre said that Dad did not recognize or remember either one. She parked the car in front of our old family house and waited but Dad kept saying that we had lived at a different house.

This was upsetting, but I was skeptical. Why was she telling us this? The old house was an emotional landmark for all of us, but it no longer resembled the one we had lived in. It had been extensively renovated. The only thing they couldn't change was the ugly yellow fire hydrant sitting out front, right by the sidewalk.

Phoebe reacted to Deirdre's story with surprise: *It's strange how different Dad can be. We visited him yesterday, when I dropped by to bring him some of my homemade bread. Dad seemed fine. He was up to date on all the current politics and delighted to see us.*

That's the Dad I saw.

Deirdre repeated her message: *It was very upsetting to see Dad in such rough shape.*

That's when Bill spoke up. "Yes, I agree with Phoebe. Dad is much better in a relaxed environment, like when he is at home. Whenever I see him, he's got it together and knows what's going on. By the way, he may not be crazy for not wanting to take blood thinners. That drug was ranked as the FDA's second-most dangerous drug of the year."[3]

At this point, Deirdre's husband jumped in with both feet. Chuck is a hard-nosed guy with a buzz cut who doesn't waste words. He was shocked: *How could anyone believe that Dad still has it together? Maybe, it's because Franke and Bill are not on the receiving end of the ten to fifteen emergency phone calls we get every day. Heck, on one day, we counted forty-one calls in just six hours!*

Really? Calling repeatedly sounds like something Teresa would do, not Dad. But nobody should be put away for making too many phone calls anyway.

Then Chuck delivered his ultimatum: *This is a crisis situation. And it has reached the breaking point. Get on board, we're all getting tired.*

Phoebe tiptoed back into the conversation: *Could Perla could work a few more shifts?* Perla had been providing support to Dad and Teresa for the last couple of years.

But Deirdre nixed that: *I've already added more hours.* And from her tone, presumably we couldn't afford more. Then she rhymed off a series of calamities that could befall Dad if we didn't get him 24/7 care:

He could suffer a stroke or a heart attack.

He could get robbed after going to the bank with his wallet full of cash.

He could get hit by a car crossing the busy street.

He could take the wrong medications.

He could break his hip if Teresa pushed him.

I didn't believe that any of these dire events were likely but the claim that Teresa at 4 foot 6 inches could be a physical threat to Dad seemed especially odd. Just reading Deirdre's list of imaginary tragedies made me exhausted. No wonder they were burning out. They believed that Dad was suffering from serious dementia. But I didn't. Dad may have slipped, but he certainly hadn't fallen off the deep end.

Then Deirdre berated us for using her "see attached" update as a springboard for family chit-chat: *I have a long list of things to accomplish today, including picking up Teresa within the next hour. End of discussion.*

CHAPTER THIRTEEN

Behind My Back

October 1, 2013

I FEARED THAT DAD WAS BEING SET UP FOR SOMETHING HE didn't want.[1]

This was weighing on my mind as I spoke with a reporter from *Inside Climate News*. We were discussing my upcoming show in Washington and Canada's efforts to silence environmental voices. Of course, I didn't mention the new battle looming in my life.

With the interview done, I headed out for my regular five-mile walk. Even though it was October 1, it still felt like summer, so I was wearing a lime-green top, grey shorts and running shoes. I walked over to Yonge Street, the main corridor in Toronto; it's a ribbon of asphalt running through the centre of the city from the lake shore through downtown, up to our leafy residential neighbourhood and out to the suburbs and beyond. In our area of North Toronto, Yonge Street was populated with retail storefronts—small grocers, restaurants, dress shops, nail salons, and coffee shops—in low-rise brick buildings. Bill and I had grown up in the area, and we were comfortable there.

I breathed in the fresh air and reminded myself of all the good things in my life. I felt lucky to be busy with so many opportunities. Nevertheless, as I was walking along, I started worrying. Deirdre had taken Dad to the doctor and was pushing to get him placed in a nursing home. I didn't believe her anecdote about Dad's forgetfulness. It seemed like some of my siblings had decided it was time and were making excuses or exaggerating things in order to justify their plans.

To ease my anxiety, I decided to drop by Dad's place to ask him what he wanted. His condo was about a mile away from our home, in a modern six-storey building, right on Yonge Street. He was not expecting me, but I wanted to head off this trouble if I could. I rang the buzzer to his condo and said hello.

"Franny? Is that you?"

Dad liked to call me by my childhood nickname, even though he knew I preferred Franke. I adopted it from my Auntie Frank, who had lived in Vancouver, BC. Sadly, I never met her as she was estranged from her sister, my grandmother. I liked "Franke" much better than my given name, Frances; now almost everybody, except for Deirdre, calls me Franke.

"Yes, Dad. Can I come up for a visit? I won't stay long."

Dad buzzed me up, and I took the elevator to his fourth-floor apartment. He opened the door, looking vigorous. He was wearing a collared golf shirt, a light-blue cashmere sweater and dark slacks. He gave me a warm hug and invited me in, telling me that Teresa was out at her programs. He cleared away the newspapers from the table and straightened the place mats on top of a burgundy tablecloth. His "Lady and the Unicorn" board place mats were a whimsical find from an extended trip Dad and Mom took to Europe decades ago, without Teresa.

Across from the table, there was an ornate French cabinet, an antique heirloom from my grandmother. Dad stored his camera equipment in it, securely locked, along with some mementos and papers. On that same wall, but closer to the entrance, Dad had hung one of my paintings, a large canvas of two dancing, nude figures. It was abstracted, but you could catch the energy of their movement through the swirling brush-strokes and vivid colours.

The condo was comfortable and compact. The main room was open concept, with the kitchen near the entrance and the living room at the far end by the floor-to-ceiling windows. The dining area was in the middle, separated from the kitchen by a small counter. On one side, there was the door to Teresa's bedroom and on the other side was the door to Dad's.

Teresa had weekly music lessons on their upright piano, which stood against one of the living room walls. On its maple top were framed photos of Mom and Dad on their wedding day in 1948. Scattered around the room were dozens of family photos. Our family had been very prolific and by that time, Dad was a grandfather and even a great-grandfather. Teresa was the only one of my siblings who was single.

He offered me a cold drink, but I held up my stainless-steel water bottle. "I'm good, Dad. Brought my water with me." We settled in to talk. Dad was happy to see me and asked about my latest news.

"Things are really hopping," I said. "I've never been busier. Tomorrow night, I'm giving a talk at a tribute to Chinese artist Ai Weiwei at the art gallery. My talk is about the Canadian government's silencing of scientists and dissenting voices—like mine."

Dad chuckled approvingly, "I always knew you were a smart cookie. This doesn't surprise me at all."

And then I told him about my show in Washington, which was scheduled to open in just over a week, but there were complications: the U.S. government was shutting down over a budget fight.

Dad nodded and smiled, "I'm sure it will all work out. I have faith in you." It was a sentiment he often repeated. When I asked for his advice, he would share his opinion and then say, "I know you'll do the right thing. You always do." I figured he said the same thing to all my siblings, but it still made me feel good. I appreciated that he was trusting me to make the right decision.

With the small talk out of the way, I felt ready to ask him the big question, "How are things going for you and Teresa?"

Dad shook his head and looked down. I sensed despair, which was very out of character for him. He was a romantic optimist, even in his law practice. If a married couple showed up asking for a separation agreement, Dad would counsel them on getting back together. I marvelled at that.

Slowly, Dad started to tell me what was bothering him. The day before, he'd visited the doctor with Deirdre and she had asked the doctor to complete the papers for his admission. I could see it was painful for Dad to talk about this, and he was simmering with anger.

"I think that people are working behind my back," he said, looking me straight in the eyes. "I think the kids are trying to send me to an old age home and then send Teresa somewhere."

I was relieved that Dad knew, but what could I possibly say that would help? I figured I could only speak for myself. "Yes, Dad," I answered, "but I'm not in favour of that. I think you should stay here at the condo."

Dad was getting more and more agitated. He continued speaking, his voice getting louder. "I won't allow it. I'll tell you that! I will not go to a nursing home."

I felt sad that my once-strong father had to fight for his right to continue living in his own home. I tried to reassure him, "Dad, I promise you I will do everything I can to help you stay here with Teresa."

"We're a team!" he said with exasperation. "Why can't the kids understand that we help each other? I want to stay here. I want Teresa to stay here with me."

Unfortunately, the "kids" he was referring to (Siobhan, Deirdre and Conrad) had control over his medical and financial affairs. I didn't know what legal power he had retained. All I could tell him was that I supported his wishes. However, Dad was still feeling threatened. He insisted that the power of attorney documents that he signed years ago did not allow people to put him in a nursing home against his will.

"If you kids force me," he said, "I will take legal action to stop you. I will not be forced into an old age home. If necessary, I am telling you, I will exhaust my estate to defend myself."

I took a deep breath. This was good news to my ears. Despite his occasional memory lapses, Dad was aware. I was relieved to see him fighting back. As a retired lawyer, he knew how to defend himself and his threat to change his will made sense. But the fact that he was considering legal action against his own children—my siblings—was heartbreaking.

I told Dad again that I wanted him to stay at the condo as long as possible, and that I would write to my siblings and tell them so. He was happy to hear me say that, but he was still upset. Dad gave me another hug as I left, and I continued on my walk with the worries twisting in my mind.

When I got home, I responded to Deirdre's "list of calamities" email. I wrote a note telling everyone about my visit. I said that Dad was concerned that people were trying to put him in an old age home and send Teresa somewhere. I told them he had threatened legal action to stop this plan.

Dad's wishes were crystal clear. "Dad is adamant that he wants to stay at the condo," I said. "I'd like to see us all work together to make sure that happens."

But the only one who responded was Phoebe. Skillfully, she managed to agree and disagree with me: *It would be wonderful if Dad could continue living at the condo, but it's not realistic. Dad needs a significant amount of support and Deirdre and Chuck are already overburdened. We should work together to solve this as a unified group.*

A unified group to overrule Dad? Phoebe's brush-off only strengthened my resolve.

CHAPTER FOURTEEN

Do Not Talk About That

October 7–10, 2013

"FRANKE JAMES IS ABOUT TO DO THE VERY THING SHE SAYS the government tried two years ago to prevent: take her art and message abroad."[1] My oily American eagle had landed on the front page of the Toronto Star's entertainment section, and they were having fun with my name: "Franke James Goes to Washington."[2] I loved the whistle-blower reference to *Mr. Smith Goes to Washington*. Siobhan, Phoebe, and Teresa were wowed to see it, but Deirdre and Conrad didn't comment.

Earlier that year, I had pitched the idea of a protest art show to the Natural Resources Defense Council (NRDC), a U.S. environmental non-profit. The NRDC was on a mission to convince President Obama to stop the Keystone XL pipeline. A street-level exhibition—showing that Canada was silencing debate on climate change while simultaneously pushing dirty oil—was just what they needed. It was a fun guerrilla tactic against Big-Oil's PR machine.

We had been working for months to make this happen. That summer, I had received an email out of the blue from a writer claiming to be Dr. David Suzuki. I laughed out loud. Who was pulling my leg? I wrote back, "Ha! Wouldn't it be nice?"

"Franke James goes to Washington" as it appeared in the Toronto Star [3]

Five minutes later, the writer responded, "Excuse me? Hmmm, I'm at my cabin on the island. Please call to confirm."

So, I picked up the phone and called to confirm that it really was Suzuki. As soon as I heard his warm deep voice, all the memories came rushing back. As a teenager listening to him on the radio, watching him on TV and, then just a few years ago, seeing one of his public talks. Suzuki told the audience that we were living in a very important time because we were going to determine the fate of the world. He implored everyone in the room to act now, to do it for our children.

It was after that talk that Bill and I had made the big decision to sell our only car. For years, I'd been worrying about the disconnect between my being a climate activist and driving a gas-guzzling SUV. Hearing Suzuki talk was my inspiration to finally deal with it. So, in my story about selling the car, I drew a portrait of him as the mythical green man, a gnarly tree fiercely defending nature itself.

During that first call, Suzuki said he was eager to help. He offered to join my campaign to expose Canada's censorship on climate change matters. I was amazed and grateful. And it all came to be. Here we were, three months later, together in Washington DC, delivering our message to the President of the United States—well, via the media, that is.

At the National Press Club, we were flanked by some of Canada's best-known environmental activists: Tzeporah Berman, Tim Gray, and Danny Harvey. We were ready to deliver our message: Stop the Keystone XL.

Suzuki was the first to speak. With wavy grey hair and wire-frame glasses, Suzuki wore a black cotton shirt embroidered with an Indigenous red orca. His sleeves were rolled up as he leaned towards the microphone. He was the megastar the media wanted to hear from, and he was itching to speak. He pounced.

"There is a systematic attack on science and democracy taking place in Canada. But scientists cannot and will not be silenced. Not when we are facing an irreversible climate catastrophe like the tar sands." With gravitas, he said the evidence documenting the pollution of the tar sands was being suppressed and that we could not trust Prime Minister Harper.[4]

We were aiming at Harper's credibility and his empty promises. The first posters were up on the streets of Washington, and they were getting attention.

It was thrilling to see the posters on the street and read the reactions in the press. Leaders hate to be mocked. My caricature of the Prime Minister as a trench-coat-wearing oil barrel was getting laughs. It was inspired by an article in *The Guardian* that said: "Canada is the dirty old man of the climate world."[5]

Nicolas Kristoff put it well in *The New York Times*, "Authoritarians are pompous creatures with monstrous egos and so tend to be particularly vulnerable to humour. They look mighty but are often balloons in need of a sharp pin."[6]

At the National Press Club in Washington: Bill Burton, David Suzuki,
Franke James, Tzeporah Berman, Tim Gray, and Danny Harvey.

I looked out at the room and saw people quietly scribbling notes. I
hoped that some would side with the planet, but I knew we would not
get an easy ride. *The Globe and Mail*, Canada's self-described "national
newspaper" and voice of the status quo, had sent a reporter. Paul Koring
quipped, "To listen to the panel, America's northern neighbour has
become a repressive regime where free speech is silenced, and the government has aligned itself with the interests of a single industry—oil."[7]

On the face of it, *The Globe* was reporting what we said, but between
the lines it oozed contempt. How could anyone call the government
of Canada *repressive*? As far as *The Globe* was concerned, that was
preposterous.

Yet we had the floor, and this was our best opportunity to convince
President Obama to kill the pipeline. It was my turn to speak.

"Most people don't realize that Canada is censoring and muzzling all
sorts of people," I said. "Most Americans think of Canada as the friendly
neighbour to the north, but the truth is far different. The Canadian government is sacrificing human rights to oil company profits."[8]

"Canada is the Dirty Old Man" poster in Washington

As expected, no one from the Canadian government attended our event. But they did respond. Later that day, the Canadian government announced that they were going to spend $24 million in a "rapid response" advertising blitz to combat the bad press on the tar sands.[9] *The Globe* noted that my "stark" posters were "appearing on a handful of Washington bus shelters in a small, crowd-funded effort intended to counter Ottawa's multimillion-dollar pro–Keystone XL campaign."[10]

Maybe I should have been discouraged, but I was thrilled that our little band of scientists and activists was making them nervous. Despite all the odds, we were getting traction in both Canada and the U.S.

The Hill, Washington's political newspaper, wrote, "Anti–Keystone XL pipeline posters blasting Canada's oil sands and carbon pollution have cropped up on the streets of Washington, DC." In an interview with *The Hill*, I said, "Ironically, being told not to talk about climate change by

"Do Not Talk About Climate Change" poster in Washington

Canada's government was the inspiration for my 'Oh No Canada!' show in DC. We need to talk about climate change, not look the other way and pretend it's not happening."[11]

Although there were many, many people looking the other way on climate change, it was exciting to see my "Do Not Talk" poster in plain sight of Capitol Hill. I had flipped the government's censorship on its head by speaking up—and it felt very good.

CHAPTER FIFTEEN

What If Dad Dies?

October 23, 2013

SIOBHAN WAS FUMING. FOR WEEKS THE FAMILY HAD BEEN silent, which was a relief because I was busy. Finally, we were home in Toronto, and I was sitting on our deck watching the action at our bird feeder. The finches and chickadees were singing, chirping, and almost laughing when suddenly a big blue jay swooped in and chased them off. Typical.

I flipped open my laptop. Managing Teresa's future was back on the family agenda.[1]

I had been asking my siblings to include both Teresa and Dad when planning their futures. This was based on my own sense of fairness and how I would want to be treated. But if I could go back in time, I would arm myself with a phrase that I've heard many times since: "Nothing about us without us."[2] That's the mantra of disability rights activists in their fight for equality and justice. Inclusion advocates Eli A. Wolff and Dr. Mary Hums describe the process: "People with disabilities have a voice that should and must be at the table from the beginning of any planning process and should never simply be an afterthought."[3]

Siobhan had been on the phone with the care agency for Teresa. The caseworker told Siobhan that Teresa was on the list for a group home, but she would never get to the top because she had a large family, and *surely* there must be someone in the family who could take care of her.

Oh, really? Well, that was enough to get Siobhan leapfrogging over the caseworker to call the higher-ups, who essentially told her the same thing. That's how Siobhan came to her unhappy conclusion: *Teresa would never get a group home spot because she has family.* But then, miraculously, Siobhan announced a solution: *A "crisis placement" in a nursing home. The CCAC is on board, and it could happen within two weeks.*

What? Two weeks? My worst fears were coming true. I had hoped that my siblings would drop their plan, but instead, they were racing full speed ahead. Siobhan said that they were also getting Teresa tested for early-onset Alzheimer's disease.

I felt sick. I hadn't seen any evidence of Teresa forgetting stuff.

Then Siobhan raised the stakes: *What if Dad died today? Where would Teresa go?* Siobhan's question was unpleasant but practical. Of course, nobody lives forever. I remembered the play *Rare* and how one of the actors cried about losing their father.

If Dad died today, Teresa would be devastated and would need us more than ever. I would invite her to stay with me until we set up proper support. However, Siobhan insisted that we could not do that. And she repeated her warning: *If you take Teresa for one night, she is yours forever!*

Siobhan said we must do something immediately: *Teresa cannot stay at the condo. If there's a crisis, we don't want to look out-of-touch and foolish. Putting Teresa into a nursing home is not ideal, but it's not terrible.*

I rolled her words over and over in my head. If the situation was reversed, Siobhan would—as Dad would often say—be screaming bloody murder!

CHAPTER SIXTEEN

See the Liability

November 3–6, 2013

FANTASTIC! MY SISTER-IN-LAW, CANDI, WAS FULL OF PRAISE: *This story couldn't be better unless it was about Teresa herself.*[1] The story was about a woman with Down syndrome from Canada's east coast in Halifax, who had just moved in with her older sister. It had parallels to our situation, the main difference being that none of Teresa's siblings— including me—were ready to take her.

The fact that we heard about this story must have been destiny. Bill and I were in Calgary for the launch of my "Do Not Talk About Climate Change" posters. Bill was out for a run when he spotted a billboard about Nicholas, a young man who had a girlfriend, a job, a great life, and Down syndrome.

The poster, which was part of the outreach campaign by the Canadian Down Syndrome Society, challenged everyone to "See the Ability." And for Bill and me, it provoked an epiphany.

When we returned to Toronto we saw the next story in the series. Mary Frances, a woman with Down syndrome, had moved in with her sister Jean after their parents had died. Jean told the story:

The transition from sibling to guardian has been a somewhat bumpy one for myself and Mary Frances. You see, I
am the oldest of six siblings, and Mary Frances is the youngest.... I was taking on the task of caring for my youngest
sister—the family treasure—who has Down syndrome.[2]

This resonated with me. Mom and Dad always treasured Teresa.
Dad often said no matter what happened to him, he wanted Teresa to
be happy. I agreed, but I still couldn't see myself, or any of us, stepping
up for Teresa. And yet I was hopeful that this heartwarming story could
somehow inspire us to do something great for Teresa. When Bill suggested we share the story with my family, I was all for it, relieved that this
was something good to talk about.

"See the Ability!" Bill wrote. "It's Down Syndrome Awareness Week.
And here's a story that everyone will want to read."

Bill, Deirdre replied, *if you and Franke can find it in our hearts to take
Teresa, then you are both blessed.*

I bit my tongue. Deirdre was slyly poking us, knowing full well that
we were not planning to do that.

"Yes," Bill answered, "we are all blessed to have Teresa!" Then he
shared another option: "Teresa and I met another woman with Down
syndrome today. She's five to ten years younger, a big hockey fan (the
Maple Leafs when they're winning), and a little bit more independent.
Apparently, she is living by herself."

Candi played along, cheering for the Maple Leafs and asking: *Is Teresa
looking for a roommate?*

Phoebe joined in, praising Bill for his walks with Teresa, but worried:
But what will happen when the older sister passes away?

I was perplexed by this. Any of us might die before Teresa, but that
shouldn't stop us from helping her now. I tried to redirect things: "Down

Syndrome Awareness Week is an opportunity for us to shift our focus to see what Teresa can do. Our belief in her abilities can help us imagine and actually create a bright future for Teresa, one where she is happy, independent and has friends within the DS community, and the love of all her family."

Candi agreed and spoke glowingly of my mother's dreams for Teresa. Then she said: *When Teresa behaves, she's wonderful. But when she refuses to do what she's told, she's impossible!*

Of course, Teresa is not a child and doesn't like to be bossed around. But still, there was a glimmer of hope. Candi offered to help: *I would be happy to make time if there was something I could do to support Teresa.*

Phoebe sighed: *It would be nice if Teresa could live with one of us, but it's just not realistic.* Then, saying that she was all ears, she quietly deleted Dad from the email chain.

"It would be cool," Bill said, "if we could look at Teresa and see the ability instead of just seeing the liability."

But where would Teresa live? Phoebe asked.

I'd asked Dad and Teresa that many times, and they always came back with the same answer, "At the condo." So, I added Dad back into the email thread. I knew the group would be annoyed, but I wanted him in the loop. I said, "Right now, Teresa and Dad are living together well, and they are a big help to each other. It would be great to have them at the condo as long as possible."

The challenge we were facing was negative thinking. I wanted to blow the doors open—maybe a brainstorming session could help us get unstuck? Bill agreed, so I pitched it to the family by email. I asked each person to imagine "Teresa's best possible future" and answer three questions:

1. What's your Vision?
2. What are the Hurdles?
3. What is the Action Plan?

Phoebe replied first. Her vision was soothing. She imagined Teresa enjoying life, well supported, and protected. Phoebe's hurdles included Dad's declining health and his inability to care for Teresa. Her action plan sounded promising: *Teresa deserves a fulfilling life in an appropriate place.* But her solution was not so upbeat: *We have to put Teresa into a nursing home. There are no other options.*

She was singing the same song as everybody else, but being Phoebe, she added a spoonful of sugar: *If Teresa did go to a nursing home, and she continued with her programs, visiting with her friends, dropping by to see family, she could be quite happy using it as a home base, where she just eats and sleeps.*

I had hoped that our brainstorming session would spark some new ideas. And, to my annoyance, Phoebe had deleted Dad from the conversation again. Undaunted, I forged ahead and asked the others.

Conrad responded next: *Quit wasting time with words! Either step up or shut up.* His response was rude and a sharp departure from the brother who had helped me in the past. I wondered if he was feeling sensitive about his decision not to take Teresa, but I zipped my lips and invited the others to comment.

Hank, my widowed brother-in-law, seemed ticked at me too. *If you think your dad is fine, then you, and your husband Bill, both need to buy tickets to "Reality Ontario."*

This was insulting, but not out of character. He continued: *Your Dad's time is running out. Perhaps the only reason you are unaware of Dad's decline is because you are not on the receiving end of Dad's daily phone calls about his missing keys and other assorted poppycock.*

My head hurt. Conrad was angry. Hank was dismissive. Phoebe sounded like a sunshiny Mary Poppins, but she was pushing the same prescription as the others. Why did I see things so differently? Weren't my siblings raised by the same parents as me? The same ones who had steadfastly refused institutionalization. To me, Dad and Teresa were still doing well. With the right support, I thought they could stay in the condo. It was a choice. Many families keep their loved ones at home right to the very end. Why couldn't we?

Then Hank laid out his plan. First, his vision: *The highest possible standard of health, comfort, and happiness for Dad and Teresa.* Then his hurdles: *Franke, and any others, whose cheery optimism is preventing the family from making the necessary decisions.* And finally, his three-point action plan:

1. *Put Dad in the Veterans' Wing at Sunnybrook Hospital.*
2. *Put Teresa in a nursing home.*
3. *Take me off your mailing list.*

I was gritting my teeth, twitching to straighten him out. Bill tried to calm me down. "Relax. Hank is a clown. His old police buddies must have loved him."

"But look at his action plan!" I said. "It's awful! And he doesn't want to discuss it anymore."

However, the family conversation wasn't over. Candi, in her booming cruise-ship style, jumped in again. Any fond memories of how Mom and Dad had devoted themselves to Teresa seemed forgotten. She accused Dad of ranting and bullying and threatening to lock Teresa up in a nursing home.

Wait, what? Wasn't that what my siblings were threatening to do? And it was so unfair because Dad couldn't object or defend himself as Phoebe had removed him from the email chain. And lest I be tempted to add him again, Candi gave explicit instructions: *DO NOT INCLUDE DAD. This just makes things worse and sabotages the family's exit plan.*

My stomach was in a knot.

"A correction is needed," Bill replied. "Dad has been a wonderful caregiver to Teresa for almost fifty years. He has devoted his life to her. And whenever I have seen him, Dad has treated Teresa wonderfully. Dad certainly deserves our respect. In fact, I think it would be best if both Dad and Teresa were included in this discussion. They are the ones who will be most affected by the 'exit plan.' And their voices should be heard.

No one is denying Dad's dedication to Teresa, Candi insisted. Then she pivoted and pointed her finger at me: *Do you have a plan? If you don't have any practical solutions, you should just step aside. And you'd better listen to the majority, or else this will get very messy.*

I shuddered. Why was the group trying to push us around?

Bill tried to get things back on track. "Candi, glad that you agree that Dad deserves our respect."

By that time, Candi was peeved: *Any further conversations are pointless. Nevertheless, I will continue working with your sisters, who have dedicated themselves selflessly towards producing a happy ending.*

A happy ending?

That's the bottom line. And we all know who will be doing the hard work! Candi ended breezily: *We're off to see the Eagles in concert tonight.*

"Eagles?" Bill replied. "Great! 'Hotel California' is the perfect song for a nursing home." And he added his own riff on its famous line: "You can check in whenever you want, but you can never leave."

CHAPTER SEVENTEEN

Mount Everest

November 4, 2013

"TERESA HAS LOTS OF ABILITY."

"Then take her—"

"Siobhan!" I exclaimed.

"When Dad dies," she said.

"You're being ridiculous."

"No," she said, "take her. Take her!"

"No! You're being ridiculous," I repeated.

I was on the phone with my older sister, and she was jumping on my every word.[1] She knew I had no intention of having Teresa move in with me. She was daring me so I'd back off.

I had called her after getting advice from the Canadian Down Syndrome Society, whose "See the Ability" campaign had sparked our family firestorm. I was keen to tell Siobhan everything they'd told me.[2]

Even though I had grown up with Teresa, I knew I still had to learn how other people with Down syndrome were living. Seeing *Rare* had made me wonder if we were shortchanging Teresa.

The staff at the Down Syndrome Society were upbeat about disability rights. I started researching online and found news stories about a woman with Down syndrome who had been forced into a group home by her parents. Jenny Hatch didn't want to live in a group home and fought back. She went to court to assert her right to decide where she lived. It was a difficult battle, but she won and has become a champion for all people with disabilities.[3]

Now, armed with this knowledge, I felt more optimistic. I was ready to pitch my siblings and give them some realistic options. We were *not* reinventing the wheel. Lots of families were supporting their disabled relatives to live in the community. I was confident we could do it for Teresa, too.

Nevertheless, as I was getting myself mentally prepped to call Siobhan, I started to worry. Why were my siblings so desperate? Could I convince them to change their plans?

I recalled the shock I'd felt two years earlier when I first heard that the government was secretly interfering in my art show. The bureaucrats probably thought I was powerless. That's when I started acting like an investigative journalist, recording all my calls, and filing Freedom of Information (FOI) requests.

The situation with my family felt eerily similar. Did Conrad's and Deirdre's roles as substitute decision-makers *really* allow them to do whatever they wanted—regardless of what Teresa wanted? Things could go very wrong, very fast. I would be kicking myself if the worst happened and I had just stood by and watched.

I was standing at my treadmill desk in the comfort of Darcy's old bedroom. It was a lovely room with a big window looking out onto our backyard and a large skylight on the sloped ceiling that faced the front.

I held the silver recorder in my hand as I weighed the pros and cons. If this all blew up, I would need a witness to what had *really* happened. By now my siblings had stopped answering my emails. It seemed like they didn't want to put stuff in writing. I needed to start creating an audio record. Otherwise, it would just be my word against theirs. I'd be road-kill, and I would have failed to save Teresa.

But still, I was facing a gut-wrenching decision. I knew how to do this. I'd done it before. But I never thought that I'd be put into a situation where I might have to blow the whistle on my own siblings. Was I misinterpreting things? I reminded myself that making a tape was like an insurance policy. I wouldn't need to use it unless things went haywire.

So, with my recorder connected to my phone and these confusing life-changing events swirling around me, I made the decision. I steeled myself, and—still on the phone with Siobhan—I pressed record.

"How am I being ridiculous?" Siobhan asked.

She had done a good job of throwing me off, even before I could get started. I took a quick breath and tried again.

"Let's back up," I said. "We have three options. One, she can go to an old age home. Two, she can go to a group home. Three, she can—"

"There aren't any spaces in group homes," Siobhan declared.

"I'm just telling you," I pushed back. "We have three options—"

"How can that be an option when there are 3,200 people in the same line for group homes? Seventy-two of whom are declared in crisis?"

"Siobhan, listen to me. We have three options—"

"Fine!" She kept talking over me. "A nursing home. A group home—"

"I'm not saying they're all good," I interjected.

"And you want to run a private nursing home at Dad's condo?"

"Guess what? We're not chained to Dad's apartment," I answered. "Not by any means."

"Franke, it's not us saying Teresa has dementia. It's the other people," Siobhan said. "We all want what's best for Teresa. We're all dying at the thought of putting her in an old age home. Not a single one of us wants to do it. But if Dad dies tonight, where will Teresa go?"

I didn't believe they were *dying at the thought,* and I didn't believe that Dad was in imminent danger of passing away. Siobhan was trying to distract me from making alternate plans for Teresa's future. We kept talking and I finally got to option three: "I'm going to investigate the possibility of Teresa living with another person with Down syndrome."

"But with how much supervision?"

"Teresa doesn't need 24/7 care!" I insisted.

Siobhan's voice rose higher and took on an air of authority. "You would allow Teresa to live with another Down syndrome person who is equally mentally handicapped?"

I bristled. She was trying to dismiss Teresa with a label, as if she had no ability to do anything by herself.

Siobhan continued, "You would just abandon the two of them in an apartment to their own devices?"

"There are lots of people with Down syndrome who live on their own," I said. "Why not try this for Teresa?"

"Because we're talking about what Teresa is *capable* of," Siobhan insisted. She sounded like an irritated schoolteacher. "Please explain to me why she's not taking care of her period? Because that's as basic as it gets."

"But—"

"She's not using toilet paper," Siobhan continued. "She's not brushing her own teeth."

I wanted to get Siobhan to see Teresa's potential, but she wouldn't even think about it. And besides, I didn't know if there was *any* truth to what she was saying about Teresa. You certainly don't put someone away because they have poor hygiene. I steered back to my immediate concern.

"It would be nice if we could keep Teresa and Dad together as long as possible."

"I want to keep Dad in the condo, period," Siobhan said. "I don't want Dad in a nursing home. I've looked at two in the last five days, and it would kill Dad to go into either one of them."

She paused and then said, "We're gambling. And that's the part that's killing me. Dad could die today. Dad's senility could get so bad that the police are called, and he's carted off to Sunnybrook."

Carted off to Sunnybrook? What a weird thought! Who would call the police on Dad?

"There has to be a plan in place for Teresa," she said. "And Teresa has to be placed before Dad dies."

"Siobhan, you know what?" I said, not hiding my frustration. "My gut feeling is that as much as you and Deirdre and Phoebe are all pushing the idea of the old age home, I don't think it's the right choice for Teresa. We have to—"

"Do you think any of us like it?" she interjected.

"I haven't finished speaking," I snapped. "I'm looking at options because I don't believe that a nursing home is the right choice."

"Why weren't you looking at these options with me two years ago when I started?" Siobhan asked. "When I did this completely on my own. Where were you? You're acting like I, suddenly, decided to put Teresa away. I've looked at everything!"

"Siobhan," I said, "you think that a nursing home is the best option. But I don't think it is. And I'm entitled to my opinion."

"Of course you are," she answered, "and what I'm saying is—"

"I'm looking at options that are different from yours. And it's not a useless exercise."

"I never said it was useless," she said.

"The option that I'm considering, which I think is possible, is that Teresa would live with another person with Down syndrome."

"You don't think I looked into that?" she said. "I looked seriously at it. And I thought, Oh, this could be fantastic for Teresa, until I found out what the pitfalls were."

The pitfalls?

"It would involve tremendous family support," she said. "This is beyond us because we're all old. We're all retiring, and we can't be monitoring Teresa while she lives independently. Sure, Teresa can move into an apartment, but I don't want to be the point person."

"Your plan is a very neat solution. It's the *easiest* thing for all of us," I said, taunting her.

"It's only good if it works for Teresa," she said, catching my sarcasm. "I feel such guilt because of Dad," she said, opening up a little. "I'm furious with Dad and Mom. This is *their* child. Dad should damn well have planned for Teresa, and he didn't. What he did was deliberate. And it was all designed so that one of us would take her."

It was obvious that Siobhan wasn't happy with Dad's plan for Teresa, *but it was his plan*. He wanted one of us to take Teresa.

"I'm so furious at being put in this position," Siobhan said. "I can't sleep at night. I'm having nightmares, and they all revolve around Teresa and Dad dying."

Then she told me about her fears. About how she had been told that on the day Dad dies, we would need to drop Teresa off at a fire station or homeless shelter. Because if any one of us took her into our home, Teresa would immediately lose her spot on the crisis list. When she heard this, Siobhan asked them, "What kind of a monster do you think I am? That I would put my sister in a homeless shelter?"

I was dumbfounded. We were all well off. There was no way we could let that happen. But I held my tongue, and she continued.

"But the agency people just said it again, if you take her home—even for just one night—she's out of the placement queue." And so, Siobhan reached her inevitable conclusion: "Teresa has to be placed before Dad dies. I have looked at every single option and this is the one that has come up by default. I don't like it. And I feel terrible for Teresa. But unless someone says, 'I want to take Teresa and have her live with me for the rest of my life,' we're screwed."

I responded bluntly, "Siobhan, I really don't believe you."

"Then take over," she replied. "I didn't spend the last two years on this to have you come in at the last minute with 'I have an idea' because I already had that idea."

I batted back. "There's something called *consensual decision-making*, but you're not doing it."

"When you first came up with this," Siobhan replied, "I said that I had already looked into it. It's not viable. But then I told you, 'Go. Run with it!' "

"I am looking into it right now!" I said.

"Run with it," Siobhan said. "But you're running up a street with a dead end."

All I could think was that a nursing home was the real dead end. On average, people who moved into a nursing home died within 2.3 years.[4]

"Do you think I want to put her in a nursing home with ninety-year-old people?" Siobhan asked. "Do you actually think that's what I want?"

I stammered, "You know what? The thing is…"

"No," she interrupted. "I want to bring Teresa to my house. And I want her to live with me because I really love her."

Long pause. I waited, surprised to hear Siobhan's wish. Where was this leading? Her children had moved out, so Teresa could take one of their bedrooms. I imagined Siobhan waking up every morning, making an extra egg and more coffee, and then sharing breakfast with Teresa as they discussed their plans for the day. It was certainly possible, and it could work.

"I can't stand the thought that she's going to leave the only home she's known with Dad and go into a seniors' house," Siobhan said. "It's tearing me apart."

A seniors' house? I winced at her euphemism. "I suggest that we look at this other option," I said, trying to stay focused in the midst of her conflicting statements.

"This is higher than Mount Everest," Siobhan said. "This is insurmountable. It will not work."

She just kept saying *no.*

"Okay. That is what you believe," I said. "You believe it firmly. And you know what? I don't believe it at this point."

"You don't believe it because you haven't done it."

"So, I'm going to have to look into it."

But Siobhan wouldn't let go. "I've talked to all these agencies, and I've asked, 'Where do they go?' "

"We're going around in circles, Siobhan."

"Hold on," she said. "What they said is, disabled adults usually end up living with their siblings—because there's nothing else."

"The fact is that Teresa could live in an apartment with someone else," I said. "It is a viable option. And we should look into it."

"Go and look at it," Siobhan said. "I wish you well."

CHAPTER EIGHTEEN

They Can't Send Her Back

November 11, 2013

IT WAS TRICKY FINDING MY WAY THROUGH THE LABYRINTH, especially as my siblings hadn't provided any contacts.[1] However, I was piecing together the social services puzzle and discovering new options: Teresa could live in a HomeShare, which was a government-funded program to help people live in the community. Wow! It could be a great fit for Teresa.

The agency people suggested that we start with a person-directed plan. This was like the brainstorming session Bill and I had with my siblings, but with one big difference: the "person" is an active participant. It embodied the slogan, "nothing about us without us." Teresa would be helped to set her own goals, identify the hurdles, and create her own action plan.

So, bolstered with this new-to-me information, I called my sister Siobhan again. It was not new to her. "I have been dealing with these people for three years, so you're not going to pick up anything that I didn't." Then she dismissed person-directed planning as too *airy-fairy*.

I started to tell her about alternative housing options. "Teresa would live with three or four adults in a—"

"Been there. Next."

"She could be on the list for HomeShare. To me, this is a better option than a nursing home."

"But they are not going to incorporate Teresa into their life. They're merely to provide a bed and food, and that's it," Siobhan answered. "It does not sound like a very nice environment."

"But Siobhan, I don't think the nursing home sounds like a very nice environment."

"Have you been to one?"

"I've been doing research on—"

"No, no, no," she interrupted again. "Have you been to one?"

She was bringing this up because she knew I didn't go on their tour. I challenged her, "This would be a public nursing home? We wouldn't be paying for it, would we?"

"They pick up the full cost," Siobhan confirmed.

"There's a big difference between the fancy ones and the public ones, where she would just get basic living."

"But you realize that she's not eligible for the upscale ones?"

"We couldn't afford it anyways," I scoffed.

"Why not?" Siobhan asked. "We can afford absolutely anything by selling the condo. I don't think any of us care if we inherit a cent. We want the money being used to take care of Dad and Teresa."

I was skeptical. I said, "She would be much better off in an apartment or a group home."

"The problem with the group home or apartment is that if it doesn't work out, they will send her back. She still belongs to us. They can't send her back from a nursing home."

What? It sounded like she wanted to get rid of Teresa permanently. I objected, "Teresa won't qualify unless—"

"She already has qualified."

"On what basis?"

"She's forty-nine years old and has Down syndrome."

"You can't do that! What about Teresa's human rights?"

This didn't make sense to me. I knew that Teresa's rights were protected by both the Canadian Charter[2] and the UN Convention on the Rights of Persons with Disabilities.[3] "But Teresa has a legal right to decide where she lives," I said. "Have you thought about having a conversation with her?"

"Franke," Siobhan said slowly, "Do I seem like I'm just incredibly stupid?"

I had hit a nerve.

Siobhan's voice was hurt and angry. "Do you realize you've challenged me on my research? You've challenged me on my compassion for Teresa. And on my motives."

"Siobhan, I'm serious about Teresa."

"This is terrible that you're doing this to me! Of course I've talked to Teresa."

"And what did Teresa say?" I asked. "That she'd rather live in a nursing home?"

Siobhan mimicked Teresa's voice, making it sound like she was a child: "I want to live with you, Siobhan." Then she asked, "What did you think she would say?"

"We've got to help Teresa understand that staying with us is not an option," I said.

"It will be heartbreaking," Siobhan said. "This is going to be the most horrible thing that we do as a group."

I gasped. This was getting worse and worse. I would *not* be part of that group.

"Teresa is going to hate wherever she goes," Siobhan continued, "because it's not her home. She's going to want to go back to the condo to live with her daddy. Or she's going to want to live with one of us."

Of course Teresa would want to stay with us, because we had always been the centre of her life.

"Well," I said, trying to find a way through this very disturbing conversation, "I would like to see us all come together and examine the options. The best option is something like a group home or an apartment with a supportive roommate."

"Hold on," Siobhan said firmly, "I think that's beyond her at this point. She needs supervision. She's never left alone. And I don't think she should be—"

"Teresa doesn't necessarily need as much supervision as you think," I insisted.

"If Dad went to the hospital, would you be comfortable leaving her in the condo alone?"

"We all need to decide together and—"

"Unfortunately, Franke," Siobhan interrupted, "we can talk to Deirdre and Conrad, but they're the ones who make the decisions about Teresa."

"But Teresa has the legal right to decide what happens," I objected.

"No, she doesn't," said Siobhan, sounding solemn.

"Yes, she does!" I protested.

"And why would you think that?" Siobhan asked.

"Because the power of attorney does not take over her legal right to decide where she lives," I told her.

"And when would it take over?" Siobhan asked.

"If Teresa was declared incompetent?" I guessed.

"That is what has been done to Teresa," she said.

"When did you decide that?" I was shocked.

"I did not decide it," Siobhan answered. And then slowly, emphasizing each word, she said, "I did not do this. The CCAC interviewed her. The CCAC determined that Teresa could not decide for herself."

I was shocked to hear this. I gathered that Deirdre had some forms signed for Dad, but I didn't realize they'd done it for Teresa too. "Teresa has a lot more potential than you're recognizing!"

"Listen, I think Teresa is a fabulous person," Siobhan explained. "And don't get me wrong. I am not trying to incarcerate her."

"Siobhan," I said, "nursing homes are a horrible solution."

"Why would you say that to me?" Siobhan asked.

"Because I'm looking into it!"

"We own three nursing homes!" Siobhan retorted. "I mean, do you have no respect for us at all?"

What? I didn't know that Siobhan and Jared owned a nursing home, let alone three. This was a shocker ... and it explained why she knew so much.

I pushed those thoughts aside. "Why are you so determined to get Teresa into a nursing home?"

"Because eventually, if she lives to be eighty-five, Teresa will need a nursing home," Siobhan said.

It was mind-boggling to suggest placing Teresa more than thirty-five years in advance. I blurted out, "But there's all sorts of controversy about—"

"The decision is Deirdre and Conrad's," Siobhan snapped. "Whatever they decide, they decide. I do not have a vote. And I don't withhold information." She paused, then added crossly, "As the owner of three nursing homes, I think they serve a purpose. I don't think it would necessarily be a bad thing for Teresa."

CHAPTER NINETEEN

Are You in My Corner?

November 12, 2013

SIOBHAN'S BOMBSHELL—THAT TERESA HAD BEEN FOUND "incompetent"—rattled me.[1] And it seemed like she was the brains behind the whole thing, and yet she said it was Conrad and Deirdre who were making the decisions.

I didn't believe what they were saying about Teresa, so I asked them to show me the "psychological report" claiming that Teresa had Alzheimer's. After four days, and two reminders, Conrad finally responded. He didn't have it and they wouldn't get it for months.

Then I asked for the report in which Teresa was declared incompetent. Conrad didn't have that either.

I shot back. "We need full disclosure to make the right decision for Teresa." I was not under any illusion that Conrad and Deirdre would suddenly embrace transparency, but I had lots of questions.

The warning signs were everywhere and making front page headlines. The *Toronto Star* wrote, "Abuse and rape uncovered in nursing homes." The article cited 3,200 incidents, including a report about a woman with dementia who had been raped in her bed.[2] The complaints were similar to the abuse that disabled residents had suffered in the institutions of years past.

Conrad, Deirdre and Siobhan didn't seem concerned, but maybe Phoebe would be, especially if she read the ghastly stories. I sent her the *Toronto Star* article, and I called to ask if she'd read it.

"I saw it," she said, "but I didn't look at it. I was so busy at work today."

"It was only one of many stories," I said, disappointed. "The sum-up on nursing homes is that they're overcrowded, underfunded and understaffed."

"Oh, I agree 100 percent, but it's the only thing we've got." She hesitated a moment, then asked, "Is there anything else available?"

"Of course!" I said. "There are lots of other options. Group homes are definitely a possibility."

"Not according to Siobhan."

"Siobhan has blinders on," I said. "And this is not like a private nursing home where you'd pay thousands a month. This is publicly funded."

"I know it's awful, but—"

"It's a horror show!" I said. "And if you research nursing homes in the *Toronto Star*—people are bullied and abused."

"I believe it," she said. "But the only thing is: do we have an alternative?"

"There are so many other alternatives!"

"If you guys can find one, you'll be heroes. Everybody would love it!"

I doubted that but I let it pass. "Guess what? I did find something. A housing program called LIGHTS. I emailed Siobhan, but she hasn't responded."

"I think she was going away this week."

"Whatever. LIGHTS is just one of many options. And now that I've looked into nursing homes, I wouldn't even consider it for Teresa."

"That's why we were trying to encourage people to visit before any decisions were made. And you were super, super busy with your books at that point."

That was her spin. Yes, I was busy, but I had *refused* to go because it was wrong for Teresa.

Phoebe was rejigging the story to smooth over my objections. She continued, "But the nursing home was so awful. Awful. And Deirdre felt the same way." And then she wiggled and backtracked. "They're not all awful, though. Some are better than others, apparently, but I don't know."

My sister was a master at waffling. When I objected again, she said, "That's great! You're so creative. And if you can find something that's good for Teresa, it would be wonderful. Everybody would love it. But it has to be something that actually exists."

I ignored her insinuation that I was on a wild goose chase.

"Number one," I said, "we should be sitting down with Teresa and bringing her into the conversation. So that she can start thinking about moving out in the same way we did when each of us moved out."

"I don't think we'd have a hard time convincing Teresa to do that," Phoebe said. "But we'd have to find a place for her."

"That's why I need to know that you're in my corner. Because it seems like Deirdre, Conrad and Siobhan are all opposed."

"I don't think Deirdre is," Phoebe said.

"Good," I said, doubtfully.

"I don't think Siobhan is opposed either."

"I'm looking into the group home option," I said, hoping to sway her. "I've started contacting people. Teresa has so much potential. She just needs more encouragement and a positive environment."

"Franke, go! Run! If you can do it, fabulous!"

"But we need full disclosure from Siobhan and Deirdre."

"They haven't been answering emails," Phoebe said. "I think they're afraid to put anything in an email."

I was glad Phoebe had noticed this too. Then I asked about the other troubling news. "Siobhan told me that Teresa has been"—I hesitated for a moment—"declared incompetent?"

Phoebe answered in a hushed voice, "I know!"

"Is this true?" I asked. Siobhan had sounded so final. I was worried that Teresa had lost her right to make her own decisions, even about ordinary things, like where to live or what to eat.

"I don't think it is," Phoebe said. "Listen, I love Siobhan dearly, but sometimes she says things to me, and…What is the truth? I don't know. And it's the same thing when people say Teresa has early Alzheimer's. Where are they getting this from?"

"I don't know," I said, relieved to hear her echoing my doubts.

"And I don't either," Phoebe said. "I think that this social worker asked Teresa some questions, and she wasn't…I don't know."

"I think that Siobhan is doing her a disservice by getting Teresa declared incompetent."

"Siobhan is trying to protect Teresa by getting her put under government care," Phoebe said. "So, we've got to give her credit for that."

I skirted that thorny issue and said, "Bill and I are trying to find another solution."

"Teresa might be better off in an apartment with a roommate," Phoebe said.

"Yes!" I said enthusiastically. "There are lots of other options. We can do much better."

"Franke, you say that now, and I applaud you. But you may end up like Siobhan and Deirdre throwing up your hands and saying, Oh my God! The only thing we have is a nursing home."

"I don't think so," I said firmly. I would move heaven and earth to prevent that.

"Well, I hope that's not the case," Phoebe said.

"We need to have full disclosure," I repeated. "How much money do we anticipate that Teresa will have?"

"Deirdre can give you that information," Phoebe answered. "But if you call Deirdre, just don't get all hyper with her. Just be very calm because she can fly off the handle. She does have a lot of knowledge about the finances." Then Phoebe shared her thoughts about Dad's future estate. "Everybody has said they're perfectly willing to let all of Dad's money go to Teresa. I don't think anybody's waiting for any inheritance. As far as I'm concerned, Teresa can have everything."

"That's good," I said. Our mother always said that we should never expect to inherit much money because Teresa needed it. I returned to the main point: "I can't investigate these options unless they share the information with me."

"You're going to have to phone Deirdre," Phoebe said. "I think she will be very forthcoming. And I think Siobhan is the same. They just don't want to do stuff by email."

"Talking with you is encouraging," I said. "It's giving me a feeling that it's worth investigating."

"Oh my God! Of course it is!"

"Because, when I talk to Siobhan, it's like the nursing home is the only option."

"I know," Phoebe said, "but we always have to remember that's just the way Siobhan thinks. And she *suckers* me in so often."

I nodded as she continued.

"And it's always great to talk to you because you're just so positive, and you've got so much energy. Deirdre, on the other hand, can flip out like ... You never know. But recently, she has been pretty good with me."

"Good," I said, still hoping that despite her vacillations, she was in my corner. "The point is that none of us want Teresa living in our homes. That's the bottom line. Right?"

"Yes," Phoebe agreed.

"And I don't want to see Teresa going to a nursing home. That would just be death!"

"Yeah."

"She could very easily be rebellious in that environment. She could end up in a lot of trouble. This is not good for her. This is *not* what we should be doing."

"Franke, I agree with you. And if you can figure out something, seriously, it would be fabulous. Just fabulous!"

We ended the call. I appreciated being able to confide in her.

Phoebe was the older sister I had always turned to in times of trouble. When I was little, she would babysit. One day when I was young, maybe four years old, my parents were out and Phoebe was in charge. I was in the living room playing a rocking game. I was perched up high on the back of our chesterfield, with a skipping rope around my waist. Deirdre was holding the other end of the rope. The game was for me to lean back as far as possible, and then she would pull me back up. I went back and forth like a seesaw, getting into a good rhythm and giggling. This was fun until the rope slipped and I tumbled backward behind the couch, hitting my head on the cast iron radiator. Crack! I screamed, and blood gushed out.

Phoebe came racing into the living room and carried me into the kitchen. She put ice on my throbbing head and dialed for help. I was drifting off. But through my foggy consciousness, I felt her shaking me and calling me. I can still hear voices urging me: "Don't fall asleep or you might die." I was lying on the kitchen floor as I opened my eyes and looked up. Phoebe was holding me in her arms, comforting me. "You'll be okay," she seemed to say. And I knew I would be fine. They took me to a doctor, and I got a bunch of stitches and a stern lecture from my mother, but I will never forget that bang on the head.

Suddenly what Phoebe said—this social worker asked Teresa some questions—hit me. Did Siobhan tell us the social worker was coming to do a competency test for Teresa? That got me searching through my emails. I found two.

A few months earlier, Siobhan told us that the CCAC had determined that *in their opinion* Teresa could not make her own decisions about going into a nursing home. I shrugged that off. I didn't want Teresa in a nursing home anyway. But I totally missed the significance. I assumed that the CCAC wanted to meet with Dad about providing support for them to stay at the condo.

In that email, Siobhan also laid down the law for Conrad: he must tell Dad he was not taking Teresa. The CCAC insisted on it since Dad was legally in charge.

But something didn't add up. Siobhan had just told me that Conrad and Deirdre had control of Teresa's powers of attorney. How the heck did they remove Dad? And how the hell did they get themselves appointed? Maybe if I offered, I could be Teresa's attorney?

CHAPTER TWENTY

A Bulletproof Plan

November 13, 2013

"THERE'S A VACANCY COMING UP." CONRAD WAS ON THE phone, telling me how things work.[1] "But they don't look at it like that. They look at the worst-case scenario."

Bill and I had spoken with PLAN Toronto, a non-profit agency that helps people with disabilities live in the community. They were brimming with ideas for Teresa. I called Conrad, but as far as he was concerned, these were just empty promises and false hopes; Teresa had been on the wait-list for more than five years.

Now, Conrad said, the family had the silver bullet: "Having a ninety-one-year-old father, who is in crisis, is a worst-case scenario. It can't go on the way it's going. Dad is in no shape to take care of Teresa, and it's getting worse."

While I could agree it was getting harder for Dad, I challenged him on Teresa. "She has lots of opportunity ahead of her."

"She does, Franke," Conrad agreed. "But the thing is, initially, Candi and I were going to take Teresa. Then Siobhan said if you take Teresa, she's yours for the rest of your life."

"Okay," I said. That's exactly what Dad expected.

"Siobhan was not lying," Conrad said. "Every single person we've talked to has said the same thing. We were just going to take her for a short term, and then integrate her into a different thing. But it cannot be done."

That's not what Dad expected. And he'd promised financial help so Teresa wouldn't be a burden.

"And so," he continued, "we have to say we are in a crisis situation and that it's getting worse every day."

"But there are group homes rather than nursing homes," I protested.

"Yeah, that's fine. But we've been through this umpteen times," he said. "You have to go to one of these meetings to believe it. You're dealing with about five or six different organizations all at the same time. No one wants to take responsibility and ownership. You just beat your head against a wall."

"So, who has power of attorney for Teresa right now?" I asked.

"Deirdre and I." Then, unexpectedly, Conrad said, "If you're interested and want to take over the power of attorney, I have no problem."

"I am interested," I responded. "I've discussed it with Bill, and we would like to do it."

There was a long pause.

The power of attorney is the legal tool that Conrad and Deirdre were insisting gave them the authority to make all the decisions for Teresa. The way it works is that you appoint someone to act as your attorney, and they become your substitute decision-maker. For example, I could appoint my husband, Bill, as my attorney. If I was in dire health, then Bill would act as my representative, speaking with doctors. And because I would have appointed Bill as my attorney, he could make all the necessary decisions for my health and finances. Of course, the attorney is supposed to be guided by the person's known wishes and always act in that person's best interests.

Since presumably Teresa had been declared "incapable" by the CCAC, she could not decide where she lived. So now the person designated on her power of attorney document would have to make that decision. From what I knew, Teresa had originally appointed Dad as her power of attorney. But somehow, over the last three months, Conrad and Deirdre had taken over that authority. I didn't understand how it worked—and I had never seen Teresa's power of attorney documents—but I assumed that if they could change it once, they could change it again.

"We're very concerned," I said.

"And you don't think we are?"

I scrambled, "I think that you are, but I'm just saying—"

"Years have gone into getting to the stage we're at now. And we are so close—"

"But have you done any research into nursing homes?" I asked.

"Yes, I have. But don't forget. We have Jared at our disposal. Jared *owns* three nursing homes," Conrad said, with emphasis. I figured that Conrad was implying that Teresa would get special treatment because of family connections. But that didn't make me feel any better.

"I'm horrified to think that Teresa could go into a nursing home and—"

"She cannot live in a group home," Conrad interrupted.

"Why?" I said pointedly.

"We've gone down that road."

"Why?" I repeated.

"Because she is mentally about the age of five," he said.

That's not true. Teresa reads and writes. Labelling Teresa as having the "mental age of a young child" was insulting and it disempowered her. The whole theory of mental age is harmful. For many decades it's been used to discriminate against people with intellectual disabilities.[2] The theory makes them into perpetual children and denies them civil rights which they're entitled to as adults, such as minimum wage.

Conrad continued: "She cannot be left unsupervised. It's more than abundantly clear. And she's failed every assessment that she's taken."

I wondered what assessments he was referring to. In the real world, Teresa had lived successfully with Dad for forty-nine years.

"Well, they have different types of group homes," I suggested.

"We've looked at them," Conrad answered. "Teresa is not a candidate. Trust me."

I was shaking my head. They had come up empty-handed, and yet they didn't want me to investigate? I said, "Bill and I are both interested in solving this. If you want to sign over your power of attorney to me, that would be great."

"Okay. I'll discuss it with Deirdre."

"It seems like she's under a lot of pressure—"

"She *is* under a lot of pressure!"

"Then she wouldn't mind giving up her power of attorney." I waited.

"I will talk to her about it."

CONSIDERING THE SHAKY ground that we were on, it's ironic that I have Conrad to thank for the most significant romantic relationship in my life.

As a university student I went to art school in the Maritimes. Each spring I would return to Toronto and get a summer job. I was a gopher at my dad's law office, a waitress at a beer garden, and a smiling order-taker at McDonalds. But, of course, there were long summer evenings. After my third year in art school, Conrad offered to introduce me to the brother of his new girlfriend. They figured we'd get along because we were both artists. Her brother had just returned from a year of travelling in Europe and Africa. He sounded intriguing, and I agreed to meet him at a bar. I had a friend with me, and we could make a quick exit if necessary.

When we arrived at the bar, he was sitting there with one of his friends. Bill got up and shook my hand and I thought, Wow, what a nice guy and what beautiful blue eyes. How come I've never met him before? I was charmed but still wary. My friend and I sat down, and we ordered drinks. Everything was going smoothly; we were laughing and joking until I knocked over a tall glass of beer. It was embarrassing. I'm not usually clumsy. Unfortunately, the beer spilled all over Bill and soaked his jeans. But Bill just laughed like it was no big deal. By the end of the evening Bill reached over and put his hand on top of mine. Holding it firmly he looked into my eyes and said very directly, "We should go out together soon."

By the end of that summer, Bill and I were head over heels in love. On the other hand, Bill's sister and Conrad had broken up. But I'm glad they dated because Bill was a keeper. We married the next summer. Our interests and values have always been aligned.

THE NEXT DAY, Conrad called. "You will never be the power of attorney. You can't be."

"That doesn't sound right," I said. "People do it all the time."

"You can't do it now," Conrad insisted. "Go ahead and call Deirdre. That's what she told me." And with that, he swept the issue off the table. Then he rhymed off a dizzying, alphabet-soup list of organizations. I had no idea what the acronyms stood for or how the various organizations fit together.

"Can you put the names into an email for me?" I said. "You're rambling them off very quickly."

"I can't. I'm not going to waste my time," he answered. "Deirdre and I have put a lot of time and effort into this. We are working in Teresa's best interest. But you've never offered to help with this until now, at the eleventh hour. And it's too late."

"Conrad, for many years, you swore up and down that you—"

"Yes, I was going to take Teresa," he said brusquely.

"And now you're not," I said. "So, this is November. You told us that news in the summer."

"Yes."

"So you dropped this at the eleventh hour—not me."

"Why have you never come forward?" Conrad challenged, his voice rising. "When we asked, you never volunteered. Never! Once. Only once..."

"That's not true," I said. "We've done lots of things."

"Walking?" Conrad scoffed.

"Yes!" I said. "The Terry Fox Walks and the Sick Kids Walks."

"Wonderful." It's hard to say "wonderful" with irritation, but Conrad managed to do it. "That's wonderful, but that's all you've ever done."

"Teresa's physical fitness is much higher now than five years ago," I insisted. His dismissal of our weekly walks was irksome. He placed more importance on visits to the doctor than on getting Teresa out walking in the fresh air.

"That's wonderful," he said. "Do you honestly think that Deirdre and I will do anything contrary to what you would do for Teresa?"

For a split second, I hesitated. But feigning politeness would not help Teresa, so I answered honestly and bluntly: "Yes, I do."

"I'm sorry if you think that way, but you don't have a choice."

"Conrad," I said, "it seems that Teresa has been declared incompetent?"

"Teresa *is* incompetent," Conrad insisted. "She's been incompetent her entire life. She is mentally handicapped."

I flinched. He was so dismissive. But I didn't correct him. I acknowledged it as his description of Teresa's intellectual disability. "She is," I said, "but she's not incompetent. She could live with a supportive roommate, but she needs coaching."

"That might have happened in 1980," he said.

"The coaching that Bill and I have given her has made a world of difference," I said. "Teresa's in better shape. And she's happier about going for walks than ever before."

"That's great," he said dryly.

"Why don't I send you some links to the nursing home articles that I've read?" I asked. "You will be concerned, too."

He paused for a moment, then asked, "Do you and Bill want Teresa for the rest of your lives?"

"We would like to help Teresa."

"As do we all. Answer the question!"

I knew that Conrad was goading me. But I would not be pressured into thinking that we had run out of time to do the right thing. "We can do so much better."

"The whole thing is," Conrad said, "Disability Services of Ontario, the DSO, does not want Teresa placed in a seniors' home."

That was good to hear. But his wording caught my ear. He used same the euphemism Siobhan had used.

Then Conrad described their extremely long meetings with the DSO. At the big meeting Deirdre had told everyone that when Dad died, they would have no choice but to drop Teresa off at the nearest fire station. The staffers objected, saying we had a large family. But Deirdre kept saying no and warning that Dad's placement at K-Wing, the veterans nursing home, was imminent. And finally, the DSO relented. "The bottom line," Conrad said, "Teresa has now been put in crisis mode."

"There are so many other solutions," I said with disappointment. Then I asked, "Have you contacted the people at LIGHTS?"

"I have no idea," he said.

"LIGHTS could help us find a home and support Teresa in our community. They do this all the time. Just imagine the ideal: Teresa would live in a comfortable apartment with a supportive roommate."

"You'd have to come up with a remarkable person because you're talking 24/7," Conrad said. "And even with all these grandiose ideas, it won't work until we get over the initial hurdle—Teresa has to be placed before Dad dies. Period. And to get the ball going, Teresa has to get thrown into the system."

"I hope we're agreed that Teresa will not go into a nursing home?" I said.

"Short-term she may," Conrad said. "We'll have no choice about that."

I was not making any progress. "I see a lot more ability in Teresa," I said. "She has more on the ball than you're giving her credit for. We should be trying to give her the best possible—"

"That is what we have been doing!"

"A nursing home is not a reasonable place for a forty-nine-year-old."

"Teresa has to be placed before Dad dies," Conrad insisted. "The DSO is trying to scare us right now. They're waiting for one of us to say we'll take her. That's when the whole thing falls apart."

"Personally, I think she would be a lot better off at the condo with a supportive—"

"You can't do that until after Dad dies!" he snapped.

"Maybe she could stay at Dad's condo permanently?"

"Well, she can't," he replied. "I want to see what the state can provide, before I make a decision to turn this money over to keep Teresa in a condo."

This money, which Conrad controlled, was *Dad's money,* and Dad wanted Teresa to stay at the condo.

"If you read the news articles, the investigations into the nursing home industry are—"

"Shocking," Conrad interrupted. "I agree with you."

"It is shocking! It's like, how can we set Teresa up to get bullied and sexually abused?"

"We have to be an active part of her life," he said. "And if she's not okay, get her the hell out of there! And in the nursing homes that we went to, like Wheiry Lodge, the people were so bloody old. No one could abuse Teresa. They couldn't catch her. They're all in walkers and wheelchairs."

"Conrad, you think that's funny. Just last week, there was a news story about a guy who murdered one of the other residents."[3]

"Yes, I did see that. We have to be very vigilant. Look, we're up against the wall. We can't do anything. We have a plan in place. And we must wait to see what the government can come up with."

I continued to object. "Keeping Teresa in an apartment with a supportive roommate is—"

"You can't do that before Dad dies!" Conrad insisted. "We need to have a bulletproof thing in place. And we do. We can do all kinds of things once Teresa has been placed, but we can't do anything before that." And then he tossed me a crumb, "Go see LIGHTS. See what they come up with. I would be willing to sit down and talk with them."

CHAPTER TWENTY-ONE

Crisis at the Condo

November 21, 2013, 6:30 p.m.

C ONRAD SLAMMED DOWN THE PHONE. I DIDN'T KNOW WHAT his problem was, but I needed to talk to my brother.[1] So, I called him back.

I was excited. Bill and I had spoken with LIGHTS that morning. They had lot's of housing ideas for Teresa. Now I needed Conrad, or my sister Deirdre, to sign the consent form. Teresa's care agency would not speak to me or LIGHTS without getting my sibling's consent.

Although Conrad had blasted me, I thought perhaps he was having a bad day or didn't understand that I just needed his signature. It would take him two minutes. I dialed him again. When he picked up, I said, "So, I wanted to ask you about—"

"Go and deal with your father right now!" Conrad's voice was getting louder and more strained with every word. I could hardly believe it was him.

"Conrad?" I asked.

"GO AND DEAL WITH DAD," he exploded. "I am not having a discussion until YOU see what we are putting up with!"

"I have spoken to Dad," I insisted.

"Go and help Phoebe! OR FORGET IT! I WILL NEVER TALK TO YOU AGAIN!" Conrad was yelling at the top of his lungs. "THIS ENDS NOW!!"

I heard the click and the beep-beep of the dial tone. What a jerk.

Conrad's anger was confusing. On the surface, he was upset because Dad was upset about a missing photo. The mystery of the missing photo had been going on for a few days. I had already spoken to Dad and Teresa about it. It didn't seem like something to freak out over. But Conrad was having a meltdown. So, I shook my head, took a deep breath and called Dad to see what was happening.

Phoebe answered, "Dad's being...not very nice."

"Can I speak with Dad?" I asked.

Dad got on the phone, and I asked him what was going on.

"Listen," he said, "this picture came along. Very nice. I wanted to put it over the piano, but Teresa took it into her room and has refused to give it back."

"Dad, I spoke with Teresa about it," I interjected.

Dad continued, "She's dealing the wrong way with me. As I said, she's really annoying me." He hesitated and then said, "I'm sorry, but she'll just have to leave."

"She's going to have to leave?" I was shocked. "To go where?"

"To one of those group homes."

"Uh, okay," I said. My mind was reeling but I needed to keep my wits about me.

"If I leave, she'll have to go anyway," Dad said. "I've had it. I can't put up with it anymore."

This wasn't the Dad I knew. It was unbelievable for him to say that Teresa should move to a group home. I was trying to process what was happening in this swirling sea of emotions. I could feel his frustration. He really believed that she had taken the photo. While that was plausible, it seemed more likely to me that he was mixed up. My fear was that he had lost not just the photo, but his mind.

However, I calmed myself with the knowledge that the slide into dementia—if that's what it was—is gradual. It's not like a light switch, on or off. The process takes many years. In the final stages, people lose the ability to communicate coherently and that certainly hadn't happened. I believed that what Dad was experiencing was like a storm, and when it passed, he would be back to his old self. Some of our elderly relatives had been supported to stay in their own homes right to the very end and they were far more befuddled than Dad; they could not even recognize their own children, whereas Dad was just at the mild stage of losing his keys, his wallet, and in this case, a favourite photo.

At that moment Dad needed support. If I had overseen his affairs, I could have helped him to stay at his condo. Unfortunately, there wasn't much I could do. Dad had put his trust in Conrad and Deirdre, who were now planning to put him into the veterans nursing home. Maybe it wouldn't be that bad? Phoebe and Conrad had both said it was a fitting reward for Dad's years of service, that he'd have the companionship of other World War Two vets and he'd enjoy the antique camera collection there too.

"So, it sounds like you may be ready for K-Wing?" I said holding my emotions in check.

"Yes," he said.

Hearing him say that was disappointing. However, I wasn't going to let it rattle me—I could cry later. I needed to put one foot in front of the other. If Dad wanted to go into K-Wing, that was his decision. Maybe he was agreeing to it because he was upset, and later he'd change his mind. But I wasn't giving up on Teresa. I needed to figure out how to help her.

We continued talking. I told him I had spoken with Teresa a few days earlier and that she didn't know where the photo was. This just irritated him, and he insisted that she had taken it. I asked him gently, "What is the photo of, Dad?"

"I don't want to get into that right now," he answered quickly.

"But what's the photo of?"

"You kids sent it over to me," he said. "I'm really upset. I can't even think straight. So don't bother talking to me."

I laughed nervously. His avoidance suggested that the picture might be a figment of his imagination. Despite everything, he was still polite. He admitted being upset, which was far more courteous than Conrad.

"But I'll tell you this," Dad said gruffly, "she's not having any more coffee in this house until I get it back."

When Phoebe got back on the phone, I said the thing I dreaded: "It sounds like Dad is ready to go to K-Wing."

"Absolutely," she agreed.

I asked if there was any progress on that front.

"Hopefully next week ..." Phoebe hesitated. "I don't know." Then she changed the subject. "Teresa and I tidied up her room. We went through everything. There is no picture to be found."

"I think that this picture is imaginary."

"Of course it is," Phoebe said. "I called Conrad. I hope he comes over."

"I called Conrad and he yelled at me," I said dryly.

"Oh!" Phoebe said.

"And he hung up. Then I called him back. And he yelled at me more and hung up again."

"Why?" asked Phoebe.

"Because he's furious. He said that I should go over there and help you."

Style-wise we were opposites, too. When we were young, Deirdre painted her bedroom brown, which may have been trendy, but I found it depressing. When I finally got my own room, I painted it bright white and chose a red shag rug. I had a big easel at the bottom of my bed for my oil paintings. Everything seemed just right to me.

As you would expect among seven kids, we didn't always get along. With only one shower to share among nine people, there was a lot of banging on the bathroom door. And Monopoly games could end in tears, with the board turned upside down and the loser marching off in a huff. But those spats were always resolved, and my core belief remained unshaken: our family was united by common values and lots of love.

I was standing at my treadmill desk, holding my silver recorder, and thinking of the best way to approach Deirdre. It had been an action-packed day: the meeting with LIGHTS, Conrad's hang-ups, and the mix-up over the missing photo. I knew Deirdre could be prickly, but I summoned my courage and dialed her number. When she picked up, I said, "I'm wondering if you were able to look at the permission form?"

"I saw it." Her curt answer told me this was not going to be easy.

"I'd like to get permission so that I can share the information with LIGHTS."

"Look," Deirdre said, "Conrad is going to call you about this. Wait to talk to him."

There was no point in mentioning that I had already called Conrad and he yelled at me. I moved on to the main point. "So, you don't want Teresa to live in the condo?"

There was a long pause—I waited. Deirdre had not replied to my invitation to meet with a disability lawyer. I wanted all of us to discuss setting up a Henson Trust, which could allow Teresa to receive money, or get Dad's condo, without losing her government benefits. (This contradicted the family myth I'd been told countless times—that Teresa couldn't inherit much because the government would just claw it back.)

"We already have a plan for where Teresa is going to live," she said carefully. "It's not going to be at the condo."

"Is it going to be in our neighbourhood?" I asked.

Another silence.

"Don't know," Deirdre said curtly.

"So, it's not going to be nearby?"

"We don't know yet," she said.

"It's unlikely," I said.

"Could be," she said.

I challenged her, "It's very unlikely it will be in our neighbourhood because—"

"Then you'll just have to walk farther," snapped Deirdre.

I took her comment as mockery of my environmental activism, implying that we shouldn't have sold our car and I shouldn't have written a story about it. But there was no point in getting detoured on that.

"Teresa is an important part of our life," I said firmly, "We won't be able to have that relationship with her if she moves out of the neighbourhood."

"I can't help that," Deirdre said.

"Why?" I asked.

She answered slowly, enunciating each word: "I am doing the best job that I can do." She paused. "I am trying to deal with Dad and Teresa. It's a *huge* responsibility."

Deirdre was directing both their lives and had to balance all sorts of things, including finances. If Teresa lived in a nursing home, it would be cost-free—paid for by the government. However, if she continued to live in the community, she would need additional money from Dad. As his dependent, Teresa was entitled to some degree of financial support. Of course, all of us would ultimately inherit less money. .

"I spoke with LIGHTS," I said. "It's possible to have Teresa stay at Dad's condo. I would like to explore that opportunity."

"I don't think that's going to happen."

I took a deep breath.

"Why?" I asked.

"The situation in the condo is getting worse and worse," Deirdre said.

"Dad needs to go to K-Wing. I can agree with that," I said. "What I don't agree with is Teresa being shipped off to a long-term care institution."

"We will make the best decision that we can for Teresa."

"The best decision is to—"

"I've already done my homework."

"Teresa could be very happy living at the condo," I said. "And I would like to look into this with everybody's blessing."

"You don't have my blessing," Deirdre said. And then a torrent of words and hurt feelings rushed out. "When you first reached out, Bill twisted my words around and made me look like a fool."

Whoa! I had no idea she was holding a grudge. Almost a month earlier, Deirdre had teased me, saying we would be *blessed* if we took Teresa into our home. Bill had answered, saying that we were *all blessed* to have Teresa. Which was a lovely truth, but somehow Deirdre was insulted.

"I don't appreciate that," Deirdre said. "I don't have to phone back and write to people if this is the way they're going to treat me."

I could hear the sweep of Catholic sacrifice and guilt. Deirdre was the martyr, stoically toiling away for the family, while I was the ungrateful sister spoiling her plans.

"I do the best job I can do," Deirdre insisted. "You're not looking at the whole picture. We have a verbal report that Teresa cannot live on her own. Teresa needs 24/7 support. Her mental acuity has declined drastically. She could be on the verge of Alzheimer's."

"But Deirdre," I said, "nursing homes are overcrowded, underfunded, and—"

"Have you seen any of them?" she said, poking me.

"Have you done any research into them?" I responded.

"Yes, I have. I've seen the articles on the internet," Deirdre said. "I talked to people. And I've gone and looked at quite a few nursing homes to see what they're talking about."

"I don't know why you won't allow Teresa the opportunity to live at the condo. This would be ideal for Teresa."

"Franke, I don't…I'm worn out," Deirdre said. "I'm sorry, I'm done for the day. You can talk to Conrad."

"I do not support Teresa moving into an old age nursing home," I insisted.

"That's fine, Franke, but you don't get a vote."

What? I thought.

"You're not the power of attorney," she said. "You're not a substitute decision-maker."

I was stunned. Deirdre was insisting she had all the power and I had none. I pushed back. "Teresa has at least two, possibly even three more decades of life. Putting her into an old age home is not in her best interests."

"Wherever Teresa lands," she answered, "it is going to be the best possible thing that we can work out."

"I think that we could have Teresa stay at the condo—"

"You've already said that," said Deirdre, talking over me.

"And I would like to—"

"You know what?" Deirdre interrupted again. Her voice brightened. "The best scenario? Teresa lives in your daughter's room. And she has her living room in your son's room. You work from home. It would be wonderful."

"Pffft," I scoffed at Deirdre's provocation.

"It would be fantastic for Teresa," Deirdre said happily. "If I had the space, I would take her." Then, in a serious voice, "But I don't. So, it's not going to happen. I have to find a better solution."

CHAPTER TWENTY-THREE

A Crack in Everything

November 21, 2013, 7:30 p.m.

"FUCK, FUCK, FUCK! THEY'RE REALLY GOING TO DO IT. I CAN'T believe it. And she told me I had no power to stop them." I was racing downstairs, talking and swearing to myself.[1] As soon as I saw Bill, the words exploded from me.

"They're really going to do it!"

"Do what?"

"Put Teresa in a nursing home!"

The story came rushing out. I told him about my call with Deirdre, Conrad's stonewalling, and the missing photo. "I was worried about it all, so I asked Teresa to come over to our place."

"For dinner?"

"For the night, just to give Dad some time to get back to his old self."

"What?" Bill asked with mock horror. "For just one night?"

I laughed, "Yes, I know, it's against Siobhan's one-night rule, but that's just crap. And besides, Teresa didn't want to come over. She wants to stay with Dad. And that's the problem because Dad is on the fast-track for K-Wing."

"Your dad is not that bad. He could stay at the condo."

"But tonight, he was so confused. Blaming Teresa for taking the missing photo. I think it was all in his imagination."

"How do you know?" Bill asked. "It sounds like something that Teresa would do."

I laughed and shook my head. This was classic Bill, challenging me to re-examine my thinking. "Maybe," I said. "But the main point is that Dad is having trouble coping."

"But he has not fallen off a cliff."

"Well, he might get pushed."

"Can't you object?"

I glared at him.

"Sorry, I know but—"

"Deirdre is insisting that Dad's power of attorney gives her absolute authority," I said.

"It doesn't seem right."

"Dad appointed them. And once he goes, boom! Teresa will be next. She will zoom to the top of the crisis list and then be plunked into a nursing home."

"That is the worst-case scenario."

"That's their bulletproof plan. As long as no one cracks."

"There is a crack in everything," Bill said, with a nod to Leonard Cohen. "That's how the light gets in!"

"The funny thing is, Deirdre dared me to do it. She said that the best scenario would be if Teresa moved into Darcy's room."

"She was teasing you."

"Yes, but they've all said it. But if we offer to take Teresa, their plan will shatter."

Teresa and Dad enjoying dinner at Franke's home, six months earlier

"Well, maybe it's time to surprise them," Bill said, his blue eyes twinkling.

I looked at Bill, thinking of our many adventures with Teresa, going for walks, visiting art galleries, having dinners. We always had fun together. "Yes, it would be a great offer."

"They would have to agree, because it's their duty to act in Teresa's best interest," Bill said. "And then the agencies would have to take her off the crisis list."

I loved Bill's willingness to do the unconventional thing. But this was a huge step—a life-changing commitment. I was nervous.

"It would shock them," I said.

"It would stop them cold." Bill said. "Teresa can live with us."

Bill was willing to do it. He had been hinting at this possibility for a while. He was the one who spotted the Down syndrome article about the two sisters who moved in together.[2] He was the one who sent that story out to my family. And when they all shot back, he didn't back down.

All this made me a little teary. I looked at him and I said, "It would be ideal for Teresa."

"It's what your dad always wanted. He's asked us many times."

"Yes, but I never thought that we'd be the ones."

Bill is such a generous person, but this was a big decision we were contemplating. I sighed. Were we ready to do this? Over the last few months, my siblings had repeatedly challenged me to take Teresa whenever I objected to their plans. We'd always said no, there must be better options. But now, the spectre of Teresa being sent to a nursing home was motivating us to say *yes*.

I felt torn between protecting our life and marriage as we knew it and protecting Teresa. I mustered a few cautionary words: "It would change everything in our lives. And we would have to be ready to make a long-term commitment. She may never get a spot, but Teresa needs us now."

"I know," Bill said. "We have to step up."

"The agencies want someone in the family to take Teresa."

"Does Teresa get support money from them?" Bill asked.

"I think so. And Dad has always promised help too. So maybe there would be something like that. But Conrad and Deirdre are not forthcoming."

"No kidding," Bill shook his head. "But I'm sure your dad will help."

We sat there, silent for a minute. I looked at our posters and our artwork hanging all around. We had everything just the way we wanted.

"What about our freedom?" I asked. "Right now, it's just you and me. We can do anything and go anywhere."

Bill hesitated on this.

We were both thinking of all the places we had been to recently— Halifax, Washington, New York, and Calgary. We were enjoying the freedom to pursue our dreams. Our lifelong goals to become successful artists were finally coming true for both of us. Would we have to give up all this to take care of Teresa?

Bill looked at me and said, "Teresa will open the door to new things."

"I love you." I pulled him closer and kissed him on the lips. And then ... I grabbed my laptop. "It's the right thing to do. Let's put it in writing so they can't ignore it. We're going to blow their bulletproof plan to smithereens."

We sat on the couch and typed out the letter together. I started by hitting *reply all* on the last family email and changing the subject to "Teresa's Guardians."

"Good," Bill said. "That will get their attention."

And then we wrote a brief note with our offer:

> Bill and I are interested in discussing the option of taking full responsibility for Teresa for the rest of her life.
>
> Would you please reply with financial information on how much support we can expect from Dad's estate? I recall that when Conrad and Candi were going to take Teresa that it was substantially more than just the money from the Life Insurance Policy which Teresa will receive.

It was straightforward and addressed their driving concerns. Bringing Teresa into our home would demand a lot from us, but it really was the best-case scenario. Hopefully, it would put an end to my siblings' desperate train wreck of a plan.

At 8:48 p.m., I hit send.

CHAPTER TWENTY-FOUR

The Kindness of
Their Hearts

November 22, 2013

T HE NEXT MORNING, SILENCE. NOT A PEEP FROM DEIRDRE OR
Conrad.[1] Our life-changing offer to take Teresa for "the rest of her
life" was left unanswered. I felt a sense of doom as I read the morning news.

The *Toronto Star* had just published another story about a Toronto
nursing home. This one was ordered to shut down because of the filthy
conditions and mistreatment of vulnerable residents.[2] A reporter had
posed as a down-on-his-luck drifter and spent a week living in the nursing
home as a resident. "What he witnessed was enough to make anyone
sick," *The Star* wrote. And now, after three years, the province was finally
shutting it down. I shuddered as I read that one of the neglected residents
had Down syndrome.[3]

Then we got the first response to our offer. I was cheered to see an
email from Phoebe: *You are wonderful for even offering to take over the care
of and responsibility for Teresa. But I hope that it doesn't come to that.*

Her reply was hush-hush, sent in a private, "no subject" email: *I really
think you should go along with Conrad and Deirdre's plan, because it may
not be as bad as it looks.*

Obviously, she hadn't read the story in that day's newspaper.

Then Phoebe unloaded all her worries about the crisis at the condo. Apart from Dad's upset over the missing photo, what really shocked her was Teresa's determination to stay put: *If there had been a fire, I would have had to knock Teresa unconscious, and then try to drag her out.*

Yes, Teresa wanted to stay at the condo, and she is very territorial. And yes, it would be a challenge to convince her to move to our house. But if Dad was going to K-Wing—which Phoebe was now suggesting was imminent—I was pretty sure that given the choice, Teresa would want to live with us.

But Phoebe seemed to be using Teresa's stubborn independence as a justification for taking away her freedom—as a safety measure. Then Phoebe repeated Deirdre's and Conrad's contradictory promise: *Even though we're putting her into a nursing home, that's not where she'll end up. Trust us.*

Growing up, Phoebe was always the nurturing type, but this was confusing. Questions popped into my head: Why was Phoebe not thinking about it from Teresa's perspective? How would she feel if she was in Teresa's shoes? Suddenly taken away from Dad, surrounded by strangers, and plunked into a home for the very old, sick and dying?

I would feel terrified and abandoned. I remember as a small child getting lost at a fairground where we'd go to ride the rollercoasters, see giant stuffed animals and clowns walking on stilts, and hear the carnival barkers. I was entranced by a puppet show and didn't notice when my family moved on to the next attraction. A woman found me crying and took me to a security guard, who then took me to what I thought was an orphanage where I'd live for the rest of my life. I was afraid of strangers and wouldn't take even a sip of soda pop. Watching kids having fun in the playground made me feel awful. I wondered how could they be happy when they'd never see their families again? After a while my mother showed up, scolded me for getting lost, and brought me home. The next summer I was on a leash, wearing a leather safety harness to prevent me from wandering off.

I felt lost again. Let down by my family. We were trying to do what Dad wanted. And what Conrad had promised to do. But somehow, when I offered to take Teresa, it was unacceptable. Why?

Phoebe didn't address this question. Instead, she issued three warnings that felt like spooky prophecies from a fairy tale.

First: *I would be sacrificing my freedom.*

Second: *If I took Teresa, all the responsibilities would fall on my shoulders alone. End of sentence.*

Third: *I should think very carefully about my offer. Especially because I had two beautiful children and, probably, in the future, grandchildren.*

I read her warnings over and over. I knew that the others wouldn't lift a finger, but the last one made me shiver.

This fuelled me to write a stronger email to the group. I reminded them that Deirdre had said it would be ideal if we took Teresa. Then I addressed the roadblocks:

1. Deirdre and/or Conrad need to sign permission forms for me to speak to the agency

2. Deirdre and Conrad need to give us full disclosure of Teresa's medical and financial status.

3. When Conrad and Candi were planning on taking Teresa, it was understood that there would be additional money from Dad's estate as they would be her caregivers. Does that same financial deal apply to us if we become her caregivers?

Teresa wearing her finisher's medal after doing a five-kilometre walk with Bill

I also included a link to the *Toronto Star* story. Then, for complete contrast, I sent a victory photo of Teresa with Bill after one of their walks. Those same walks that Conrad had dismissed, but which showed that Teresa was happy and proud of herself. How could they look at this photo and think of putting her in a nursing home?

This got Conrad's attention but not in the way I had hoped.

He attacked: *This has nothing to do with the finances. Candi and I never expected, nor were we ever offered, money from Dad. Our offer to take Teresa was given purely from the kindness of our hearts.*

What hogwash! Everyone in the family knew that Dad had vowed to support anyone who would take Teresa. And Conrad was first in line because of his promise. Why was he denying this now?

Fortunately, Phoebe challenged Conrad on this: *As I remember it, Dad promised to change his will and give all his money to anyone in the family who would step up and take Teresa.*

"I remember Dad saying that too, many times," I replied. "Wouldn't it be good if Dad's money could be used to buy the condo for Teresa? Or to buy a place of her own?"

But trying to figure out what Dad would provide for Teresa and to make future plans was impossible without seeing the files. Which brings me to Conrad's final line of his email:

As to your permission request, Deirdre and I are not prepared to grant it.

They were slamming the door on my offer. I breathed in and exhaled fully. This was it: a declaration of war. If I wanted to protect Teresa, I would now have to do battle with both Conrad and Deirdre.

This felt like a betrayal of everything that Dad and Mom had done for Teresa. I remembered a care worker telling me, "People pretend it's okay to put a person with Down syndrome into a nursing home. They pretend it's nice there, so they can forget about it."

Figuring out the psychology behind this would have to wait. I needed to keep the conversation going, so I tried to manoeuvre around Conrad's rejection with a little humour mixed with positivity.

"Ha! You know very well this is not about the money. It is about providing a happy and safe home for Teresa, where she will grow and develop to her full potential. If you are not willing to contribute to Teresa's care, that is your choice. We are still willing to take responsibility for her. Teresa's happiness is the most important issue here."

Conrad and Deirdre did not respond. But Phoebe did: *Keep an open mind. Please consider the benefits of all the options available to us.*

All the options? I had just offered to take care of Teresa for the rest of her life. Why was Phoebe dismissing that?

I wrote back, "Whatever we do with Teresa requires financial planning. But we cannot do any planning unless Conrad and Deirdre sign the consent forms. What are they afraid of? This secretiveness is not in Teresa's best interests."

CHAPTER TWENTY-FIVE

Stay with My Father

November 25-26, 2013

O
UR OFFER WAS HANGING IN LIMBO. WE WANTED TO SPEAK
with Dad and Teresa directly, so I invited them to dinner.[1] Bill
and I were getting ready when I received a new email from Deirdre. I
hoped it was a response to our offer, but no, Deirdre was acting as if it
never happened. Instead, she was giving us an update on the comings and
goings at Dad's condo.

She had a bossy efficiency that made it feel like we were being scolded
in advance: *If anyone is planning to take Dad or Teresa out of the condo, they
must give three days' advance notice, because the nurses and caregivers have
a very strict timetable.*

Just in case any of us were so reckless as to schedule an outing anyway,
Deirdre told us where to find Dad's eye drops and Teresa's ear drops.
She explained the precise routine for administering them. Every night
Dad needed one prescription drop in each eye or else he would go blind.
Teresa needed three drops in each ear or else (presumably) she would go
deaf. Plus, once the drops were in, Teresa had to hold her head tilted to
the side for at least five minutes for each ear. Really? I couldn't imagine
Teresa sitting like that for long.

Sixteen paragraphs of eye-glazing minutiae later, Deirdre wrapped up by saying they were still looking for a home for Teresa, completely ignoring the fact that I had just offered to bring Teresa into my home.

And then Deirdre dropped her bombshell: *The search for Teresa's new home has become more problematic. The doctor has completed her assessment and determined that Teresa has early-onset Alzheimer's and, therefore, needs 24/7 care.*

I was shocked to hear a doctor had come to this conclusion. As far as I could tell, Teresa was the same as she ever was. What had Deirdre or Siobhan told them? This looked like a way to fast-track her into a nursing home. And it made my offer sound completely unreasonable.

I fired off a response to Deirdre. "I would like to see Teresa's medical report for my own peace of mind. Please share it with all of us."

Deirdre did not respond. (In fact, she never shared the doctor's report with us. When we finally got access to Teresa's health records a few months later, we discovered that Deirdre had jumped the gun. Teresa was never diagnosed with Alzheimer's.)

I also realized that we had never seen the legal paperwork that Deirdre and Conrad were using to assert their authority. We had just taken it on faith, and now I was questioning that assumption too. I was planning to ask Dad about it that evening.

I shifted my focus back to prepping for our dinner party. Bill and I would divvy up the tasks: shopping, cleaning, flower arranging, cooking, and, of course, picking up Dad and Teresa—despite Deirdre's edict which had come too late.

THE AROMA OF roast chicken and savoury stuffing was in the air. Dad and Teresa were waiting in our dining room, expectantly. Teresa was smiling and happy. A centrepiece of pink tiger lilies sat in the middle of our well-worn mahogany table. It was a wonderful find from a second-hand shop: a 1940s Duncan Phyfe–style table with a twin-pedestal base and brass-capped claw feet.

On either side of the blooming lilies were tall ecru candles, which Bill had just lit. Dad had given us the candle holders as a wedding present over thirty years ago. Many times, he had told me with delight that they were sterling silver and not just silver plate (so I had better be thankful). At each place was a white cloth serviette rolled in a silver napkin ring. We had collected the rings as mementos for years and they provided a nice contrast with our gaily striped place mats. I had set out our best crystal wine glasses and everything looked festive. We were ready for the party to begin.

Dad raised his cocktail glass and exclaimed, "You've got to patent this drink! Ohh! Nothing like it!"

We all laughed as Bill announced the Drambuie and Coke drink would now be named in Dad's honour. Dad poured on more praise, "I've never tasted a drink like that! It's the ultimate!"

In between the bites, chews, swallows, and yums, Dad was telling us how much he loved the dinner. "Oh, this meal. Wow! You are good cooks." We all laughed as he continued with the compliments. "Wonderful, wonderful!"

This was quintessential Dad, which is why it was so much fun to have him over. He was so alive in the moment that whatever we were serving was always "the best."

I was capturing the night with my Nikon camera and my silver recorder. With Dad possibly going into K-Wing, I had a feeling that this was an evening we would treasure, and I wanted to ask about his plans for Teresa and himself. I set the silver recorder by my place where everyone could see it and pressed *on*. Bill gave me a look; he didn't think I needed to record this, but I thought it was far too important to miss.

I snapped a couple of photos and asked Teresa, "Have you ever used a camera before? Did you take lessons at your program?"

Teresa nodded yes. I handed her my camera, carefully slipping the strap over her head as Dad always taught us to do. I cautioned her that it was very fragile, and she promised to be careful. She looked around the room. I stepped back, curious to see her in action. Teresa pointed it straight at Dad and clicked the shutter. Done. She removed the neck strap and promptly handed the camera back to me.

I peeked at the preview to check it. Teresa's exposure was fine. She had centred Dad in the frame. His head was slightly tilted back, and he was smiling at Teresa with an air of satisfaction. His skin had good colour, and his face was set off by a crisp white golf shirt and dark V-neck sweater. Teresa had composed quite a handsome portrait. I said, "You took a nice picture of Dad. Good for you!"

Teresa was pleased to be recognized as a photographer. We continued eating and chatting, with the sounds of clinking glasses and cutlery filling the air. Dad exclaimed again, "What a wonderful meal! Oh, only you can do this. Wow!"

"Great," I said, knowing that Dad would rave about any of my siblings' cooking if he was at their homes. I enjoyed his compliments, nonetheless. I would never tire of hearing his appreciation.

"Well, it's a great treat to have you over! Now, what happened during the Grey Cup?" I asked, knowing he had postponed our dinner so he could watch the game.

"Oh, that was a laugh," said Dad. "Oh, my word."

Immediately I knew that the Hamilton Tiger-Cats must have lost.

"It all went to the West," Dad laughed. "Boy, they were awful!"

"I think Teresa switched sides," said Bill, laughing. "She told me yesterday she was rooting for Saskatchewan."

"Right!" said Teresa with some glee. "That was a good one!"

Dad, Teresa and Franke at dinner

The dinner conversation turned to city politics in Toronto, specifically the seamy mess Mayor Rob Ford was in. I was curious whether Dad had been following the news.

"So, Dad, have you been following Rob Ford at all?" I asked.

"Oh yes, they're giving him a tough time."

Bill and I burst out laughing.

"Pardon?" Dad asked. "You don't agree with me?"

Neither of us wanted to wade into explaining Ford's sordid saga.

But Dad was ready to defend Mayor Ford: "Oh my God. You'd think if somebody wanted to have a drink—"

"Yeah, but crack cocaine?" I asked.

"Oh, I can't get over it," exclaimed Dad. "One drink, and boy, you've ruined everything."

"But what about the cocaine?" I asked again.

"Well, okay," Dad said, shaking his head.

"Your dad's very tolerant," Bill joked.

"Oh, my goodness," I laughed. Dad wasn't tolerant of my use of marijuana when I was a teenager. "I don't think the alcohol is a problem, so much as the drunk driving."

"It wasn't very wise," Dad conceded. "Poor Rob Ford!"

We all laughed, then moved on to other topics. I asked Teresa about her day programs.

"I like the Scott Mission. We're packing bread."

"And how many loaves do you pack?"

"I pack four," she answered. Teresa had won an award for being one of the best workers.

As I cleared the dinner dishes away for dessert, I asked Dad to tell me about the silver napkin ring in front of him.

"Oh this!" said Dad. "That's got my initials engraved on it. Wow!" He read out each letter proudly, then held the ring up to his eyes and examined it as a jeweller might. "It was expensive! And oh boy, it's been around for a long time."

"Yeah," I said. "Wow, ninety-one years!" I placed the ring in a silver box with all the others we'd collected. This one was certainly the most precious of all.

"Oh my, that was a nice meal, sweetie," Dad said. "I really enjoyed every bit of it."

I thanked him and said we still had dessert and coffee coming. Silently I was rehearsing how to tackle the tough subject that was on my mind. I needed to ask Dad two things—what he wanted for Teresa and who was making the decisions.

"Dad, I've been hearing stories that you might be going to Sunny-brook's K-Wing? The veterans' wing?"

"I'm going to what?" Dad scoffed. "No way!"

"No?" I asked. I was relieved to hear that Dad had reversed his decision. He was back to his old self.

"Somebody else might think it's a good idea. But no, not from my point of view." Dad was shaking his head. "I want Teresa and me to be together. I don't want to go off to one of those places."

"Okay, it's good to hear that," I said. "You're happy at the condo? And you like all of the people that are coming in to help you?"

"I'm slipping a bit, but I'm holding my own," said Dad. "I don't want to go anywhere else."

"I need my dessert," Teresa interjected.

"It's coming!" Bill called from the kitchen.

"I don't want Teresa going off somewhere," Dad said. "If you hear that story, just tell them no. I'll do my damnedest to stay where I am."

I nodded, then turned to Teresa and asked, "If you had to go somewhere else to live, where would you want to live?"

"I'll stay with my father."

"What if Dad was at the hospital?" I asked.

Dad answered, "Teresa and I are a team."

"We're a team," Teresa echoed. "I want to stay with my father."

"We don't want to be split up. And I don't want her going off to one of those places."

"Bless you, Daddy," Teresa said.

I tried another approach. "Teresa, do you remember the play *Rare*?"

"Teresa doesn't want to go anywhere else," Dad said with some annoyance.

"I know." But I pressed on with the touchy topic. "There were people with Down syndrome there, right?"

"Right," said Teresa.

"And some of them lived on their own, right? Can you ever imagine living on your own?"

"No, I can't," said Teresa flatly.

I was not doing very well in guiding this conversation. I tried again. "What would you do if you *had* to live on your own? Would you want to live with other people who have Down syndrome?"

"I want to stay with my father," said Teresa.

"Forever?" I asked.

"Why is it that I get to a certain age," said Dad with exasperation, "and they decide to put me into one of those damned homes? I don't want that. I want to stay with Teresa, where we are!"

"Right," I said.

"It's better for Teresa. It's better for me," Dad said, adding, "I do pretty well."

"You do," I agreed. I turned to Teresa. "Dad is ninety-one— at some point he won't be around forever."

"I know," said Teresa.

"Where would you want to live?" I asked. And then we went in circles again with Teresa saying over and over again, "Stay with my father."

"I guess it just means that I have to stick around for a while," said Dad laughing.

We served coffee in our colourful mugs. Each one was painted with a different fantasy animal. It was a menagerie of monkeys, winged creatures, tigers, dragons, rabbits, roosters, and elephants.

"Oh, that's nice coffee," said Dad, sipping his coffee. "Thank you. Teresa and I are a team, and we are just enjoying being together."

"Right," Teresa chimed in.

"Some of the kids think that we should go someplace else. But I don't want that. I've lasted this long. When I go, I want to be done. Finished. Boom."

"Right," said Teresa.

"I don't want to go anywhere," Dad continued. "We're managing to pay the condo fees. We're in a place that we like. We're able to handle everything. As far as I'm concerned, I like it as is."

"Here comes dessert," Bill said as he brought in a piping-hot apple pie and ice cream.

"Oh, isn't this perfect? Just what we need to finish off," Dad said. Then he turned to me and asked, "So, what's your opinion? Do you think I should be trying to get ...?"

This was the Dad I'd always known. I appreciated that he was seeking my opinion. "I think it would be nice for you to stay at the condo with Teresa as long as possible."

"Yes, it's good for Teresa. And it's fine by me."

"But Dad," Bill asked, "would you consider going to K-Wing at Sunnybrook Hospital? If they asked you to?"

"I don't want to go off on that," Dad answered.

"But it's the veterans' wing," Bill continued, repeating what Phoebe had said would appeal to Dad. "It's got all kinds of stuff, like cameras."

"I want whatever's best for Teresa," Dad said.

"Well, some people are saying that Teresa would be better off if—"

"No," Teresa interjected.

Bill turned to Teresa, "Eventually, you've got to learn to live by yourself."

"No!" Teresa said.

We laughed. I understood Teresa's desire for things to stay the same, but change was coming, and she would need to adapt.

Dad summed it up by saying, "Whatever's best for Teresa, I am for it. But I hope that she stays with me."

"Right," Teresa said.

"It seems to me," Dad continued, "We've got to knock ourselves out to do what's best for Teresa, whatever that is. I'll go someplace. That doesn't matter. The main thing is Teresa."

AFTER DESSERT, Dad and Teresa took a taxi back to the condo. I was feeling the positive buzz. Dad and Teresa were so happy living together, coming over to visit, and enjoying life. But I was worried about my siblings' "exit plan." It just didn't fit in with what we had experienced that evening. I sent my siblings an email and photos so they could see what I saw.

"We had Dad and Teresa to dinner. It was fabulous," I wrote. "During dessert, I asked Dad about K-Wing. Dad said he has no interest in going and is very happy at the condo."

Phoebe answered: *I'm so glad you had a wonderful dinner, but those happy times do not reflect the reality of Teresa and Dad's life, which is rife with tension and problems—they really do need 24/7 care.*

Then she emphasized the benefits: *K-Wing is not really a nursing home. Once Dad arrives, he will be treated like a celebrity. And because K-Wing is close by, we can visit whenever we want. I know this will be difficult, but now it's time to let go.*

I didn't know what more to say. I had talked to Dad and Teresa. They were both opposed. I had told my siblings that Dad was opposed. And I told them I was opposed. But the rest of my family just continued on, ignoring everything I said.

I wrote back, "My question remains: How are you planning on breaking the big news to Dad and Teresa of their 'exit'? Are you planning to surprise them?"

Phoebe answered for the group again: *Conrad and Deirdre are working with the doctors and staff at K-Wing. They will manage the transition smoothly. However, both Conrad and Deirdre have emphasized that we should not speak to Dad about this, because it would cause undue worry.*

"Undue worry?" I asked. "It's certainly not undue worry, if it's going to happen." Then I challenged Conrad and Deirdre directly: "Please let all of us know how you are planning to ease the transition. Secrecy and surprise are sure to result in unnecessary mental anguish for both Dad and Teresa."

CHAPTER TWENTY-SIX

Teresa and Dad Update

November 27, 2013, 5:00 p.m.

I NSTEAD OF WORKING, I WAS REREADING WHAT I'D SCRIBBLED in my journal three days earlier: "Deirdre and Conrad are going to put Teresa in a nursing home. Phoebe and Siobhan are going along with it because, 'What else can we do?'"[1]

Closing my red journal, I tried to put my fears aside. I had to face the facts. I was not in control of the family drama swirling around me. Dad had named Deirdre and Conrad on his power of attorney years ago, so they had the legal authority to represent him. Not me. I had to let go. I needed to focus on my number-one job: getting my "No Keystone XL" essay done. My exhibition was still up in Washington, and creating a story about it could give it a lasting impact. Despite the family turmoil, I was making progress. My inspiration was President Obama's statement on climate change: "I am willing to work with anybody ... to combat this threat on behalf of our kids."[2] I could be an anybody. And with that idea, I started to sketch out a storyboard.

It was early evening. Bill had just left with his dad and brother to see *Les Misérables*. I was glad to have a few hours to get some work done, but as I opened my laptop, I noticed a new email from Conrad: *Teresa and*

Dad Update. I hesitated. I didn't want to get thrown off track, but what if he was replying to my offer? My mouse hovered, then I clicked.

Deirdre had received a phone call from a nursing home. They had a bed available and recommended that Teresa be admitted immediately.

Damn! They'd found a spot for Teresa. They couldn't be doing this.

I read on.

Oh my God. They've already done it.

My heart started beating faster. Conrad said he went to the condo with Candi, picked Teresa up, took her out for a special breakfast, and then drove her to a nursing home in downtown Toronto, where she was admitted at 10 a.m.

I felt sick. Teresa had no idea that this was going to happen.

When Teresa left the condo that morning, she must have thought she was going to her day program. That's certainly what Dad thought. She must have been thrilled when they took her out for breakfast. I bet she ordered her favourites. Fluffy pancakes with butter, lots of maple syrup, fresh-squeezed orange juice, and coffee. A delicious treat.

Conrad must have told her something on the way down, but I still think she would have been completely surprised when they arrived at that strange building called Aiker Place. I imagine her objecting, refusing to go in: *No, this is the wrong place. This is not my day program.*

Conrad did not describe Teresa's initial response in his family email, but he seemed satisfied that they had done the right thing. Perhaps to head off my fears about Teresa's well-being, he volunteered some surprising info: *Siobhan's husband, Jared, knows the owner and is on the board of directors.* (Later, the authorities would claim that absolutely no influence was used to get Teresa the bed at Aiker Place.)

That day, five of them pitched in to help. Each had a role to play. Siobhan was there to welcome Teresa, Conrad and Candi when they arrived. Deirdre and Chuck had dropped by the condo to pick up some clothes for Teresa. Dad must have wondered what they were doing. Teresa's belongings were stuffed into plastic bags and brought to the nursing home. Each article of clothing was fixed with a permanent label with her name and the institution's as if her clothing, and Teresa herself, were now the property of Aiker Place.

Deirdre and Conrad signed the paperwork, and Teresa was admitted as a permanent, long-term resident at Aiker Place, in a shared room, #312-1. Teresa had her own bedroom at Dad's condo. And she would have her own bedroom if she came to my house. It was infuriating that Conrad was putting a smiley face on this terrible situation.

While the paperwork was being processed, Candi, Chuck and Siobhan made phone calls, notifying all concerned: the day program, the pharmacy, the cab company, and others. It seemed like everyone knew what was happening except for Dad, Teresa and me.

Teresa must have been shocked, not understanding what was happening. I imagine she would have argued: *I want to go back to the condo. I want to stay with my father.* She would have repeated it over and over again, demanding that she be allowed to return home. Whatever she said to Conrad, it made no difference. That day he left her there.

Dad knew none of this. He was still at the condo. And he was expecting Teresa to return soon. Instead, Conrad and Deirdre arrived to tell Dad what was happening.

According to Conrad, Dad was not pleased: *Dad said that we had taken away his very reason to live and he might ask God to take him to heaven. Then he threatened to sell the condo and give all the money to charity, just to spite us.*

My heart bled for Dad.

But Conrad appeared unconcerned: *Candi and I will be attending a fundraising dinner tonight, so I have asked Perla to work late, and Chuck has agreed to sleep over at the condo with Dad, just in case.*

Alone at Aiker Place, Teresa must have been in a state of shock. But Conrad claimed that she was handling the transition quite well. He said that the care agency had sent in specialists who were working with Teresa to help her adapt to the new environment.

What rubbish, I thought.

But Conrad was pleased: *Tonight is bingo night at Aiker Place.* He ended with a request, which seemed aimed at me as the disrupter: *I hope that everyone will work together to make the transition as smooth as possible.*

He signed off: *Love, Conrad and Deirdre.*

I was heartsick.

I checked the time. Bill was probably still on his way to the theatre. I called and he picked up, saying they were almost there.

"Okay, I'll just give you the headline," I said. "They put Teresa into a nursing home today."

"What? No way!" I heard a loud sound as Bill thumped the dashboard with his fist.

"Yep, they did it. Conrad just sent out a family email. They took Teresa out for a lovely breakfast this morning and then checked her into a nursing home. They didn't tell Dad until after it was done."

"That sucks." There was a moment of silence. Then Bill asked, "Have you called your dad?"

"Not yet. He must be heartbroken. It's a terrible shock."

"And what about Teresa?"

"She must be so scared. In a strange place, surrounded by strangers, and she was told that she could never go back to the condo again."

"That is so fucking wrong!"

"We have to do something," I said. "I don't know what, but we need to do it fast."

CHAPTER TWENTY-SEVEN

All Hell's Breaking Loose

November 27, 2013, 8:00 p.m.

DAD SOUNDED OVERWHELMED, HIS VOICE QUIET: "YES, DEAR?"
"I just got the news that Teresa has gone to a nursing home."
My voice was strong, my words were factual, but my heart was aching.[1]

"Boy, am I burned up about that." Dad's voice rose quickly, "Conrad announces this! I said all hell will break loose! And he said no, they have the power of attorney to do that. And I said no, power of attorney does not allow you to do that. I told him I want Teresa back immediately. In this home. I don't care what it costs. I want her back!"

Dad sounded feisty, like the father I'd always known. Yet I feared that his power was hanging by a thread. Conrad and Deirdre had put him in a box labelled "demented." It appeared they believed that Dad was so detached from reality that he wouldn't even know what they had done, and if he did find out, he would be powerless to stop them.

"Dad, I support you. The thing is—"

"I don't care what it costs but I want her back in her own home. If there's something that she needs, okay, we'll get it. But to just announce that this is what they've done."

"Deirdre and Conrad have been working on this for months and months!" I said, relieved to have it out in the open. "I have opposed it. It is not the right thing to do."

"It's not. I'm really upset about this. I will not allow it to happen. I'm going to ..." Dad hesitated for a moment, then like a cagey lawyer he said, "Well, I won't announce what I'm going to do. But it will cost. And if necessary, there won't be any money for the family. I'll give it all to charity if I have to!" This was the same warning that Dad had made to Conrad earlier that day. "I want her back home immediately. To come here and just announce that Teresa has been moved away—"

"It's horrible," I said.

"Well, they are all going to lose, but I want Teresa here," Dad said angrily. "If she doesn't come home, I'll make a new will, I'll tell you. But they'll get nothing. I will sell this property."

Dad was furious. I wanted to help him, but first, I needed to understand who held the legal authority.

"Dad, did you sign guardianship for Teresa over to Deirdre or Conrad?"

"No!" he answered emphatically.

"Okay, so do they have power of attorney?"

"They don't have a right to use the power of attorney like that. They're out of their minds. They better get a lawyer in a hurry. They're going to need one."

"I really wanted to keep Teresa at the condo with you. I told them that, but they would not listen to me."

"Well, they better listen," Dad said. "When Teresa is here, she's got somebody with her every day. I'll get somebody to sleep here, if necessary. I want her back now!"

"I see no problem with you staying at the condo with Teresa," I said. "That's the way it should be."

"What!?" Dad asked, surprised. "I'm not moving anywhere."

"They're trying to put you into K-Wing," I warned.

"I will not go," he said.

"But that's what they're trying to do," I said.

"They can't do it," Dad answered.

"But Deirdre and Conrad say that they have your power of attorney. And they're going to put you into K-Wing."

"No!" Dad interrupted. "The power of attorney doesn't mean that! They don't know what they're talking about."

"Well—" I tried to answer.

"I'm not moving out of this place. And I want Teresa back. If it doesn't happen—all hell is going to break loose. I don't care if I have to sell this house and use every penny of it."

"Dad, I agree with you. The way to undo this is to yank the power of attorney away from Deirdre and Conrad."

"They can't use it for this reason."

"Yeah, but Deirdre and Conrad think—"

"I've really gone after Deirdre. She is in agreement with me, absolutely. She doesn't want this."

"What?" My jaw dropped. Dad still thinks Deirdre is on his side?

"Yes."

"No!"

"Yes," Dad asserted.

"No way!" I said. "Deirdre has been working for months and months to make this happen."

"Then she changed her mind in a hurry," Dad said.

"You know what? She doesn't tell you the truth. Personally, my advice is to yank the power of attorney. Withdraw it from Deirdre and Conrad."

"If that's necessary, I will."

"You should." It was obvious to me that they weren't following Dad's wishes about Teresa's care. And now Dad was feeling such pain. But at this precarious moment, how could I help? I took a giant leap: "What I would suggest is, you give the power of attorney to me because you can trust me."

"No," Dad answered. "I just won't give anybody a power of attorney. They need my signature."

"Okay, that's fine." I didn't want to push him into signing anything, but it made it more difficult to help. What I said then was unlike anything I'd ever said to him in my life. My voice faltered, the emotion breaking through. "But Dad, what I'm telling you is that out of everybody in the family," I said, trying to hold back tears, "I am the one, honestly, who cares the most about you and Teresa."

"That's right, sweetie," Dad said consolingly. "I've just been giving Deirdre a bad time—so I'm not giving you a bad time—but I sure gave Deirdre a bad time. But she didn't say she did it."

Good grief. He still couldn't see what was happening.

"Deirdre and Conrad have been scheming about this for months!" I said. "When we had you over to dinner on Monday night, I talked to you about K-Wing and I asked about Teresa because I was afraid that this was going to happen."

"I'd better let you go," Dad said.

"What?" I felt unsettled as we ended the call. But there was nothing more I could say.

CHAPTER TWENTY-EIGHT

The Morning After

November 28, 2013, 8:00 a.m.

D AD WOKE UP THE NEXT MORNING TO THE REALITY THAT
his nightmare was not over.[1] Teresa was gone. The first person he
saw was Mr. Get-on-board-we're-getting-tired, Chuck. Dad immediately
demanded that Chuck and the others bring Teresa back. He threatened to
call the police if they didn't.

My siblings' transition plan was a disaster.

Conrad arranged to drop by after his dental appointment to calm
Dad down. He sent out an email update: *My second meeting with Dad
went well. Dad said he would not be selling the condo and giving away all
his money to the poor. And he would not be contacting the police to report a
kidnapping. However, Dad is still asking God to end his life.*

How could Conrad say his visit went well when Dad had said that?

Dad also told him that he was feeling extremely lonely since Teresa
had been taken away and that he wished Mom was still with him. Conrad
took that as an opening to suggest that they "consult" with Mom up
in heaven. Previously, Conrad had—like the others—argued that Dad's
belief that he could talk with Mom was absolute proof of Dad's dementia. But on that day, Conrad apparently had a miraculous conversion and

told the family that he "sincerely believed" that Dad could indeed communicate with Mom.

So, Dad and Conrad held a séance at the condo to contact Mom's spirit. Conrad reported: *Mom told us that Teresa should be in a nursing home so she can live independently. This answer—and the look on Dad's face—was all the evidence I needed to believe that Mom's spirit was really there.*

I was not impressed by Conrad's stunt. I could not imagine Mom ever saying that.

After their séance, Conrad and Dad decided to speak to someone who was alive—Teresa.

The night before, Teresa was sleepless and frantically trying to reach Dad. She did not have a phone, so this was a challenge. When she finally got access to a telephone, she called the condo repeatedly. But instead of getting Dad she heard a strange voice, so she hung up, assuming she had the wrong number, and called again. That strange voice belonged to Chuck, who was on duty at the condo. At first, Chuck was stumped, but then he realized that it must be Teresa and managed to tell her, before she hung up again, that Dad was asleep. After that, Teresa stopped calling. However, according to Conrad, Teresa did not sleep a wink that first night and kept her roommate up as well.

Conrad said that the first phone call between Dad and Teresa was very emotional: *Watching Dad speak to Teresa brought tears to my eyes. After the call, I reminded Dad that he was Teresa's lifeline and that he needed to stick around until Teresa was settled in.*

Then Conrad raised the subject of K-Wing. Dad said no, he wanted to stay in his own condo. Conrad reassured him: *If you don't like it at K-Wing, you can always move back.* As an alternative, Conrad asked Dad if he would like to live in his basement apartment, which had previously been slated for Teresa. Dad declined again, saying he didn't want to be a burden. Conrad told him bluntly: *Yes Dad, you are a burden. But it would be more expedient and convenient if that burden was located in my basement.*

PHOEBE SAID SHE DIDN'T KNOW anything about Teresa's surprise exit: *The news hit me like a sledgehammer. I knew they were planning to take Dad to K-Wing, but I thought they would keep Teresa at the condo, for at least a few more weeks. I was so upset I could hardly sleep last night.*

I sighed and said, "It's terrible and cruel."

Then Phoebe said that Siobhan had called her to say that she had wanted to give us some advance warning, but that Conrad and Deirdre had insisted that we not be told.

This confirmed the months of uneasiness and mistrust I'd felt.

My thoughts shifted to Teresa. I imagined how frightened she must be, waking up in a strange place, far away from home, feeling abandoned.

I called Dad.

"Oh, I'm having a tough time," he said.

"But you still want to get Teresa back?"

"Of course I do," he said anxiously.

"Okay."

"And now they tell me I have dementia. I feel okay. I can read stuff. And I can talk to you and all the rest of it. But nevertheless, they say I've got dementia. I don't know…but apparently, I'm in terrible shape."

Dad's anger from the night before had dissipated. It had been replaced with despair, self-doubt, and questions about whether his mind was to blame. He didn't understand why they had put Teresa in a nursing home. I didn't understand either.

It wasn't his mind that was breaking—it was his heart. As tough as things were, we couldn't give up now. I told him, "Dad, I'm going to speak to a lawyer."

"About what?"

"About how we can get Teresa back for you."

"Gee whiz." His voice ached with pain. "I really want her back...And I'm sorry to be such a bother, but God, it's such a shame."

I knew that the lawyer would need to see the paperwork.

"Dad, do you have a copy of the power of attorney that Deirdre and Conrad signed?"

"I don't know where it is. I don't know where anything is...I feel so badly."

He was very sad and confused by the events, but he continued, "Damn it all. I'm ninety-one. Maybe I won't get to ninety-two. Who knows?" He paused for a moment. "In any event, anything you can do for me, I appreciate it."

I breathed in, feeling a sense of relief that he understood I was trying to help him. "We're talking to a lawyer. I want you to keep us posted. Because they might come and try to take you away to K-Wing."

"They might take me?" Dad asked. "Oh, that damn thing! K-Wing? I don't want that."

CHAPTER TWENTY-NINE

Summer Camp

November 28, 2013, 6:30 p.m.

I T'S LIKE GOING TO SUMMER CAMP. THAT'S HOW CONRAD framed it:[1] *Visits to Teresa should be postponed. She needs time to adjust and visitors from home could just make things worse.*

Did he expect me to believe that? There was no way I was going to abide by their stay-away order. I was determined to visit Teresa, but first I would meet with Dad at his condo.

When we initially got the news, I reached out to people in the disability community. They each asked the question: How did Deirdre and Conrad take over as Teresa's power of attorney? I'd been trying to find that out, but we still didn't know. We needed to see the document. So that was the third item on our agenda, to see if we could find a copy of Teresa's power of attorney at Dad's place.

When we arrived at Dad's condo, Perla welcomed us. She had a warm, motherly presence, and had been providing support for Dad and Teresa for the past year. We'd known her for much longer because she had previously worked with Bill's family. My ears perked up when she told us that she was there when Teresa was taken.

Bill asked, "Who took Teresa away? Was it Conrad and Deirdre?"

And so, Perla told us her story. "They arranged it so that Teresa thought she was going to her day program. When I brought her downstairs, we saw Conrad's car and Teresa asked me, 'Where is the taxi, Perla?' And I said, 'Maybe it will be a special trip for you. They're picking you up and dropping you off at your program.' And so, when I said goodbye to her, I just turned my back, because I didn't want Teresa to see me… crying. And before I came up, I just stayed there, for a while there."

Tears were welling up in her eyes, and mine too, as she finished the story. Dad walked in, looked at us, and handed Bill a box of tissues. "You could use some Kleenex, buddy."

I felt emotional, but I was determined to untangle the mess. I asked Dad, "Do you have a copy of the power of attorney?"

"I don't know where it is," he answered. "What do you want it for? I want to cancel it."

"We want to show it to a lawyer, to find out if you can revoke it."

"They can't do anything without my consent," Dad insisted.

"They have already done it," Bill said.

"I want Teresa home," Dad said. "Or I'm going to call the police on them. They had no right."

"I know," I said, "but they've done it. Teresa has been declared incompetent." Then, thinking about their exit plan, I warned him, "Whatever you do, do not go to K-Wing. Do not go to K-Wing."

But Dad wasn't listening to me. He had started searching through his files. Bill was hunting for a stapler, so I joined the search going through stacks of boxes and folders in Dad's office. "Where did I put that thing?" Dad asked, talking as much to himself as to us. Then the phone rang.

"Shoot!!" I said. "Is that them?" They could be downstairs in the lobby, ringing to come up. "Is it Conrad and Candi?" Dad nodded. "Don't tell them we're here," I whispered.

Dad picked up the phone. "Yes, Conrad."

He was silent for a moment, then said, "I want her home."

Bill and I stood by watching, listening, hardly breathing.

"You can do whatever you want," Dad said. "But I will call the police if I have to." He listened, then said, "Who? No, I did not. I did not say that."

He listened again.

"No," he answered, "I don't know where they are."

Was Conrad asking about us?

"I'm really annoyed about this," Dad said. "Anyway, I have to go." And he ended the call abruptly. Dad looked back at the files and shook his head muttering, "It should have been here. It's just a question of where I put the bloody thing." Dad continued searching through his files.

"I wonder if Deirdre has it?" Bill suggested.

"I'll call her right now and see if she's got it," Dad said.

"Oh!" I interjected, "Maybe you should call her after we're gone."

"Deirdre will do anything I ask her," Dad said.

"Dad," Bill said, "Deirdre engineered this—taking Teresa down to the nursing home. It's her plan."

"We could show you emails, Dad," I said.

"Deirdre?" said Dad with surprise. He still didn't believe it. Deirdre had been his trusted right hand for decades.

"Yes, Deirdre! The thing is I have been fighting for you to stay here. And for Teresa to stay here. I even said that we would take Teresa and let her live at our house."

"But Deirdre refused," Bill said.

I looked at Dad and said, "You need to redo the paperwork to allow someone else to be her guardian."

"To make the decisions," Bill added.

The printer whirred in the background as we spoke.

"I may be retired, but I'm still a lawyer," Dad said, shaking his head. He still needed time to think about it. "I'm upset about the whole thing."

"Well, you should be upset," Bill said.

"It's horrible what has been done to Teresa," I said.

It was getting late. We needed to get to Aiker Place before their official visiting hours ended. I promised to call him with a report.

"Yeah, okay," he said, then he turned and continued the search through his files for the missing papers.

CHAPTER THIRTY

Heartbreak Place

November 28, 2013, 7:30 p.m.

"IT'S JUST PAST THIS FUNERAL HOME," BILL SAID AS WE WALKED
from the subway.[1] "That's where they took my grandparents when
they died." Then he pointed down the street to a four-storey brick building. "See, there it is."

Aiker Place looked like a nondescript apartment building with a
plastic sign over the entrance. Nearby there was a church, a few drab
apartment buildings, a small inner-city park, and panhandlers on the sidewalk. It was depressing to imagine Teresa living in this neighbourhood.

For the last twenty-four hours we had been phoning around, getting
advice. We called our lawyer, Nikolas Vincente. We spoke with Bill's
activist friends in the medical community, who introduced us to Lois
Sampson, an elder rights activist. Everyone was concerned but nobody
had an easy solution, especially if Deirdre and Conrad had the proper
legal authority, as they insisted.

I was nervous as we walked up to the entrance. The official word from
Conrad was that visits should be delayed. I hadn't asked if that applied to
us, and I was afraid that Aiker Place might bar us from visiting Teresa.
But I tamped down my fears. We had to give it a try. Lois had given us

three tips: Dress conservatively. Be polite. Record everything. With my silver recorder turned on in my purse, we walked into the reception area.

This felt like a medical institution of some sort. It was definitely not home. We approached the front desk and said we're here to visit my sister who had just been admitted. I tried to appear calm, but my pulse was racing as the nurse checked her computer and turned to me with a pleasant smile. She confirmed Teresa's room number and waved us towards the elevators. I was relieved—one hurdle cleared.

We rode up to the third floor and stepped out near the nurses' station. It looked like a bustling hospital: medical equipment, wide hallways, railings, linoleum floors, and uniformed staff in scrubs walking back and forth. The nurse pointed us down the hallway towards Teresa's room, past an elderly man slumped in a wheelchair.

Teresa was sitting cross-legged on her bed. She grinned broadly as we walked in. "Franke!" she said. "Teresa!" I answered and rushed over to give her a hug. Next to her bed was a row of big plastic shopping bags stuffed with her clothing and belongings. I was pleased that she hadn't unpacked yet; I took it as a sign that she did not want to stay.

Behind her a thin white curtain was pulled across the room to separate her space from her roommate's. They shared a small washroom with a toilet and sink. I guessed there must be shower facilities somewhere nearby. This was a huge change from her home, where she had her own bedroom and a private bathroom, plus her own computer, a desk and a large whiteboard covered with all her notes. None of these things were allowed in the shared rooms at Aiker Place.

"We dropped by Dad's place to get a couple of things for you," I said, trying to sound as cheery as I could. Seeing her there was shocking; she looked so young and out of place. My heart ached. This felt like a betrayal of everything I'd been taught. And every value I held dear.

"Let us know anytime you want something," I said. I looked around the room. How could I begin to explain to Teresa why she couldn't go back to the condo—and why she had to live here?

Why had the government even allowed it? At that time, I thought that Teresa was the exception. I would soon learn that she wasn't. When the large institutions closed, some of the former residents were integrated into the community, but eventually thousands were put into nursing homes. They were out of sight and out of mind, segregated from society just as people with intellectual disabilities had been for centuries.

"So, where's my undershirt and my underwear?" Teresa asked.

"Let's see if we can find them." I said, as I started searching through the jumble of bags beside her bed. Deirdre and her husband, Chuck, must have been in such a hurry they forgot the basics of what she'd need.

"Maybe Conrad will bring them down," Bill suggested.

"I need my undershirt and my underwear," Teresa insisted.

"Okay, we'll get you whatever you need," I promised, glad that we could help her in small ways.

"Do you know our phone number?" Bill asked.

"Yeah," Teresa said, and she rhymed it off. "It's in my brain." Indeed, Teresa has always had a great memory for phone numbers, birthdays, and anniversaries.

"Do you have a phone?" Bill asked.

"No, I don't."

This would make it hard to communicate with her. But maybe she would be allowed to use the one at the nurses' station?

"I think I brought a small camera," I said, rummaging in my purse. "This isn't a very good one, but it's better than nothing." I snapped a photo of her on the bed, "You are wonderful!"

Teresa sits on her single bed at Aiker Place

"Thank you," Teresa said, smiling. She still looked like a teenager. She was wearing a baseball cap, a grey tracksuit with an iridescent zipper, and silver-grey Velcro runners.

"You are a terrific model."

"Franke!" she said, laughing. Suddenly a jumble of memories flooded back. Mom and Dad were avid camera buffs. We had photo albums and slide carousels galore. I remembered the photo of our summer line-up at my Aunt Rose's and Uncle Bob's cottage on Lake Huron. In that picture, we're all smiling. Mom has a camera around her neck, and Dad has a camera bag over his shoulder. Teresa is in the front row holding a red flyswatter and I'm wearing a pink cotton dress. It was one that I sewed myself thanks to my mother. She taught me how to choose a pattern, cut out the fabric, operate our Singer machine, and sew it all together into a dress. But more than that, her lessons taught me the importance of doing things right, and then how to fix things that go wrong. So many times, I'd make a mistake, curse at the unmade garment and my own stupidity, and then rip out the stitches and do it all over again. Eventually I'd have a new outfit to wear.

Like Paul Simon's song, we had a Kodachrome childhood. Some photos stand out in my head: Lynne wearing full makeup and an exotic costume for a high school play of *The King and I*; Phoebe in a long floral dress, doubled over laughing with her arms hugging herself; Deirdre treading water in the lake while drinking an orange crush; Siobhan as a curly-haired toddler in shallow water, giggling with delight; Conrad leaning over and speaking softly to Lynne's new infant son. And then Teresa as a teenager, dressed in her school uniform. That photo was framed and sitting beside her empty bed at Dad's condo.

And now, we were visiting Teresa in a nursing home? This sure seemed unfair. We all had comfortable homes and loving families. Why did they think this was good enough for Teresa?

When I asked Teresa what she was doing, she just said that she was keeping busy. I prodded, "Keeping busy, like what?"

"I want to stay out of trouble," Teresa said.

I was surprised to hear that. But Teresa instinctively knew that she had to "be good" to survive. Her daily decisions, such as what to eat, when to sleep, when to shower, etc., had sadly been usurped by the institutional structure of Aiker Place.

Years later I would learn about Jonathan Marchand, a young Quebec disability-rights activist who fought against his own forced placement in a nursing home. He called it "dehumanizing" and explained, "Whenever there's a conflict between your well-being, your rights and the rules...it's always the latter that wins. In an institution, you need to keep the peace and you need to stay in your lane, to stay quiet. They want you to be obedient... You've got to do what they say."[2] The consequence of not

*In the rush to put Teresa in the nursing home, her framed school photo and
her Sick Kids bottle with her finisher medals in it were left behind*

being "obedient" was to be physically or chemically restrained. I didn't
talk with Teresa about the worrisome implications.

"Out of trouble? So, what sort of things are you going to do?"

"I just have to sit and enjoy myself, being here."

Some people with Down syndrome, like those actors in *Rare*, might
have rebelled, but Teresa was frightened and trusting. The injustice made
me angry, but I could not snap my fingers and set her free. So I said, "We
could come and visit you regularly." And then I asked, "Will you give us
a call every night?"

"Yes, I will," Teresa answered.

"Would you? Yeah, that would be great." I was starting to feel emotional. I had been putting on a brave face, but I could feel the tears welling
up. "We would really like that. In fact, I would love that."

"Yeah," said Teresa.

"Sorry, I kind of miss you," I said, no longer able to stop the tears, and wondering how we were ever going to get her out.

Teresa comforted me, "I love you."

Tears were streaming down my face.

Teresa hugged me, "Don't cry. I'm right here." She looked at me, "Franke, why are you crying?"

"I miss you," I said, weeping.

"I miss you too," said Teresa.

I couldn't talk. I was so upset.

Teresa comforted me again, "Franke, don't cry. Come here. I love you."

Then she asked, "How is my father?"

"Well, we saw him. And he misses you," I said. "He wants you back home."

"Is my father getting better?" Teresa asked.

"Huh?" I said, not sure how to answer her question. "He misses you."

"Yeah, I miss him," Teresa said. "I'm going to call him tonight. You don't have to worry. Here," she said, reaching over and hugging me. "I'm right here. It's okay. I'm still yours." Teresa was so sweet and caring. Bill motioned us together and suggested we take a picture. I handed him my camera.

"Sit next to me," Teresa said, patting the bed.

"All right," Bill said as he took the photo. "Click three times for Teresa."

I looked at Teresa who was coping much better than me. "I'm upset. But you're not upset?"

"I'm trying to hide my feelings," she said.

"Why?" I asked with surprise.

"It's about my father," said Teresa.

"Why would you hide your feelings?" I asked again.

Teresa and Franke sitting on Teresa's single bed at Aiker Place

"Siobhan told me the news of what happened to my father."

"What happened to your father?"

"I don't know," she answered. "But she said they're taking him to Sunnybrook Hospital."

"No!" I said. "He's not going!"

"That's what Candi told me," Teresa answered.

"I know, but Dad doesn't want to go."

"And he said no?" she asked.

"Dad said no."

"Thank goodness!" Teresa said.

Teresa was trying to be a good trooper about it all, but it struck me that she had no understanding of what had been done to her. She had no awareness that a nursing home was for end-of-life care. If she stayed, she would be surrounded by sickness and death.

I kept coming back to the thought that we couldn't leave her there. It was the wrong place for her. It closed the door on what Teresa could do with her life.

"How about if I take a picture of you and Bill?"

"Yes. Me and Bill," Teresa answered.

Bill sat down beside Teresa. His eyes were red, and he was sobbing. Teresa put her arm around him. "Bill? Bill, do you have to do that?"

Bill tried to pull himself together.

Teresa said, "Bill, Come on! Take your hat off."

I took the photo. Bill and I were basket cases, weepy, teary and upset. But Teresa just looked at us and said, "You guys!"

"We're crazy," Bill said.

"I'm fine," Teresa said.

"You're fine?" Bill said. "Well, Teresa, you are a miracle! That's all I can say."

"I'm good at recovery," said Teresa. "But I need a new telephone."

"Will they allow you to have a telephone?" Bill asked.

"That reminds me, I have a cell phone right here," I said, pulling it out of my purse. "Do you want to call Dad right now?"

Teresa agreed, so I called Dad and handed the phone to Teresa. "Hi, Daddy, I love you," she said. "I want to come back on Friday morning."

We sat quietly as Teresa listened to Dad. I could also hear voices from the hallway. Someone was yelling and complaining, calling loudly for a nurse.

"I want to come back on Friday morning. I love you." Then she gave the phone back to me. Dad asked if we were going to bring Teresa home. "Not today, but we're going to try," I promised. It was time for us to leave. And I was feeling weepy again. How could we leave her here? Teresa was so defenceless.

Bill asked Teresa, "Do you think that you're going to stay here for a long time?"

"Just a short time," she answered.

"How long? Like a couple of weeks?"

"Just until Thursday or Friday morning," Teresa answered.

"But some people are saying that you can never go back."

"I want to go back," Teresa said.

"You have to let people know," Bill said. "If you don't tell them, you'll just stay here."

The sound of people yelling from down the hallway was becoming louder. I would not want to live here. I asked Teresa if she'd been able to sleep the night before.

"I was crying and scared," Teresa said. "I want to go back to the condo."

"Well, then you have to tell people that," I said. "Because right now, the plan is for you to stay here forever."

"Forever?" Teresa said. "That's too long."

A male resident was shouting in the background.

I looked at her and said, "Teresa, you have to let people know what you want. It's what YOU want. It's what YOU want."

Teresa answered, "Stay at the condo."

I WAS GLAD that Teresa wanted to go home, but of course we couldn't get her out without permission. It was heartbreaking. But what could we do? Teresa had been formally admitted. It didn't seem right at all. The staff were not trained to take care of a person with Down syndrome. I couldn't understand who would approve this placement. Publicly the government was opposed to this type of placement.

Just two months earlier the Ontario government had settled the Huronia survivors' lawsuit out of court. They agreed to pay $35 million collectively to 3,700 former residents and formally apologize.[3] This was the same institution for developmentally disabled children that Pierre Berton had warned about in 1960.[4] Forty-nine years later, they finally closed the place.

When we got home, I wrote in my red journal: "After going to Aiker Place today, it's obvious that it's unhealthy and inappropriate for Teresa. All downhill. No growth." There was nothing for Teresa to do there. She would literally be bored to death.

CHAPTER THIRTY-ONE

Kidnapped?

November 29, 2013

"TERESA IS NOT COMPLAINING." I SAID, "BUT IT'S DEFINITELY not a good place for her."

"No, of course it isn't," Dad answered.

Bill and I had called Dad to tell him about our visit to Aiker Place.[1] And then he told us about his chat with Conrad. "I told him that he had kidnapped Teresa. And oh boy! He really got mad about that."

"But with the power of attorney, Conrad had the legal right to take her," Bill cautioned.

"No." Dad didn't believe this.

"Yes!" Bill insisted.

"No, he doesn't!" Dad answered sharply.

"But Dad—"

"You know more law than I do," Dad laughed.

I was amused by their verbal sparring and Dad's gentle put-down. But for all Bill's certainty, I wasn't so sure he was right. We had not seen the documents, but we had seen a lot of funny business. Bill kept pushing. "I'm just telling you the way things work. For whatever reason, they have the legal power."

"Who has the legal power?" Dad asked.

"Conrad and Deirdre," Bill answered.

"Yes, I gave them the power of attorney," Dad said. Although we still hadn't found Teresa's, we had found Dad's power of attorney documents, which appointed Conrad and Deirdre. Dad asked, "But what does that have to do with kidnapping?"

"If Conrad and Deirdre have power of attorney over Teresa, they can decide where she lives," Bill said, "And since they have it over you, if you're deemed incompetent, they can decide where you live."

"The fact is the court has to decide," Dad objected.

"No," Bill said, "you've signed a document."

"She has been kidnapped," Dad insisted. "No question at all."

"Bill," I said, stepping in, "I don't think it really matters at this point."

I could see that Dad had been traumatized by this whole thing. Although Conrad and Deirdre would argue that they were just acting as substitute decision-makers, they had taken Teresa away without a word of warning. For Dad, it was a complete shock emotionally.

Bill also seemed to recognize this. "Okay, talking from a practical life experience, it does *feel* like they kidnapped her."

"Yes," I said. Then I focused on a possible solution. "Dad, if you want to undo this you have to revoke their power of attorney."

"I'm going to," Dad answered.

"And why don't you tell Conrad and Deirdre that you want Teresa back?" I asked.

"I want her back!" Dad said firmly. "And if we don't get her back, I'm going to get a lawyer."

"You should get the lawyer to write a letter to Conrad saying you're revoking the power of attorney," Bill said, still trying to redirect Dad's thinking.

"But they can't use power of attorney that way," Dad insisted with exasperation. "They have to follow my directions."

As I understood it, Dad had a point. There are many complex legal issues surrounding the power of attorney. First, the authority of an attorney only kicks in if the person who granted the appointment is incapable of making their own decisions. Capacity is a sliding scale about a person's ability to make decisions about finances, health care, living arrangements, and personal care. And a person's capacity could fluctuate. One day they could be unable to make any decisions, lying in the hospital unconscious, and then a few weeks later they could regain their capacity. Secondly, the attorneys were supposed to act in the person's "best interests" and follow their "capable directions," as Dad had just said.

My siblings simply insisted that they were acting in Dad's and Teresa's best interests. That seemed to be enough to justify what they were doing. Bill and I felt that if Dad labelled it kidnapping—even though that is how it felt emotionally—it would seem way too extreme.

"This is going to be very complicated," Bill sighed.

But Dad just kept going. "Once Conrad hears the word 'kidnapping', he will get Teresa out of there fast. And boy! That would really shake the dickens out of me if that happened!" Dad laughed. Then he added, "However, I don't want somebody to say that we're threatening this. Maybe that isn't a good thing."

Oh good, Dad was backing off, at least a little.

HEART WRENCHING. That's how Phoebe described it.

I was looking at my photos of Teresa from the day before. She was smiling up at me. Her innocent face, her fresh peaches-and-cream complexion, her blue eyes sparkling. There was just a thin curtain separating her from the next bed, where a woman lay, appearing to be near death.

Phoebe was trying to calm me down: *This whole transition could have been handled so much better. But now, the fact is that Teresa has already moved out.*

This was a preposterous assertion. Teresa did not "move out" voluntarily. Her right to decide where she lived was taken away.

But Phoebe believed in the system: *The agencies are working on it and they will find Teresa another spot. And since Dad is going to K-Wing, we have to find something for Teresa. So, whatever we do, we must not upset the situation—it could take years to get Teresa back to this place.*

I didn't want Teresa to get back to *this place*. We needed to get her out of there as soon as possible.

Phoebe kept pushing: *We should just leave things as they are. It could all work out, really. Teresa is smart, and even cunning, and with our support she will figure out a way through this.*

Ironically, this was the polar opposite of what Conrad had said.

The Teresa I saw was trusting and vulnerable. She didn't understand that her freedom had been taken away and her future written off. Without a strong advocate, she was powerless. I felt terribly disappointed.

Phoebe urged me to reconsider: *We should give Teresa a few weeks to adjust to life in her new home. We need to let go. What's done is done.*

No, I was not going to step back. What was done needed to be undone.

"I'M VERY SORRY to hear about this terrible situation," Dr. Abi-Jaoude wrote.

Our efforts to reach out to the community were getting results. The doctor was a psychiatrist at the University of Toronto. Our friend, Dr. David Healy, had told him about Teresa's plight. Dr. Abi-Jaoude wrote, "It seems to me that the issue is not one of misdiagnosis. Regardless of whether a person has Alzheimer's, Teresa, her father and the rest of the family should be treated with respect."[2]

We also spoke with Lois Sampson, an elder rights advocate. Teresa was not a "senior" but she was now living in a nursing home. Lois gave us practical advice on challenging health care institutions. "It's important," she said, "not to proceed or make decisions based on assumptions. Right now, you have no proof of anything Franke's siblings are telling you. You must get the documents."[3]

Lois continued: "One other thing, just because someone is not legally authorized to do something, it doesn't mean they won't try. So, even if someone doesn't have a valid power of attorney, they can often take actions that will be accepted by authorities who are likely to side with them. That happens a lot.

"Often, these cases are like dire games of chicken," she said. "Whoever can get away with whatever will be the winner. Those who use intimidation and deceit often achieve their goals over those who play fair."

There had been so many red flags by now that my trust was totally broken. I suspected that Teresa's admission papers and health profile had errors which made it appear—just as Conrad, Deirdre, and Siobhan had said—that Teresa needed to be in a nursing home.

This whole thing was so frustrating. The only thing we had was Deirdre's word. But, as Lois said, there was no proof that anything they said was true.

I WANTED TO COLLECT my thoughts before I phoned Dad. An image of him from two summers earlier jumped to mind. It was a wonderful occasion. Almost everyone in our large extended family was gathered around to celebrate his ninetieth birthday. Siobhan was hosting, and it

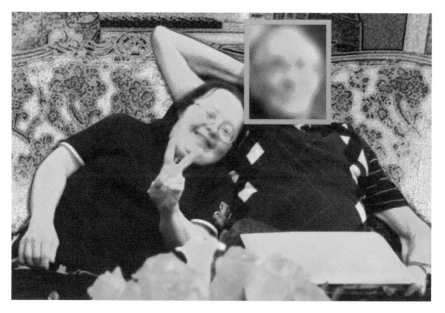

Teresa and Dad, relaxing at his ninetieth birthday party hosted by Siobhan

was a beautiful July day. Dad was beaming with happiness, health and confidence.

So much had changed since then, and now as I imagined Dad sitting alone in the condo, I worried. I called him: "Dad, if they try to take you over to K-Wing, don't go."

"I wouldn't go to K-Wing. They can't push me around that way."

"I just got an email from Phoebe, and they want you to go on a tour. Don't go. Or you won't come back."

"I wouldn't go near it. There's no way. But I will call the police if they give me a rough time with Teresa." His voice grew louder as he spat out the words, "Here she is—at a nursing home!"

"She is," I said. "And she's been there since Wednesday."

"Damn!" His voice was whistling with anger. "I'm really going to raise Cain. A nursing home! Dammit! I'm going to get her out of there."

"But how can you?"

"I'll tell the police what happened."

"I don't think that the police can help in this instance. You need to change the power of attorney."

"The power of attorney—that doesn't mean nothing!" Dad replied, exasperated and uncharacteristically using bad grammar. "They can only do something after I give them authority."

"But Dad—"

"Listen, I'm really upset now." Dad was steaming. "I want somebody to bring me down there! And I want to get her out of there."

"You know what?" I said. "Maybe we should take you down to Aiker Place?"

"I'll go with you if you want to go down."

"Yes," I said. "And we could try to get Teresa out."

We were both quiet for a moment, thinking.

"Of all the things to do!" he said with exasperation. "Of all the things to do! Teresa was perfectly happy here. With her own bedroom and all the rest."

"She was," I said, feeling sad that I had failed to head off this calamity.

"You watch me move!" he said, ending the call.

As soon as I got off the phone, I rushed downstairs and talked to Bill. He agreed it was a good idea, but he was worried. Weren't Deirdre and Conrad still in charge? Probably, I said. But the alternative was seeking guardianship through the court system, and that could take six months or more. If we went down to Aiker Place with Dad, he could ask to see the paperwork, and maybe there would be another way. We both believed that Dad would have the moral authority as Teresa's father and her primary caregiver. Maybe that would be enough.

We called Dad back. He was all riled up.

"I'm just so upset. I'm telling you," Dad said. "I'm going to show you what I can do. I'll get a lawyer."

"We are getting a lawyer for you," Bill answered. "But we can't get one until Monday."

"I'm telling you. I'm set to go to the police."

"I know, but the police will not help," Bill said.

"Yes, they will. They took her."

"I know, but they had legal documents," Bill said.

"They have nothing that could allow them to do that."

"They have the power of attorney," Bill said. "It's enough that the police will not arrest them."

"Teresa had her own home here. And everything!" Dad was fuming. "I'm so upset. What an awful thing to do! She was going out three or four times a week. It was just perfect. Look what the bastards have done!"

"Well, you know what?" I said. "I wonder if we should take you down there tonight?"

"What?" Dad asked.

"Take you down to Aiker Place," I said.

"No, not tonight. I'm too upset." Then he asked, "Where can I get Conrad?"

"It would be better to talk to a lawyer," Bill suggested.

"I'm going to the police," Dad said. "And I'm going to call Hank."

"No!" Bill was alarmed.

And I was too. I said, "Hank wants Teresa in the nursing home!" Dad must have thought that my brother-in-law could help because Hank had worked on the police force for decades.

"And Hank said you should be in K-Wing," Bill added.

"They wouldn't get me into K-Wing," Dad answered confidently.

"That's their plan," Bill said. "The thing is ... They're a bit tricky."

"That's all right," Dad said. "I'm not practising law, but I've still got a little bit of intelligence left."

"You have a lot of intelligence left," Bill said. "And you can stand up to these people."

"That's why I wanted to get a hold of you," Dad said. "Because I knew you were trying to do something."

"Right," Bill said. "The thing is, we called a lawyer."

"We called two lawyers today," I interjected.

"Actually, three lawyers today," Bill laughed.

"Yes, three," I said. "But we haven't found the right one—"

Click-click.

"What's that?" I asked.

Click-click. The sound of call waiting.

"Somebody is trying to get me," Dad said.

"Okay," I said.

"Bye," Dad said, ending the call.

"Call us back."

An hour later, he did. We were out. He left a message: "Please call Deirdre."

My heart sank.

CHAPTER THIRTY-TWO

Against Medical Advice

November 30, 2013, 11:00 a.m.

"WHAT IS YOUR POSITION ABOUT TERESA?" DAD ASKED. "Are you trying to help us? Or are you on the other side?"[1]

"I'm trying to help you," I said.

Dad sounded calmer than the night before. I knew this was a confusing time for him. He didn't know whom he could trust. I explained the situation simply. "Deirdre and Conrad put Teresa into a nursing home. We want to take you down there today to see Teresa. Is that okay with you?"

"Yes," he said. "If I could get a few things done here, yes."

"Okay," I said. "You left a message that you'd spoken with Deirdre last night?"

"I'm going to speak to Deirdre today."

Phew. "Don't bother speaking with her yet. Wait until you see Teresa for yourself."

Dad wanted immediate action and was ready to pull out the big guns. "I'm going to the press," he said. "I've tried to make arrangements to go to the *Toronto Star*."

"Just hold on to your hat," I said.

"That will blow this thing sky high!" he said.

"It would," I said, laughing at Dad's bravado. "But listen, let's go down to see Teresa first."

"Okay, but then I will carry on with the *Toronto Star* because what has been done to Teresa is just dreadful." It did seem like a story for the *Star*.

"They have written lots of columns on the terrible crisis in nursing homes," I said.

"That's what I want," Dad said.

I told him that I'd sent *The Star* articles to Conrad, Deirdre and Phoebe, but they just ignored them. I turned back to our immediate objective. "You and I can go down to Aiker Place today. You can see it for yourself. And I think you will be shocked."

"Yes. And I'll do something about it too," Dad said. "I'm upset about this." His voice pulsed with indignation and frustration.

"But right now," I said, trying to keep a lid on things, "just keep in mind that we're coming over. We'll be there in an hour, and we'll take you down to see Teresa."

"That's good," Dad said, relaxing a little. "It's nice to have you on my side."

MY GLOVED HAND was clasped in Bill's warm mitten as we walked over to Dad's place. It felt wintery, but it wasn't snowing. The sun was behind us, peeking through the clouds, as I watched our shadows falling ahead of us on the sidewalks of our quiet residential neighbourhood.

"This could be the day that changes everything," Bill said.

"Yes, maybe," I said. Immediately I thought of things that could go wrong. I tried to reframe his words as "the day that changes everything for the better." We were both committed to freeing Teresa. However, we were both apprehensive. My siblings' had stepped over the line, trampling

Dad is resolute as he leaves the condo to catch the cab to Aiker Place

on my core beliefs. Everything my parents had taught us about respecting Teresa's equal rights had been trashed.

When we got to Dad's apartment, Perla opened the door. I was surprised to see her, even though of course it was just part of her routine. But I was wary. I knew Perla had to follow Deirdre's and Conrad's orders; they were managing Dad's affairs and wrote the cheques.

Dad was in the kitchen and greeted me with a warm hug, saying he was ready to go. When Perla heard we were visiting Teresa, she asked to join us, so now it was a team of four.

As Dad put on his black parka and grey fedora, I remembered a photo of him in his World War Two Air Force uniform. He was a handsome young man with a bright spark in his eyes, his jaw firmly set. Dad was now standing tall with his shoulders drawn back, and I saw the same look of fierce determination in his eyes. We pulled on our winter coats and rushed downstairs to catch the cab.

It was an odd feeling to realize that my skills as an activist were now useful to Dad. I was happy about this, but it was also puzzling. If the old saying that the apple doesn't fall far from the tree is true, why was I the only one stepping forward to help Dad rescue Teresa? But I pushed those thoughts aside. Right now, we needed to get Dad down to Aiker Place.

WE DID NOT LOOK like a formidable rescue squad. The four of us were standing at the entrance to Aiker Place. It was like a motel carport, a low-ceilinged drive-through where families could conveniently stop to unload aging relatives, wheelchairs, and other baggage. I spotted the receptionist through the glass doors. What she would have seen was an elderly man arriving with a support worker and a middle-aged couple. She might have assumed that Dad was a potential client coming in for a tour. I don't think she would have guessed it was trouble walking through the front door.

At this point, we didn't know what we'd be able to achieve. Our ultimate goal was to rescue Teresa. But we didn't know if it was possible. The first step was to have Dad visit Teresa and then ask to see the admission papers. After that, it was all fuzzy.

We entered and walked across the ochre-tiled lobby. What decade was it when that colour was fashionable? The place was busier than two nights before when Bill and I had first visited. We signed in and took the elevator to the third floor. The doors opened to the nurses' station and a waft of antiseptic. We stepped out to see a gaunt, white-haired woman in the hallway, parked in a wheelchair, waiting for us like a sentinel. She showed no sign of awareness as we walked past her.

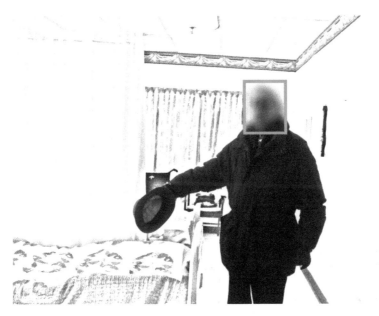

Where is my daughter? Dad asks as he gestures to her empty bed

Dad was not happy with what he saw. He was growling and muttering. "The money they think they're getting from my estate, they won't get it." As I directed him towards Teresa's room, he whispered, "First of all, I've got to get a lawyer."

We arrived at the room, but Teresa was not there. All of her belongings, still in plastic shopping bags, were lined up in a row beside the bed. Dad looked around expectantly.

"This is Teresa's room," I said. The flimsy white curtain was pulled across to separate Teresa's bed from her roommate's. The walls were beige. The ceiling was hung with industrial acoustic tiles. The lighting was fluorescent. It was practical but a far cry from the beautiful bedroom she had at Dad's condo.

Dad was grumbling unhappily. "Please sit down, Dad," I said. "We're going to be here for a while."

"I can't sit down," he said. He was upset.

While we were standing there spinning our worries, a young woman wearing a colourful sweater and jeans, her long hair tied in cornrow braids, walked into the room. Giving us a bright sunny smile, she introduced herself as Hope and said she was part of the transition team to help Teresa adjust to Aiker Place. She told us that Teresa was downstairs at lunch. And then, recognizing Dad—she had been to the condo before to work with Teresa—she said hello.

Dad just shook his head and looked grimly at the floor.

"He's not happy that Teresa was taken away," Bill explained.

"Oh, okay," Hope said.

But then Dad said, "We all want to look after Teresa, but they want to keep her here and have the government pay for it." Hope listened sympathetically but didn't say anything.

I looked over at Teresa's bags piled beside the bed and asked Hope what was going on. She sighed. "We've been asking Teresa to organize them and unpack them, but she said she's going home."

"Oh, yes." I was happy to hear that.

"I've been trying to explain to her that she is not going home," Hope added.

"Right," I said, silently praying that Teresa was right and Hope was wrong.

Then she said, "If you want, you can join Teresa at lunch and sit beside her. She's really eating down there!"

That caught my ear; Teresa was pre-diabetic and needed to watch her weight. "Does she have a limit on how much she can eat?" I asked.

"She has a limit," Hope said. "But you would have to ask the nutritionist."

We went downstairs to find Teresa. The cafeteria was a big, noisy room. Scraping chairs. Clattering dishes. Clinking cutlery. Loud voices.

The staff were serving the residents, many of whom were hard of hearing, and shouting to ask them if they wanted more coffee, more food or whatever.

We quickly spotted Teresa. She was sitting with three other residents at a plastic-topped table. It was clear she was enjoying her meal. The others were not so excited. They looked glum, sitting there silently while the staff members fed them. Teresa's youth and her ability to feed herself distinguished her. The other residents had lots of support. But Teresa didn't need that level of care; she was out of place.

When Dad saw Teresa, he zigzagged around the tables towards her. I followed him with my camera. Teresa looked up as Dad said, "Hi, sweetie." He bent over and kissed her on the head.

Teresa stood and reached for him. "Hi, Daddy!" They gave each other a long hug. I circled taking photos and marvelling at the moment. But the click-click of my camera caught people's attention. I was getting dirty looks. "I'm a photographer," I said, smiling and trying to deflect their concerns. "And this is a big moment."

After hugging Dad, Teresa sat down to finish her lunch. Dad, Perla, Bill, and I stood beside the table and gazed around the room. Teresa raised her hand to ask for a second helping of dessert. It was given with no questions asked.

I wanted to get on with our rescue mission, so I turned to Bill. "We need to see the paperwork."

"Yes, but we should talk to Teresa first," Bill said.

"Sure." My siblings *should* have asked Teresa if she wanted to come here in the first place, but they didn't. Now that she was here, we needed to ask her if she wanted to leave.

Dad leans over to kiss Teresa, then talks to her about going back home

Bill turned to Dad and gave him a nudge, "You should ask Teresa if she wants to come home."

"Ask Teresa?" he said.

"Yes," Bill said.

Dad leaned towards her and said, "Teresa, would you like to come home?"

She looked up from her second dessert and said, "I'll think about it."

Dad was a little surprised. He tried again, "Teresa, would you like to come home if you could?"

"I could," she answered.

Dad asked again, "Do you like it here?"

"I don't know," she answered.

"Or do you want to come home?" he asked.

"I want to come with you," Teresa said, looking at Dad.

"Well, I want you to come with me," Dad said, pleased. "But I can't take you today anyways."

"Actually, Dad," Bill said, "you can make a request to take her home today."

"We can make a request?" Dad asked, surprised.

"Yes," Bill answered. "We can't insist. But we can ask."

Dad was happy about this. He kissed Teresa on the cheek.

"I love you, Daddy," Teresa said, clapping her hands.

Dad bent towards Teresa and gave her another hug. "We're going to get you back home," he said, standing up again.

"I know, I know," Teresa said.

Dad looked at Bill, "If there is some way, could we do it today?"

I had spotted a nurse who looked like she was in charge, so I introduced myself and asked her if Dad could sign her out. She said sure, just go to the front desk. But then she looked at me quizzically. I had taken Lois's advice and was dressed conservatively. I was wearing a slim black zippered cardigan dress and a red rose scarf. The big Nikon camera slung around my neck might have made her wonder, though, because she asked, "Where are you taking her? Just out for the day?"

I hesitated for a moment, then said, "My dad wants to bring Teresa back home."

"From now on?" the nurse asked, surprised.

"Yes," I said firmly and smiled. I was glad that my audio recorder was turned on in my pocket. I could tell that the issue of Teresa coming home permanently was not something she wanted to deal with. She pointed upstairs and said, "Speak to the head nurse who's in charge of the third floor."

I WAS STARTING to feel anxious. We had been waiting in Teresa's room for an hour and we still didn't know if Dad would be able to sign Teresa out. We had spoken to the head nurse, who was courteous; then she left, promising to return with Teresa's file. It was taking a long time. Dad was sitting in a chair with a grim expression. Bill was leaning against the wall looking pensive. And Teresa was sitting on her bed, holding a plastic whistle in her mouth. She was demonstrating what she would do in case of an emergency. Fortunately, she wasn't blowing the whistle, which would have brought the staff running, and not in a good way.

Finally, the nurse returned with a handful of papers. She showed them to me, quickly flipping through the pages, saying, "This one is the advance directive. This one is the medical plan of treatment."

"What is this?" I asked, holding up the first sheet.

"The level of care form we would send to the hospital—CPR, all those things."

All those things? It was end-of-life instructions. This was definitely the wrong place for my little sister. "Teresa has Down syndrome," I said. "She's able to do so much. She can actually walk five kilometres! It seems to me that she could be in a group home where she's with other people of her ability."

"Yes," the nurse said.

"That's what we're concerned about," I said.

"Can Teresa leave if she wants?" Bill asked. "Is she allowed to go?"

"It's up to the family. If they want to take her out," the nurse responded.

"If Teresa's father wanted to take her out, could he do it?" Bill asked.

"If he is the power of attorney, yes, I would believe so," she said.

"Do you have the power of attorney documents?" Bill asked the nurse.

Dad's ears perked up at the mention of the legal documents. He was sitting down with his fedora on his lap. He looked at the nurse and said, "She means everything to me. We've been together since she was born. She's such a help. She's so bright."

"Okay," the nurse said.

"We want her home," Dad said.

Teresa gets ready to blow her emergency whistle

The nurse hesitated for a moment, then cocked her head and asked, "You guys didn't decide to bring her here, did you?"

"No," Bill answered. "The people that brought her here, her sister and her brother, did not tell Teresa's father that they were doing it."

That raised alarm bells. The nurse shook her head, "You need to talk to someone higher up than me about all that."

Bill pressed, "Teresa's father wants to know if he can take her out."

The nurse said, "He can call the DOC, the Director of Care, on Monday."

She was still shuffling through papers when she found one and handed it to me. "Is this signature your brother's?" she asked.

It was Teresa's admission form. I snapped a photo and passed the form to Dad.

"Conrad?" Dad asked.

"Look at the signature," Bill said, pointing to the form.

Dad studied the paper. "Who signed this?" he asked. Then he answered his own question with disbelief. "My son?"

I turned to the nurse and asked, "Do you have a power of attorney on file? It should list my dad."

"Okay, let me check," the nurse said. She took the papers and left.

Dad looked at me and asked, "Was that Conrad's signature?"

"Yes." I showed him the preview photo on my digital camera.

"He helped get her in here?" Dad asked, shaking his head in disbelief. He already knew this of course—Conrad had told him—but seeing it in writing made it all real.

"Yes," I said.

"Bastard!" he said.

"It should have been done with your consent," I said. "And with Teresa's consent."

"Gee, it's awful. It's just awful," Dad said. "I imagine they'll try to put me in next."

"That's right," I said.

"That's the plan," Bill said.

"They're trying to get you into K-Wing," I told Dad.

"I don't want to go anywhere," he said. "I'm able to look after myself. I don't need any help. If I have Teresa there, we're all set. We're a team."

"You have Perla, too," I said.

"Oh, Perla," Dad said. "She's such a help." Perla smiled and thanked Dad. She gave Teresa another hug and told us that she was heading home. I worried what she might report to Deirdre about her shift.

The nurse returned with another form.

I looked at it. Yes, this was it, the power of attorney. Excited, I read it carefully and then double-checked it.

Dad hugs Teresa hoping that he can bring her home

"Yes, Dad is the senior power of attorney," I said.

This piece of paper meant that Dad had the legal authority to sign Teresa out.

Bill turned to Dad and said confidently, "You can take Teresa home if you want."

"Yes! We want to take her home," Dad said. "Definitely!"

But the nurse interjected, "I'll have to talk to the DOC." (The Director of Care would have to approve our request for Teresa's discharge.)

"Tell them to call us," Bill answered. "We're going to take her home now."

"Really?" the nurse asked.

"Sure. Why not?" Bill said.

"All this is higher than me," the nurse said, backing off. "I can't just—"

"The point is that Dad has the power of attorney," I insisted.

"Yes," she said.

"He can sign Teresa out," I said firmly.

"Let me call the DOC." And she raced out of the room.

I crossed my fingers. It might just be possible to get Teresa out.

"She looks after me, and I look after her," Dad said, hugging Teresa. "She's everything to me, and I'm everything to her. It just breaks my heart."

It was breaking my heart too, but now I was optimistic that we could undo this mess.

"I'd like to have her home tonight," Dad said. "I don't want to take any chances."

"I think it's a good idea to take her out the way they brought her in," Bill said with a laugh. "Without warning!"

"I just want to get her out of here," Dad said and hugged Teresa again. "We all want you home!"

"Bless you. Bless you," Teresa said.

We waited again. And chatted with Hope. I told her that we were very concerned. This was not the right place for Teresa. She had another ten or twenty years to make the most of her life. Then we started talking about all the wonderful things we'd done with her.

"Five years ago, Teresa wouldn't walk around the block. But then Bill started coaching her and taking her on fitness walks. Now she can do five kilometres."

"Eight kilometres!" Bill interjected, giving Teresa a high five. "The Terry Fox Run!"

Dad was catching the excitement too. "Teresa has a great memory," he told Hope. "You should see what she can do with the telephone. She remembers all the numbers."

Franke tells the story about Teresa's personal trainer, Mrs. Kehlmann

"Right! I do," Teresa said proudly.

"She should be doing so much with her life," I continued. "You know, my mom was a real trailblazer. When Teresa was just an infant, Mom put her into an exercise program with a personal trainer. This was in 1964!"

"Wow!" Hope said with a big smile.

"The personal trainer, Mrs. Kehlmann, would exercise Teresa's arms and legs. I remember sitting outside the room, and the door was shut, and Teresa was loudly protesting. But Mom said, 'This is the best thing for Teresa. She has to exercise!' The neat thing is that by the time Teresa went to school, she could climb ropes by herself!"

"Wow!" Hope said again.

"Mom was a champion for Teresa, getting her to be the best that she could be. And so now, I will not accept this limitation. Teresa should not be in a nursing home."

Dad looked at me and said, "You two are something else. Honest to Pete, what you've done here is amazing. Whether it works or doesn't work, you are marvellous."

"We love Teresa," I said. "We just want to see her in the right spot."

Then Teresa suddenly piped up and asked, "Where is K-Wing?"

"That's where they want to put Dad," Bill said.

"But Dad wants to stay at the condo with you," I said to reassure her.

"Right," Teresa said.

"This man is your ticket out of here!" Bill said, waving his arm and pointing at Dad.

"Yes, Dad is the one," I said.

"And at home, you've got your own room," Dad added. "It's so much better than this place."

"Right," Teresa said.

"Everybody loves you," Dad said.

The nurse popped her head in and asked, "Who wants to talk to the DOC?"

"The Director of Care? Is she here?" I asked, standing up with Dad and Bill.

"Come to the phone," she instructed, waving us to come with her.

We followed her to the nurses' station, where the DOC was on the line. I introduced myself and told her that I was there with my dad and that we wanted to sign Teresa out. I said we were very concerned and asked if she would like to speak with my father.

Dad got on the phone with a friendly hello. He was trying to be positive, but as he continued to speak, I could hear the pain in his voice. "Really, she is such a marvellous daughter! We are a team at home. She really helps me, and I help her. And the whole family is a team. We really want her home so badly." Dad listened as the DOC spoke for a minute and then said, "Oh, my hearing is not quite as good as it could be. Can you just repeat that question to my daughter?" And he handed the phone to me.

The DOC warned that if we signed Teresa out, it would be against medical advice. She suggested that it would be better to wait until next week.

"But my dad could sign to get her out now, right?" I asked.

The DOC conceded we could but again asked us to wait.

"This is not the right home for Teresa," I said. "If we had experts here who know about nursing homes and people with Down syndrome, they would agree that putting a forty-nine-year-old with Down syndrome in a nursing home is not the right placement."

Again, the DOC acknowledged my point but said there could be an underlying medical condition that would make it necessary.

"There isn't," I insisted, sticking my neck out. I told her that Teresa's placement was based on misinformation. I did not believe that Teresa had Alzheimer's or needed 24/7 care. And I was darn sure that her crisis placement would never have been processed if the government knew I had offered to take her into my home. I also emphasized that it was done without my father's knowledge or permission. "That's why, ever since Teresa was admitted, he's been trying to figure out a way to get her out. And so we came down, confirmed that he has the power of attorney, and he would like to sign her out."

"Right now?" the DOC asked.

"Yes," I said. Then she asked to speak to the nurse, and I handed her the phone. After she finished, the nurse told us that she needed to email the doctor for his advice on Teresa's discharge.

"But the DOC did say that Dad could sign Teresa out," I insisted.

"But it would be against medical advice," the nurse answered. And she asked us to wait for the word from the doctor.

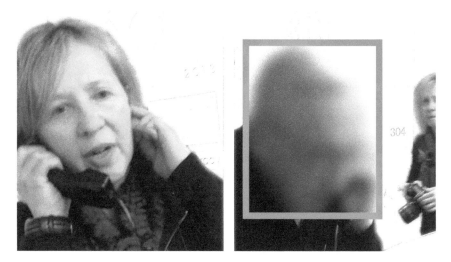

Franke and Dad on the phone pleading with Aiker officials

Fifteen minutes later, we were called back to the nurses' station. But it was not the doctor as I expected—it was the CEO, the Chief Executive Officer of Aiker Place.

The first thing she asked was if this had something to do with a board member. (Conrad had told us that Siobhan's husband was on their board.) I was pleased to hear her connect the dots on who Teresa was. "Yes, my brother-in-law, Jared, is on the board." But I kept the focus on our primary objective. "I'm here with my father to get Teresa," I said. "Dad wants to take her out today, and I'm happy to do that. I have been speaking with my lawyer today, so we can consult with him too."

The CEO may have been startled because she asked about the lawyer.

"Yes, if anything is required," I said, glad that she knew that I was getting legal advice. I told her that because Dad had the power of attorney, according to Aiker Place's own paperwork, he should have the authority to sign Teresa out immediately.

The CEO conceded this, but she objected to the timing. She asked us to wait a few days and keep Teresa at Aiker Place until they had time to properly sort things out. I imagined all the roadblocks we'd face.

"I would advise against that," I said. "This is not the right place for her. It is inappropriate. And it is unhealthy." My voice was strong and rising with emotion. "Teresa would flourish in the right group home. If she needs to stay at my house until that home is found, we will do that."

Then I asked for her contact info, and she told me again she was the CEO. I tried to be diplomatic. "This is a lovely place," I said, "but it's a lovely place for the right type of person. Teresa is the only one here who has Down syndrome and is forty-nine. Would you agree?"

She agreed that it could be an incorrect placement.

"This is so wrong," I said. "Out of desperation, my brother and sister opted for it. But there is no need for that desperation because Teresa can stay at my place. Or she can go back into the condo with my dad."

She said Aiker Place had stepped in to take Teresa only because they had heard Dad was going to K-Wing.

"He would only go to K-Wing under duress," I said. "He does not want to go."

She backed off. That was a family issue.

"A family issue?" I scoffed out loud. "My vote is for my dad to stay at the condo. And for us to have support for Dad and Teresa."

Then the CEO was surprised to hear that I had offered to have Teresa live in my home. Living with a sibling could be ideal for Teresa, she agreed. She finally gave us her okay. Dad could sign Teresa out.

I thanked her and gave her my contact info, just in case she needed to reach me, and we ended the call. I went back to give the news to Teresa, Dad and Bill.

"We got approval!" I raised my arms enthusiastically. "Teresa can come back to the condo." We high-fived each other.

"When?" Dad asked.

"Now," I said. "Right now!"

"Oh! Wow! You wonderful girl!" Dad gave me a big hug and a kiss on the cheek.

I could hardly believe it. Just a few more things, and we were out of there. Dad needed to sign the release papers, and we had to grab Teresa's things. Luckily, she had never unpacked. I looked at Dad, and I saw that his excitement was also turning to concern. What was going to happen next?

Dad stepped closer to Bill and me. The three of us stood, huddled in the middle of the room, our heads almost touching.

"You have to promise me," Dad said softly and with great seriousness, "that you will take care of Teresa if I can't."

As I tried to get the words out of my mouth, my mind was racing ahead to what it meant. This would be a giant step. There was no going back. This was going to change our lives forever, just as Bill had said earlier that day. "I promise. We'll take care of Teresa when the time comes."

"I want her to live with you when I'm gone," Dad said. "I don't want her ever coming back to a place like this. This is very important to me."

"Teresa can live with us," I said.

"Teresa is very important to me," Dad said.

"We will take care of her," Bill said.

"You count on me," I said.

"Thank you," Dad said, hugging me tightly.

Then the nurse asked us to come to the nurses' station to sign the paper. It was a one-page form titled "Release of Responsibility for Leaving the Facility Against Advice." Dad read it carefully. The nurse pointed to the spot for Dad to sign. He took the pen and signed the release with a determined flourish.

"Alright!" Bill said. "Let's get Teresa and get out of here!"

As we turned towards Teresa's room, the phone rang at the nurses' station. The nurse picked it up, said a few words, and then called after Dad, "Sir, that was your daughter Deirdre. She's driving down right now, and she wants you to wait. She'll be here in a couple of minutes."

Damn! My heart skipped a beat.

"Let's not wait," Dad said, shaking his head no.

"We're not waiting," I said to the nurse breezily. "We can chat with Deirdre when we get home."

We rushed into Teresa's room and told her it was official: "We're going back home." Teresa was thrilled. We grabbed her bags, hurried to the elevator, and I ordered a taxi on the way down. When we got to the ground floor, we raced across the lobby. Well, actually, the only thing racing was my heart. We inched our way across the lobby with Dad, Teresa and her shopping bags. When we finally made it out the front door, the carport was empty.

We had to wait. I worried, looking left and right, praying that the cab would arrive before Deirdre did. Then I saw it: a green and orange taxi. Bill threw Teresa's shopping bags into the trunk. Dad, Teresa and I climbed into the back seat, and then Bill jumped into the front. And we said, "Go!"

CHAPTER THIRTY-THREE

The Celebration

November 30, 2013, 3:30 p.m.

WE WERE OFF THE ROLLERCOASTER. THERE'D BEEN SO many ups and downs and hair-raising twists and turns.[1] And now, remarkably, things were back to normal. Teresa was once again in her own bedroom. I asked her, "How do you feel about being back home?"

"As good as new," she said, smiling at me. "But I need my clock radio."

Somehow, in the comings and goings, it had been misplaced. I found it funny that with all the big drama she'd been through that she'd noticed the disappearance of her clock radio, but—like most of us—she knows what belongs to her. She doesn't want anyone stealing her stuff. "Don't worry, we'll find it. I'm really glad to see you home."

"It's nice to be back in the condo," she said. "Thank you, Franke."

Bill had zipped out for some coffees, and we joined him in the living room for a celebration toast. Teresa sat on the piano bench wearing her purple fleece cardigan. Behind her, on top of the upright maple-coloured piano, were the framed photos from Mom and Dad's wedding day. In one photo, Mom was smiling radiantly in a long white wedding dress. Her complexion, as my grandmother would say, was like an English rose. Her

Teresa, happy to be back in her own bedroom at the condo

dark brown hair was pulled tightly back like a ballerina's, and she had a gauzy white veil on her head. She was seated with a magnificent bouquet of white calla lilies that covered her lap. Another wedding photo showed Mom and Dad together, smiling happily. As I looked at it, I thought what a beautiful couple they had made. Dad was young and handsome. I could see the resemblance to my own son, Trevor, in the intelligent sparkling eyes and the set of his jaw.

My emotions seesawed as I reflected on what Mom would think of that day's events. I could never have imagined this day, but I felt proud that we had helped Dad rescue Teresa. Bill handed out the coffees while I picked up my iPad to shoot another video.

"Cheers!" Teresa said, holding up her coffee.

Bill raised his cup to Teresa's. "Success!"

"Success!" I said, joining them.

Teresa and Dad together, happy to be home

"We got everything we asked for!" Dad said. "Getting Teresa back here, it's just so wonderful! Thank you, Franke and Bill. No question about it. You did the whole thing, the two of you!"

It was nice to hear Dad say that, but we couldn't have done it without his help. He really was Teresa's ticket to freedom. "Well, we're thrilled!" I said. "We really love Teresa. And we want to see that she is in the right place."

"Right," said Teresa, raising her drink again.

And then we talked about ordinary things, like how nice it was to see all the family photos in Dad's condo. And how we were enjoying our coffees, just the way we liked them. Bill and I had decaf, Dad had regular, and Teresa had ordered a full-power—caffeinated—cappuccino, just the way she liked it. We all laughed, and Dad thanked us again, saying, "You really did the job. You got Teresa back!"

Teresa raises her coffee cup to cheer her return home

"Cheers to Teresa," Bill said. "The champion of champions!"

Overjoyed to be back at the condo, we all knew that a cloud of uncertainty was hovering over us. Bill was the first one to say it out loud.

"Who knows what's going to happen next?"

"Well, when Deirdre checks," Dad replied chuckling, "she'll find that Teresa is back at home."

"Deirdre, Conrad and Candi are going to be unhappy," I said warily.

"I don't think that Deirdre would do anything against me," Dad said. "She must have gotten mixed up. I'll just call Deirdre and tell her I have Teresa here at home."

"They're going to say they have power of attorney over you," Bill cautioned.

"My God, I want to get that power of attorney off," Dad said. "I'll wait till tomorrow to do that."

"It might be a good idea to do it today," Bill suggested. Then he looked at me and asked, "Can you phone Vincente and ask him if there's a lawyer about?" I agreed and called Vincente, but I just got voicemail. Then we got up and went to Dad's office to see if we could find the documents.

That's when the phone rang.

Dad answered, "Hello?" And then, recognizing the voice, he said kindly, "Hi, dear." Bill and I waited silently by his side. "Pardon?" Dad asked. There was a touch of worry in his voice. A feeling of dread crept over me.

"What are you talking about?" he said with irritation. "I've got Teresa home now. She is here with me."

"Who is it?" I asked.

"Deirdre, I think," Dad said, and he handed me the phone.

"Hello? Oh, hello, Deirdre."

Deirdre started speaking so fast that I couldn't understand what she was saying, but she sounded agitated.

"Put her on speakerphone," Bill suggested, "to get her voice recorded."

I pushed the button to put the call on speaker.

"Deirdre? Can you hear us?" Bill asked.

Deirdre answered, "Yes, Bill."

"Okay," I said. I told Deirdre that we had signed Teresa out because Dad was listed as Teresa's primary decision-maker.

"I know, I know," Deirdre answered. "But what you didn't see was the other piece of paper, which is Dad's resignation."

What? Dad's resignation? This was news to us. I tried to ask her what she meant but she said, "No. Listen. I can read it to you." And she started reading loudly: "Notice of Resignation."

"But Deirdre?" I pleaded.

She ignored me and continued. "In accordance with section eleven of the Substitute Decisions Act—" I looked at Dad and Bill, but they were as shocked and surprised as me. Deirdre read on, sounding like a judge issuing her final decree. She read Dad's full legal name and said, "I hereby resign—"

"What in the world?" Dad asked.

Deirdre barrelled on: "...as the surviving attorney—"

"Deirdre!?" Dad demanded.

But she pushed on: "...for my daughter Teresa."

Dad raised his voice. "I'm going to cancel all my powers of attorney as of ..." Deirdre just kept reading. Dad spoke even louder, "As of right now! I'm cancelling all of them!"

But Deirdre didn't slow down. She raced to the finish: "... Effective immediately!"

We were stunned. We didn't understand what Deirdre had just read to us. But then she issued a warning: "If you do not return Teresa, the police will come and escort her. And you just think of how awful it's going to be for that poor little girl to be dragged back."

"But Deirdre," I protested.

"Return her!" she ordered. "I'm giving you your notice. And I'm hanging up now."

"Deirdre? Deirdre?" I pleaded.

"The police will come and get her," she warned.

"But Deirdre," I said, "you took Teresa away without Dad knowing..."

Deirdre didn't respond. We waited for another second, then Bill said, "I think she hung up." I looked at the phone, and yes, Deirdre had ended the call.

"She's going to call the police," Bill said.

"Yes," I said.

"But what? What is she doing?" Dad asked.

"She wants to call the police to get Teresa back into the nursing home," I said.

Dad shook his head, looking at us. "If they're using my power of attorney to force her back," he said, "I would say it's impossible."

We were all mystified. It seemed like a nasty trick. What was this resignation document about? Why would the police come and take Teresa? A nursing home was not a prison. And we had signed her out properly, after speaking with the Director of Care and the CEO. What was Deirdre doing?

CHAPTER THIRTY-FOUR

Return Teresa (or Else)

November 30, 2013, 4:00 p.m.

I KNEW THEY'D BE ANGRY, BUT THIS WAS A DEEPER LEVEL OF fury than I had ever imagined.[1] We were shaken by Deirdre's threats. To Dad's credit, he thought he could sort the mess out. While Teresa was busy putting her belongings back into her bedroom, Bill and I were with Dad in his home office. Dad was sitting in front of his computer with his papers laid out on his desk. Bill and I stood by his side as he dialed Deirdre's number. I held my recorder firmly, thanking my lucky stars that it could act as our digital witness. When Deirdre's husband picked up the line, I pressed start.

"Oh hi, Chuck," Dad said politely. "Something has gone crazy here! I don't know what in the world has happened, but I'm upset about it."

"It's because of what you've done!" Chuck said.

That caught Dad off guard. "What have I done?" he asked.

"You went and got Teresa," Chuck said accusingly.

"Of course I went to get Teresa," Dad asserted. "I'm really upset if you had anything to do with putting her there."

"You were wrong to do that," Chuck said. "You were wrong!"

"What?" Dad asked, startled. This was a side of his son-in-law that he'd never seen.

"And Deirdre has been such a help to you," said Chuck.

"That's right," Dad said. "And all of a sudden, she's done something like this? I don't understand."

"You've caused a lot of trouble for everyone," Chuck said.

"Call it what you like," Dad said, "I'm not going to have somebody come in here and take my daughter away from me!"

"She wasn't taken away," Chuck said.

"She sure was!" Dad insisted.

I could hardly believe my ears. How could Chuck say that Teresa wasn't taken away when that's exactly what they did? This was very confusing and upsetting.

"You have been my help all the way along," Dad said. "What have you done? What have you suddenly done?"

Chuck didn't answer.

"What in the world has come over you?" Dad asked.

"Dad?" It was Deirdre's voice. She must have taken the phone from Chuck.

"Yes," Dad answered politely.

Deirdre said, "Franke knows that we have documents to show you have dementia."

No, I thought. I certainly didn't know that. If Deirdre had any medical documents to back up her claims about Dad or Teresa, she'd never shown them to me.

However, the word "dementia" made Dad sit up straighter. It was the label they were using to disempower him. And Dad knew it. He immediately objected.

But before he could finish, Deirdre interrupted: "When the police come, they will have the documents. And they will drag this through. You don't want this, Dad."

"No. And you don't want it either," Dad snapped back. "I'm going to take every share of stock that I have, and I'll make sure that nobody gets it."

"You go ahead, Dad," Deirdre said, daring him to try.

"If you want to do it that way," Dad said. "I just can't believe that this is you."

Deirdre didn't waver: "The police are going to be there if you don't return Teresa."

"I have no intention of returning Teresa," Dad said. "But I tell you this, I'm going to get a solicitor. And I'm going to take action against you if you do this."

"Dad, the police are coming," Deirdre said. "I'm getting the paperwork together to give them. And I'm sorry that—"

"Shame on you!" Dad interrupted. "I can't believe this—"

"Shame on Franke," Deirdre insisted. "Shame on Franke. Shame on Franke! She had no business doing this." I held my tongue, not saying a word.

"What in the world?" Dad said.

"I have the legal documents to prove that I did it right," Deirdre warned. If anyone knew the importance of a paper trail, it was her.

"What in the world has come over you, Deirdre?" Dad said. "All of a sudden, you've gone crazy."

"Yep, yep. That's fine," Deirdre said, dismissing Dad's concerns.

But Dad was bewildered. "I've been so good to you. And you've been good to me. What have you done so suddenly?" Dad was shaking his head, hesitating, then he asked sternly, "Why would you want to put Teresa into a nursing home?"

"Because she will not have a home," Deirdre answered. "I'm not getting into this discussion, Dad. I answered the phone out of politeness. And now, we're done. The police will be at your—"

Dad exploded, "You said we're done. I'll show you what I can do. This is terrible. I'm so shocked by you. I can't believe it could happen."

A different voice came from the phone, "Dad?"

Dad was still speaking when the voice interjected again, "Dad, can you hear me?"

"Pardon?" Dad asked, his voice softening.

"Dad, it's Candi here. Can you hear me?" Deirdre had given the phone to my sister-in-law, Conrad's wife. She must have been listening at Deirdre's house.

"Yes, Candi?"

"Dad, we've worked very, very hard to make sure that Teresa has a safe place to live—"

Dad jumped on that: "She's got a safe place to live. Here with me!" And Dad had accepted my offer to take Teresa when the time came.

Candi waited for a second, then said, "Franke has come and upset the entire apple cart. You shouldn't be mad at Deirdre and Chuck or anybody else. You should be mad at your daughter Franke. She has done nothing to help us."

I had to agree with that. I had done everything I could to stop them.

Candi continued with her warning. "If Teresa doesn't go back to Aiker Place, the police will come to your doorstep. Then they will go to Franke and Bill's doorstep. Do you understand what we're saying?"

"Yes," Dad answered. "I'm going to get a hold of the bank right away and take all the powers of attorney away from you."

"We have all the powers of attorney," Candi said, "And you have no money that you can hold back from us."

I was surprised to hear her say that. It sounded like they had taken complete control over Dad's bank accounts. I imagined my siblings arguing that it was necessary because of what they called his dementia.

"I'm not sure what you're trying to do," Dad said. "But I will get a lawyer. It will cost money, and it will come out of your pocket."

"Dad?" Candi said. "We have talked to you many times about these plans, but unfortunately you don't remember!"

This made Dad angry—angrier than I had ever seen him in my entire life. "You don't know what assets I have!" Dad said, standing and raising his voice. "But you won't get a penny of them if you take one step right now. You won't get a penny!" This was the one weapon he had left to defend himself—threatening to disinherit them.

"We don't want your money or any of your assets," Candi said. "Maybe that's what Franke and Bill want—your money and your assets."

"I'm just shocked by you," Dad said. "I don't want to talk any further, but I'll tell you—you try to touch Teresa, and we'll never talk to each other again. But I will have a lawyer."

"Well—"

"Shame on you!" Dad said. "I can't believe you would do this!"

Candi responded with a warning: "Expect the police to arrive sometime in another half hour or so."

"Alright," Dad said. He was not backing down.

Candi continued, "They'll be taking Teresa back down to Aiker until she gets placed—"

"I'm pretty sure I'll stop that!" Dad said.

"I'm pretty sure you won't," Candi said.

"But if you succeed," Dad said, his voice rising, "I'll remove you from everything I've got in my estate! I will make sure you don't get a penny of it!" Then he slammed down the phone, ending the call.

The stress on Dad at that moment was enormous. It felt so tragic. But I admired his courage. With every fibre of his being, he was fighting to protect his daughter. This was the father I had known and loved all my life.

Bill and I were reeling. I tried to make sense of it. Why were my siblings so mad? Why were Deirdre and Candi threatening to call the police to force Teresa back? I didn't have any good answers, only bad ones. I knew that their threats felt very real. I worried that the police might give more credence to Deirdre because she was the mother of a cop. And maybe they would give her more credence simply because she called them first. That's when I came up with a new plan.

"You know what I think we should do? We should call the police ourselves."

"Yes," Dad said, his voice calm after the storm.

I called 911, and they connected me with an officer. After listening to our story, he said, "If your sister did call the police—"

"She was kidnapped!" Dad blurted out.

"Shush," I whispered, thinking that "kidnapping" might sound too extreme.

The officer continued: "The only reason that the police will apprehend someone is if they think the person is vulnerable. If they suspect there's abuse. Or if they deem that the person needs to be apprehended under the Mental Health Act for their own safety. It doesn't sound to me like that would apply here, but I'm not a doctor, so I don't know."

"Okay," I said.

"Your other sister..." The officer hesitated and then said, "I'm sensing that she told you that she had called the police to frighten you. To kind of coerce you—"

"I don't know," I said worriedly.

"When the police show up, the officers usually listen. In this kind of issue, there are usually two versions—your sister's and yours, right?"

"Right."

"They will listen to what you have to say," he said. "But it's a complicated issue because a medical professional has to determine whether your younger sister actually needs to be in a nursing home. From what you have explained to me, it doesn't sound like she needs to, but I don't know. It sounds like it's more of a civil problem than a real police problem." He finished up by saying that there were no active calls for Dad's address. He asked if we would like an officer to come by so we could file a police report. I said yes, that was a good idea. I gave him my phone number and the buzzer code for Dad's condo.

"YES, IT'S GOING to spoil our relationship." Dad was on another call. I didn't know who he was speaking to, but he was very upset. Bill was standing beside Dad recording a video on the iPad. It sounded like a female caller, who was explaining that all this was part of their plan of care for Teresa.

"By putting her in a nursing home!?" Dad said, spitting the words out. "I'll tell you—you won't get away with this!"

The caller continued but her voice was muffled.

"I won't go into K-Wing," Dad said loudly. "I'll tell you that too. I'm getting a lawyer. We'll stop that as well. I can't believe that you would do this to me!"

He must have been talking with one of my sisters or my sister-in-law.

"You better think a little bit about this. I'm going to make some changes. I'm going to immediately take you off of my will."

More muffled words.

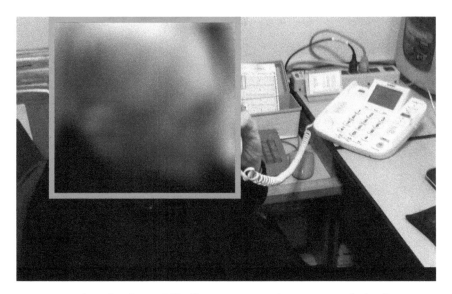

Dad on the phone, "I'll tell you—you won't get away with this!"

"I don't remember anything such," Dad said. "You call it dementia. I don't call it dementia," Dad said. "There's various degrees of dementia. Maybe somebody says I have it."

She kept insisting, saying something about a diagnosis. I was skeptical.

So was Dad. "Not that I know! Not that I know!" he answered heatedly. They were treating him as though this purported "diagnosis" instantly removed all his rights Dad continued, "I'm going to fight you tooth and nail. I'm getting an expensive lawyer. It will cost money. And it will come right out of your pocket."

The caller continued but I could only hear fuzzy fragments.

"You can't love me with what you're doing," Dad said. "I'm not going to say anything more. You say you don't care about the money. That's okay. But you won't get away with this one." He stood up, holding the phone. "I'm so upset. I can't believe that you would try to grab my daughter and take her away like that. And then threaten to do it again!"

She something about the police.

"I will never forgive you for what you're doing."

Dad ended the call.

"Was that Candi?" I asked.

Dad looked at me and said, "These people have gone mad."

WHILE DAD WAS on the phone, Teresa unpacked her bags and put everything back the way she liked it.

"Wow, you are organized!" Bill said as we walked in.

"Thank you." Teresa smiled.

Then I told her that the police were coming and they might try to take her back to Aiker Place.

"I want to stay at the condo with my father," Teresa said calmly. She didn't understand that there were forces swirling around us that we couldn't control.

"That's good," I said. "So, if the police come, just tell them that's what you want."

"I like it here," Teresa said.

"Good," Bill said. Then he turned to me. "We should do the new power of attorney thing, before the police arrive."

"Yes." We went back to Dad's office, worried that Conrad and Deirdre automatically would reject any new documents that Dad or Teresa signed. But to me, this just seemed arbitrary. Dad and Teresa had signed power of attorney documents *before*, they should be able to do it *again*. Dad agreed. We also knew it would be better to have a lawyer witness the signature, but with Deirdre's threats—the police would be arriving in the next thirty minutes or so—we needed to do something immediately.

We went online to the website for the Ontario Office of the Attorney General to read the details and download the official government forms.

Dad fills out the power of attorney forms, reading the instructions online

The two-page document looked straightforward until, after reading the instructions, we realized we needed two witnesses to appoint me.

According to the rules, the spouse of the attorney cannot act as a witness, so Bill could not be a witness. I asked Dad if he knew anyone. He said he'd ask his neighbours. He walked across the hallway and knocked at their door. Fortunately, they were home and agreed.

We also wanted Teresa to sign new documents. But Teresa was reluctant. After all that had happened, she was nervous and didn't want to sign anything. "No, thank you," she said. And none of us could convince her. So, we decided to go ahead with Dad's power of attorney and hoped that his authority—as Teresa's father and lifelong caregiver—would protect Teresa when the police came.

A few minutes later, the neighbours arrived. We had the official signing ceremony for Dad in his kitchen. I took lots of photos: more proof,

Teresa signs her power of attorney for personal care (family name redacted)

just in case. After Dad had signed his, I asked Teresa one more time, "Do you want to sign a new power of attorney appointing Dad and me?"

She had been watching Dad as he signed his new documents. Dad looked at Teresa and said, "It would really be a good idea."

"Do you want me to be your new power of attorney?" I asked.

"No," she said, "I want my father."

"That's good," Dad said.

"That's perfect," I said. "Can I be the substitute if Dad is not available?"

"Yes, that's okay," Teresa agreed.

We filled in the form, naming Dad as her primary attorney and me as the secondary. We gave the form to Teresa, and she looked over it carefully, reading the names aloud: her name, Dad's name and my name.

Then she said it was okay and signed it. Dad's two neighbours signed as her witnesses, and we were done. And the police had not arrived yet.

Phew! Dad's neighbours wished us luck and left. Then we waited. And we worried.

Technically old power of attorney documents are automatically revoked when new ones are signed. But Dad didn't want to take any chances. He took the copies of his old documents and drew a big X over each sheet, wrote in "Revoked," then dated and initialed each page. I took more photos, double-checking everything to make sure it was correct.

What was next? When would the police arrive? Were they still coming? I called the police department and asked. They said yes, the police were coming, but they didn't know when. It was getting close to dinner time, so we ordered pizza. Teresa was thrilled. We were all starving as we hadn't eaten since breakfast. When the pizza arrived, Bill served it onto four plates. I could see the stress and exhaustion on his face. It had been a hell of a day: the tremendous thrill of helping Dad rescue Teresa and then the confusing attacks by my siblings. The whole experience reinforced how lucky I was to have married Bill. Our values were aligned. He was as committed as I was to seeing that Teresa had a full life. *Somehow* this was all going to work out. We were doing the right thing and that was all I needed to think about.

We sat together at Dad's small dining room table, savouring the miracle that Teresa was with us. "Wow! This is so good," Dad said. "Thank you for all your help today! You really did it."

"Thanks, Dad, but it took all of us. We did it together." I looked at Teresa eating her pizza and said, "Isn't this better than the nursing home?"

"Yes," Teresa answered. "Much better!"

Bill serves pizza at Dad's condo while we wait for the Toronto police

CHAPTER THIRTY-FIVE

Apprehension

November 30, 2013, 8:00 p.m.

D ESPITE MY SIBLINGS' NEGATIVE REACTIONS, I WAS ELATED
that we had rescued Teresa.[1] We had finished dinner and, with
the dishes done, we were finally relaxing. I was making a video of Teresa
showing off her activity calendar to Bill. She had carried books and photos
from her bedroom and arrayed them on the table.

"Look at the Terry Fox poster again," I said, filming her.

"It's awesome," Teresa said.

Bill picked up Teresa's official photo from the Terry Fox Run. "Isn't
that a great photo?" It was an action shot from a beautiful summer day.
Teresa was marching along, swinging her arms and wearing her black
Terry Fox T-shirt. "Superstar!" He pointed to the photo. "See? She's doing
the power walk."

Bill turned to the next month on Teresa's calendar. The calendar was
a creative solution to a problem. Five years earlier, Lynne and Siobhan
had been concerned that Teresa was too sheltered living with Dad. To
get her out into the world, they proposed several initiatives. One idea was
that each family member would do something fun with Teresa at least
once a year. That was the birth of Teresa's activity calendar.

Teresa holds up her book while Bill holds out Teresa's Terry Fox Run photo

Everyone in the family planned events with her, which were then marked on her calendar. The outings were something she looked forward to. It was a success and Teresa loved it. Bill and I were especially enthusiastic. We set the goal of helping Teresa improve her fitness so she could do the Terry Fox Run. We gave her new running shoes and then went on regular fitness walks. Bill acted as a coach, motivating Teresa to get fit. We also went to cultural events with Teresa, like *Rare* and exhibits at the Art Gallery.

"There's a nice picture of Dad," Bill said, pointing to the calendar.

"Right!" Teresa said, smiling happily. She was enjoying the show and tell.

Bill flipped to the next month and said, "Look at this, the Sick Kids Walk!"

"Right, I'll show it to you." She went into her room and returned with her Sick Kids T-shirts, piling them on the table.

"Meagan's Walk," Bill said, holding it up. "That was the best!"

"Right," said Teresa, beaming with pride. Then she returned to her room and came back with a golden trophy. "And this thingy! My trophy and my medal."

"Where'd you get that from?" Bill asked.

"The Scott Mission," Teresa said. That's where she worked once a week, packing lunches to help support the homeless.

"That's so cool!" Bill said.

"Beautiful," I agreed, delighted to have this all on video. Teresa was certainly happy to be home and show us her things.

"Thank you," Teresa said, smiling.

Then we heard an urgent knocking at the front door. Bill got up to answer it. Teresa picked up her things and carried them back to her room. I kept filming, focused on Teresa, until I heard the voices. I turned towards the front door.

It was the police.

"And paramedics too?" Bill asked, seeing a stretcher and the medical team.

The first cop stepped in. He looked big and beefy, especially wearing a bulletproof vest and gun.

"Who are you?" he barked.

"That's Bill." It was Deirdre's voice coming from the hallway. She had arrived with the police. She looked through the door and saw me, "And that's Frances right there." I was wearing the same clothes as I had been all day—the black cardigan dress with the red rose scarf.

Bill asked, "What are you doing?"

"Come on out," the cop ordered. "Come out."

"You have to leave," Deirdre said.

"Can I see the documentation?" Bill asked.

The Toronto police officer orders Franke to leave Dad's condo

"No, just hang on," the cop said. Then he caught my eye and waved me to the front door, "Come on out. Come out."

I shook my head. Bill stepped back, turned and saw Teresa coming out of her room towards the front door. "Teresa!" he said.

I was startled and dropped my iPad on the table. I grabbed Teresa and pulled her away from the door. Dad came out of his bedroom into the kitchen and saw the police. He stood by my side as Bill backed up and joined us.

It was a big crew: two Toronto Police officers, two paramedics with a stretcher, my two sisters, and their husbands. They filed grimly into Dad's apartment, crowding into his tiny kitchen, leaving the stretcher in the hall. The two couples—Deirdre and Chuck, Siobhan and Jared—lined up behind the cops and stared at us sternly.

I felt confused, not sure what was happening. I had called the Toronto Police too, and they had promised to come and take my report. But this was something else.

I couldn't help but worry about the impartiality of the police, with three relatives on the force. I was hoping that they would be fair and listen to both sides.

As we faced the others, I put my hand in my pocket and felt my recorder. I was so flustered when the police arrived that I had stopped the video. But now I was concerned about how things were unfolding. I needed to document this. I took the silver recorder out of my pocket and turned it on.

The first cop said, "We want to make sure that you're okay."

"We're okay. We're fine," Teresa answered. I pulled her closer to me, worried they were going to take her away.

The cop continued, "There's an allegation that your father threatened to kill himself a couple of days ago."

I gasped. Bill spoke, "That's not true."

"It is true," Chuck countered in a loud whisper.

What the hell kind of stunt was this? Dad was not suicidal. We had just rescued Teresa, and we were celebrating. This was bizarre. But my attention was riveted on Deirdre.

She raised her arm, pointing at me. "We're being recorded!" She stabbed her finger. "Franke! She's got a tape recorder."

I stepped forward. "Yes, I've got a recorder." And I held up my small, silver recorder for everyone to see. "Is that okay?"

The cop nodded and continued, "So, based on that information, your dad is going to have to go into the hospital to be assessed."

Holy fuck! They're going to take Dad. I looked back at Deirdre again. She had repeatedly told us that the police were coming to get Teresa. This was a terrible twist. But months ago, Siobhan had predicted it. She warned me that things could get so bad that the police would be called to cart Dad off to Sunnybrook.

"That's fine, but can we tell our story? Or not?" Bill asked.

The cop ignored him. "Your dad is going to be apprehended under the Mental Health Act."

The Mental Health Act?

The cop continued. "And as of right now—"

"Sorry," Dad interrupted. "I'm ninety-one, and I'm a little bit stupid, but ..." he said, laughing at his own self-deprecation.

"No, no," the cop said, acknowledging Dad.

"I'm getting on now," Dad admitted.

The cop tipped his head towards Dad. "My pleasure. We want to make sure you're okay. Just make sure you go to Sunnybrook Hospital."

Then the cop turned and spoke to everyone. "We have the paramedics. He's not going to go in the back of the police car, obviously. But we want to make sure that he's okay ... mentally."

"But are we able to give you a statement?" I asked.

The cop shook his head, no. "We're working on third-party information that—"

"We called the police, too," I said. "Are you aware that we called the police?" It felt like we were being steamrolled.

The cop lifted his hand to silence me. "Guys!" he said. "We'll talk in a minute. Right now, I don't want to get anybody upset."

The second cop stepped forward and spoke to Dad. "Sir, we're taking you to the hospital to get you checked out."

"For how long?" Dad asked.

I pleaded, "But we should tell you what happened."

"Just ..." The first cop held up his hand again. "First, we want to make sure that he's well. Based on the information that Deirdre has told us, we have to act on it."

I objected, "But we called the police too!"

"I'm not going to entertain this and get your dad, or anybody else, upset." Then he tried to brush me off, "We'll talk in a minute."

I objected again. "I'm just concerned that they're going to the hospital with Deirdre." I was worried that she would not tell the whole story.

"No," the cop said. "We'll talk about that later." Then he looked at Dad, gestured towards the door, and asked, "Can we go?"

Dad looked at him and said, "I don't know what's going on to tell you the truth."

Bill stepped in. "They're taking you to Sunnybrook Hospital."

"Pardon?" Dad asked.

Bill pointed to Deirdre and the others lined up against the kitchen cupboards. "Deirdre and Chuck and Siobhan have all said that you are suicidal. So, they're taking you to Sunnybrook Hospital."

"That I'm suicidal?" Dad said incredulously.

"That's what they're saying," Bill said.

"What are they talking about?" Dad asked, turning and looking at his children.

The cop answered Dad's question: "Four days ago, on Wednesday, and again on Friday—" The cop stopped, turned to Deirdre and asked, "Is that right?"

Deirdre nodded and added, "And on Thursday too."

He continued, "Deirdre said that you were going to kill yourself."

What a pile of crap! I thought. Dad had threatened to change his will. And now they were saying he was suicidal.

"That I was what?" Dad asked incredulously.

Deirdre stepped forward and answered, "That you were going to ask God—" She interrupted herself and looked at me holding the recorder. "Sorry. Turn it off, Franke. And then we'll talk."

"No," I said defiantly, holding up my recorder with the red light on. I wanted her to know I was recording everything.

"You're making public statements," Bill said. "Go ahead. Make them."

Deirdre and I glared at each other.

The cop intervened. "That's fine." He looked at Deirdre, "Just tell them what you told me."

Deirdre hesitated, then began quietly, "He—"

Dad spoke up, "I don't know what you're talking about."

Deirdre answered loudly, "He said that he would seek permission from God to kill himself."

That was all the cop needed. "Okay, based on that information—"

"I don't know ..." Dad said, interrupting and flustered.

"We're not doctors," the cop said, looking at him. "We're just here to help."

It didn't seem like he was trying to help. I stepped forward again, "But did you realize they took Teresa without asking Dad?"

"That's secondary," the cop said.

"But," Bill interrupted, "they took Teresa away without telling him. And if you're asking why is he upset? There are plenty of reasons."

"I didn't ask why he's upset," the cop said firmly. And he gave Bill a withering look, letting him know that he better shut up. Bill nodded and stepped back.

I was shocked by the cop's dismissal. And I was intimidated. I knew I couldn't talk back, but I vowed to file a complaint later.

The cop continued, "There's an allegation that Deirdre has told us about. We're here to act on it. Everything else is secondary. I'm duty bound. I don't have an option."

Bill said, "What if the allegation is—"

The cop cut him off and snapped, "I'm not going to entertain a what-if."

The cop wouldn't even let us ask the question: *What if the allegation is false?* I was getting a very bad feeling about this. The cop continued, "I'm only going to entertain what was said and work on facts and issues. Legally, what do I have to do? What is righteous?"

The cop was satisfied with his own argument. He turned to the paramedics and asked them to get Dad. The two of them approached Dad from either side, taking his arms and asking if he was ready to leave. Dad just shook his head, no.

Deirdre and Siobhan approached us. Siobhan smiled and bent down towards Teresa to say hello. Teresa nervously tightened her grip on my arm. The last time Teresa had seen Siobhan was at the nursing home.

Deirdre glared at us, "You had no business taking her."

"We had plenty of business," Bill said.

"We did," I repeated.

The cop interrupted and looked at Bill, "What's your name again, sir?"

"Bill James."

"Bill, I don't want to ..." Another unspoken threat.

The paramedics prompted Dad, "Okay, so our bed's outside."

"Pardon?" Dad asked.

"Our bed is outside if you want to come."

Why were the paramedics trying to put Dad on a stretcher? He didn't need one. Dad just shook his head.

"Can I ask a question?" Bill said, speaking to the cop.

"Absolutely, sir."

"Where is Teresa going?"

The cop looked at Deirdre, then me, then back at Deirdre. "Who has the authority?"

"I do," Deirdre said immediately.

"I do!" I said.

The cop challenged me, "Do you have documentation for this?"

"Yes."

The cop was not sure. He looked at both of us, "Can she stay? Or does she have to go? Like I don't know ..."

Deirdre asserted, "My father is incapable of making a power of attorney."

"I have the power of attorney for Teresa," I said.

"Signed when?" Deirdre asked.

"And for Dad too," I said.

"Signed when?" Deirdre asked again.

"It was signed today."

"So, it's—"

"Guys!" the cop interjected, stopping the argument. "Listen. Let's just make sure your dad's fine. And get him over to the hospital."

But I kept pushing, "Do you want me to show you the documentation?"

"Sure," he said. I turned to Bill and asked him to get the paperwork out of his bag.

Deirdre turned to Dad. "Say goodbye to Teresa. You're going to the hospital."

"What are you talking about?" Dad was incredulous.

Bill answered, "They're taking you against your will."

"For what?" Dad asked.

"For being mentally ill," Bill said.

"Oh, that's ridiculous," Dad said.

"No," Chuck said. His voice was bristling with anger and certainty.

"What have I got to do?" Dad asked.

The cop intervened, "Your daughter—"

Bill continued, "Your children are betraying you."

"Hang on!" The cop did not like this. He defended Deirdre, "In good faith, your daughter has said this in front of us."

"Which daughter has said that I'm mentally ill?" Dad asked.

"Deirdre!" I said.

The cop continued, "Deirdre has made an allegation—"

"Deirdre!" Dad said, looking at her. "Shame on you!"

Deirdre glared at me.

I handed the power of attorney papers to the cop. I showed him where they named me as the attorney for both Dad and Teresa. He just shrugged his shoulders. "I'm putting the power of attorney off to the side. I'm working under the Mental Health Act."

What? Why was he pushing me aside? If he was really there to protect Dad's health, why wasn't he listening to me? I had been with Dad all day and knew exactly what had happened.

The two paramedics were still trying to get Dad to go outside. Dad wasn't moving.

"Who's going to take care of Teresa?" Bill asked again.

"That's a legal thing," the cop said, hesitating.

"We will take Teresa with us," I said firmly.

"No!" Deirdre said.

"Deirdre! I've got Teresa's power of attorney, right here." I held out the documents.

Deirdre dismissed this, "Dad isn't capable—"

"Guys!?" the cop interjected, trying to shut us up.

"But Teresa has the power of attorney over herself!" I insisted. She had the right to choose her own attorney.

"Hello? Hello?" the cop said, trying to get our attention.

"That'll get fixed Monday," Chuck warned from the other side of the room.

"Hello?" The cop stepped in between us to break the impasse. "Guys, do me a favour. Everybody, just calm down." Teresa was still hugging me tightly. It seemed like the cop might let Teresa stay with me, but he was going to take Dad away.

But Dad did not want this. Dad stepped away from the paramedics and asked, "What have I got to do? Go out and play a round of golf for you or something?" He stood with his arms spread wide, looking at us, asking everyone to pay attention. As far as he was concerned, the allegations were false—and this entire apprehension was pure cockamamie.

The cop was still trying to settle things down. "This gentleman is twice as old as I am. And I'm getting kind of sweaty." Then he looked at Deirdre and me. He said, "This legal battle for Teresa, I don't know how it's going to work out."

"I'm calling my lawyer," I said, pulling out my phone.

"Don't get your dad upset," the cop warned, watching me dial. Vincente answered, and as soon as he did, the cop asked for my cell phone. He told Vincente that Dad was being apprehended under the Mental Health Act. He stepped aside to continue the call.

Things were not going in the right direction. The paramedics were still urging Dad to leave, but Teresa grabbed onto Dad and wrapped her arms tightly around his waist. Dad said, "This is not fair to Teresa. She's been with me all her life." Then he looked up and asked, "Who brought this on?"

"Deirdre," I said.

"Franke!" Deirdre said.

"Deirdre," I said.

"Deirdre?" Dad asked, looking directly at her with astonishment.

"Franke! Franke!" Deirdre said, pointing at me. "She had no business taking Teresa."

I was surprised to hear Deirdre saying this out loud. It seemed like she was admitting that this was retaliation for our efforts to rescue Teresa.

"A piece of work," Chuck said, eyeing me from the other side.

The cop was watching us while he was listening to Vincente. He covered the phone for a second and said, "Guys? Guys? This gentleman is ninety-one."

Dad was standing in the centre of the room. He looked around at the family and asked, "These kids, how could they possibly suggest I didn't know what I was doing?"

The second cop answered Dad's question, "Nobody is suggesting that you're not mentally sane."

"Is it because I'm looking after Teresa?" Dad asked.

Exactly, I thought.

"No," the cop answered.

"What is it?" Dad asked.

"The direct allegation that we're here to—"

Dad interrupted, "The allegation is what? That I'm *non compos mentis?*"

"Can I tell you?" the cop said, getting frustrated with Dad's questions and perhaps baffled by his use of Latin and legal terminology. "Your daughter told the police that you wanted permission from God to kill yourself."

"I wanted permission?" Dad asked. This just didn't make sense to him.

"Permission from God to kill yourself," the cop explained.

"I'm sorry," Dad said. It seemed like Dad couldn't believe his own ears. He apologized, "I'm not hearing as well as I could when I was younger."

The cop repeated it a third time. "Your daughter told the police that four days ago, you wanted permission from God to kill yourself."

"That's ridiculous!" Dad said.

"That's the information that we are bound to act on," the cop said.

That didn't sound right to me. According to the Mental Health Act, a police officer should only apprehend if there is an immediate and dangerous potential of "serious bodily harm" or "serious physical impairment." The *alleged* verbal suicide threat had occurred four days earlier. Conrad had dismissed the threat with dark humour in a family email, so he hadn't seemed concerned about it. And here was Dad four days later, obviously healthy and denying he had any such intentions. And certainly, it was clear to me that there was no danger of self-harm.

"What am I supposed to do to prove that I'm okay?" Dad asked.

"Come with us, talk to the doctor," the cop answered.

"But it's terrible! My God! What have I got to do?" Dad was looking around. He was very upset. "Jesus Murphy!"

The cop said, "We have to act on it."

"I know you do," Dad said, conceding some ground. "But you can see... There's nothing wrong with my intelligence. You can tell by talking to me."

"I don't see..." the cop said.

I could see that the cop was not going to bend.

Teresa was still holding on to Dad for dear life. Dad looked at her and put his arms around her. "Am I a good daddy?" he asked. Then he looked at everyone else. "She's holding on to me like... she never wants to let go." Teresa squeezed even tighter. Dad wrapped his arms around her protectively.

I needed to stay calm. The first cop came back and asked me if we would go to the hospital and speak to the doctors. It seemed like there was nothing I could do to stop the police, so I agreed, hoping the doctors would listen. Then he gave my phone back, saying Vincente was still on the line. I told Vincente that it didn't look like the police officers would back off and I ended the call.

Teresa was still clinging to Dad. The cops asked Bill to help, asking if he could get Teresa to release her grip on Dad. Bill crouched on his knees and asked her to let go.

"No!" she answered.

"It's hard on her. And it's not fair to her," Dad said, hoping that someone would listen. But the paramedics moved in closer, reaching towards him. "There's nothing wrong with my intelligence," he said defensively.

Bill crouched in front of Teresa, speaking to her. "If you want to protect Dad, you have to let him go."

The paramedic answered Dad, "We are worried about the allegation."

"We got you out of the nursing home," Bill told Teresa, trying to reassure her.

"Sir, there is concern," the paramedic said, "because we have the words of suicide."

"You can see," Dad answered, "I'm not the suicidal type."

"Only a doctor—" the paramedic tried to answer.

"This is unfair!" Dad interrupted. "I'm not the type." But then he shrugged and shook his head. It looked like Dad was conceding. With Bill's coaxing, Teresa finally released her grip on Dad.

"Let's get it over with," Dad said with resignation. The paramedics took his arms again, turning him towards the door.

Deirdre stood in front of them, frazzled and simmering, but somehow triumphant.

Dad looked at her and said, "You should have been able to tell them."

"I did tell him, Dad," Deirdre answered.

"You told them what?" Dad asked.

"To take your death threat seriously," said Deirdre.

"What do you mean, my death threat?" Dad growled as he shook himself away from the paramedics. "I didn't make a death threat!"

"Yes, you did," Chuck said.

"Why would I make a death threat?" Dad asked.

Deirdre stared at him silently, pursing her lips.

The two paramedics took Dad's arms again and guided him towards the door. Deirdre followed.

Dad looked back at her, "What are you doing to me, Deirdre? Shame on you!"

As Dad was ushered out, the first cop came back into the living room, where Bill, Teresa and I were waiting. The cop said, "So, whatever happens at the hospital…I don't know. I'm not a doctor, but the grounds are here for the apprehension. And I have to apprehend."

He was saying it again. He had no choice. I didn't believe him.

I looked at the cop and tried one more time. "Do you want to take a statement from us?"

"Not really," he said. "I don't need a statement. The grounds are there for the apprehension." Then he turned and exited, the sound of his boot heels echoing on the parquet floor.

CHAPTER THIRTY-SIX

My Manifesto

November 30, 2013, 8:30 p.m.

"ARE YOU TAKING TERESA FOR THE NIGHT?" SIOBHAN whispered.[1]

"Yes," I said firmly, remembering her many warnings that if Teresa stayed one night she'd be with us forever.

"We'll take care of her," Bill said.

Siobhan had come back into the condo. "Can I speak to you privately, without Bill, please?" she asked, pointing towards Dad's bedroom.

"You can say anything you want to me right here," I said, standing with Teresa at my side.

"No, I want to talk to you privately," Siobhan said. "Bill, please go out into the hall if Franke won't go into the bedroom."

Bill looked at me. I nodded and he left.

So then it was just three sisters—Siobhan, Teresa and me.

Siobhan faced us. "I don't want this recorded."

"Well then, don't talk to me," I said. Teresa was holding on to me tightly.

"You're going to record this?" Siobhan said.

"Yes," I said. "Don't talk to me if we cannot record it."

Eleven months earlier, Franke visits Siobhan to wish her a Merry Christmas

---

"I want to talk to you, sister to sister," she said.

"It's going to be recorded, or we are not talking," I said.

"Franke, could you please put that away so that I can talk to you?"

"Nope," I said. "You can say all sorts of things, but—"

"Franke, I love you," Siobhan said. "And I would like a chance to talk to you without the recorder on."

"Well," I said, "let me do the talking since you don't want to."

"I want to talk to you alone," she said.

"No," I said. "What I am going to say is that you guys were in such a rush to get Teresa into a nursing home..." I paused. And then, emphasizing each word, I said, "You did not even ask her whether she wanted to go. You just took the first spot that was available."

My voice was cracking as I continued. "Aiker Place is not the right spot for Teresa. She was surrounded by people who were decades older than her, who had serious medical problems and were near the end of their lives. I walked in there, and I went: Oh my God, this is not good. This is not in Teresa's best interests. We need to get her into the right group home. Bill and I have offered to take Teresa until that spot becomes available. We love Teresa, and that's what we want to do. I don't see why that can't work."

Siobhan glared at me, but she was tight-lipped, not saying a word. I continued my monologue. "I spoke with the CEO of Aiker Place. She agreed that Teresa did not belong there. Teresa was the only person at Aiker Place who was under fifty and had Down syndrome.

"So, what you've done was out of desperation—you just took the first available spot. Maybe Jared talked to someone because he's on the board, and he's friends with the owner. I don't know, but it was NOT the right placement."

My voice rose as I spoke, "If you block us on this, we will be taking this public. We're going to go to all the different advocacy organizations. And we are going to make a really big deal of this. Because this is not right."

If Siobhan was worried that I would go public, she didn't flinch.

"You did not think about Teresa's best interests," I said. "That is wrong. She does not belong in a nursing home. I do not believe she has Alzheimer's, despite the fact that Deirdre claims to have gotten that diagnosis. We talked to other people down at Aiker Place and asked, do you think that Teresa has Alzheimer's? And they all said no, she's got a great memory. That's what Hope said. And the other woman who Teresa said goodbye to ..."

I looked to Teresa for confirmation. She looked back at me, nodded her head and said, "I did not want to be there."

Franke and Teresa, power walking on a summer day

"Teresa is very adaptable," I said to Siobhan. "We should be taking advantage of that to build a life for her that is wonderful. Bill and I are prepared to do that.

"I don't know why you would block us." I looked at Siobhan and asked her directly, my voice passionate. "Why do you want her in a nursing home?" I paused. "You won't say."

Siobhan said, "Turn off the recorder. I will—"

"No, I'm not turning it off," I said. "If you can't talk to me with the recorder on, then we can't talk. Because I need to be able to prove what you said—and what I said."

I looked at her again and asked, "What do you have to say that is so important that it can't be recorded?" I waited for her to answer.

Siobhan said, "I would like a chance to talk to you without the recorder on."

I said, "Okay, you're not talking to me then."

Teresa said, "And you're not talking to me, either."

"The recorder is evidence for me of what's happening," I said.

"Bill and I are prepared to take Teresa into our home. We offered to care for her. I don't see why you're blocking that," I said. "And if you continue to block it, we will have no relationship going forward. And I will have no relationship with you or the other siblings, unfortunately."

I felt the sting of my words as soon as I said them. Would our bond as sisters be permanently severed? I hoped that I wouldn't need to carry out my threat. I said, "We are doing what Mom would have wanted. And what Dad wants. The advocacy organizations that we've been speaking to are horrified to hear that you are putting a forty-nine-year-old with Down syndrome into a nursing home. That is wrong."

I waited for Siobhan to speak. Finally, she said, "I would still like a chance to talk to you without the recorder on."

"If you can't talk to me with the recorder on, then we're not talking," I said. "There's no reason."

Siobhan just stared at Teresa and me. Then she turned and left.

CHAPTER THIRTY-SEVEN

Nightmare at Sunnybrook

November 30, 2013, 9:00 p.m.

I GRIPPED TERESA'S HAND TIGHTLY. THE TAXI HAD DROPPED us off outside the Emergency entrance at the back of Sunnybrook Hospital.[1] We were now on our second rescue mission of the day, but Teresa's and Dad's roles had been reversed. Teresa was with us, and Dad was inside, somewhere—an unwilling victim of the province's Mental Health Act.

It was about 9 p.m. on a cold November night. Looking up, I could see the hospital's concrete wings looming over us. To the left, two parked ambulances sat with their flashing lights and sirens turned off. And behind us, a curtain of darkness fell into a wooded ravine. The Emergency department was buried in the bowels of one of the largest buildings on the site. Sunnybrook was originally a military hospital built after the war to serve injured World War Two veterans. Over the next few decades, it evolved to become a sprawling medical complex. Now, it hosted one of the city's busiest Emergency departments, fed by a steady stream of car accidents, heart attacks and failed suicide attempts.

I was nervous as we stood in front of the automatic doors. I had been wary of Deirdre recently, but now I was afraid. She had ratcheted up this family disagreement to a new level of mind-fuckery by alleging that Dad was suicidal. I was determined to undo this terrible mistake and to tell the doctors what I saw.

"Stay close," I said to Teresa as the three of us stepped through the doors and into the glare of the Emergency waiting room. There were clusters of people sitting around, urgently waiting for attention. Walking toward the Emergency reception, we spotted Phoebe and a few of my nieces and nephews—the cousins, as we called them. Phoebe gave us a small wave and a tepid smile. Like us, she was trying to make sense of it all. She tilted her head to one side and said: *It's just the reality of the situation. Dad needs to be put into a nursing home. We have to accept it*

"No, I don't believe in your reality," Bill said.

Phoebe shrugged and slumped in her chair, settling in for a long vigil. Our nieces and nephews stared at us. We were the troublemakers. It was going to take time to straighten this mess out, especially if they were getting a lopsided tale from Deirdre and Conrad.

My first task was to speak to Dad's doctors and tell them what happened. I had no doubt that my siblings would be claiming that they "truly believed" Dad was suicidal, without mentioning all the trouble they'd caused. When I finally got to the ER nurse, she said that Dad already had the maximum number of visitors. I told her I had been with Dad for the whole day and I really needed to tell the doctors what happened. The nurse was expressionless as she listened to me and tapped on her keyboard. She asked me to take a seat. Presumably, she would let the doctors know.

We walked past Phoebe and other family members—their huddled hostility was obvious—and we found a few chairs on the far side of the room. Bill got some soft drinks for us, and I snapped a few photos to document it all. He was sporting a Movember moustache and a grey goatee, looking handsome and trim in a dark shirt and baggy black pants. Teresa

The emergency room wait: Bill carries drinks, and Teresa carries her extra clothes

was wearing a purple jacket, an off-white toque and, remarkably, a smile. She was carrying a bag with her overnight stuff, just in case. It had been a strenuous day. I kept turning the events over and over in my mind. And fearfully wondering what they were doing to Dad behind closed doors. I told Bill that no matter how long it took, I needed to speak to the doctors.

A half hour later, Conrad arrived with his daughter Tiffany. Bill instinctively jumped up to greet them, but Conrad scowled and walked past, refusing to shake hands. I watched as he stopped to talk with Phoebe and then went to the nurses' desk and disappeared.

I asked Bill if he thought that Conrad had been allowed to see Dad. He didn't know. I went and asked the Emergency nurse myself. I reminded her that I was Dad's named attorney for personal care, and I showed her the signed form. She was polite and said she would speak to the medical team.

I sat back down, reassuring myself that I just needed to be patient. I told myself that my turn would come. I *would* get to speak to the doctors. As we waited, I kept mulling over what to say. I had a lot of time to think about it all. Two hours later we still had not been able to see Dad.

Bill and Teresa went outside to stretch their legs while I stayed in the waiting room. They walked over to the Emergency entrance. Teresa had always enjoyed spotting and counting ambulances during their Sunday walks. However, this day was different. Just three hours earlier, she had watched the paramedics take Dad away. Teresa walked up to one of the parked ambulances. She looked around to make sure no one was watching and then she kicked it.

"What?" Bill said in surprise.

"They took my father," Teresa said.

When Teresa and Bill returned, I went to the Emergency desk again. I was running out of patience. Maybe they weren't paying attention to me because I didn't look powerful. Was I too polite, too acquiescent? This time I was more insistent. I pointed to the signed document saying that Dad had named me as his attorney for personal care and that I had a right to speak with his doctors. The nurse nodded, but I couldn't tell if she was taking me seriously. I returned to my seat, worried. Even though I was speaking, no one was listening. This felt like a bad dream where I had no control.

A few minutes later, Deirdre walked out of emergency into the waiting area. She spoke to Phoebe first. We watched from a distance as they hugged and consoled each other, and then Deirdre turned and started coming towards us. I straightened my shoulders and walked towards her.

We met face to face in the middle of the Emergency waiting room. There were no pleasantries exchanged. She began talking immediately, angry and upset. In her bossiest big sister tone, she told me that the doctors would not be speaking with me.

I told her again that I was Dad's power of attorney for personal care.

She dismissed this, saying that Dad was not capable of signing anything. Incredibly, she blamed this whole disaster on me, and then turned and marched back through the ER doors.

I was shocked. Of course, I shouldn't have been. Deirdre ordered Teresa's health care workers not to talk to me. Deirdre told the police not to listen to me. And now she was blocking me again.

How could I help Dad if I couldn't even speak to his doctors? I couldn't just barge in. This was a hospital. There were rules and protocols, and doctors and nurses, and a security system, all designed to protect the patients. But now, this system of care had been turned upside down.

I went to the nurses' desk, but again I was rebuffed. The nurse just nodded sympathetically. Sorry, there is nothing we can do, was all she could say. The family and the doctors had made the decision. "But I *am* family!" I said. The nurse just shook her head. I didn't want her to start seeing me as the problem, so I backed off.

Another hour had passed before Conrad came out to the waiting area. Like Deirdre, he went over to Phoebe and talked to her. The cousins gathered around as they chatted, occasionally glancing at us. Then Conrad turned and strode over to speak with me. This was my chance to tell him straight up what I thought. "You deceived Dad," I said. "That was wrong."

Conrad just threw back his head and laughed. He contorted his face and repeated my words in a high-pitched, whiny voice. "You deceived Dad! You deceived Dad." It was quite a performance by my brother.

I looked him straight in the eyes and said, "It was wrong to lie to Dad." And again he laughed, pretending that I was naïve and that my words did not prick his conscience. Then he delivered his newsflash: the doctors had decided to release Dad on his own recognizance. This was good news. The doctors must have decided that Dad was fine.

But Conrad claimed that the doctors were *only* doing this because if Dad was labelled as a "suicide risk," it could prevent him from getting into K-Wing as they planned. He said the hospital would release Dad in the next hour or so, and we should go home. Then he turned and walked back into the emergency room.

I looked at Bill and said, "I want to stay until Dad is released, just in case I can speak to a doctor." Bill nodded, and we sat back down. Phoebe came by, heading towards the exit with her coat over one arm and the cousins following. *We're exhausted,* she said, hunching her shoulders and bending as though she was tired of carrying a heavy burden.

I watched as she left with the cousins in tow. And I flashed on a memory from many years ago when we were kids. The neighbourhood children would follow Phoebe everywhere; she was like the Pied Piper. And now, leaving the hospital, Phoebe was being followed by a line of her own children and their cousins. They were young adults, shocked by Deirdre's claims of their grandfather's supposed death threats and deeply concerned for his well-being. As they filed by, avoiding my eyes, it seemed as if they were blaming me for this bizarre turn of events.

Siobhan was not part of the hospital vigil, but her prophecy about Dad and Sunnybrook was on my mind.

We waited another hour. Teresa lay on the floor, using her winter jacket as a blanket, and slept. It had been a roller coaster day for Teresa, and I was glad she could sleep. But I couldn't rest. I was disappointed that I had failed to speak to any of the doctors. My only consolation was that Dad was not being held for observation. Around 2:30 a.m., we got the official word that Dad had been discharged and the others would be taking him home. We took a taxi to the condo, hoping to meet Dad.

―――――

AS SOON AS we walked into the condo, Teresa asked, "Where's my father?"

"We're waiting for him," Bill answered. "He's coming back. At least, that's what Conrad told us."

"Right," Teresa said, and she went into her bedroom.

Bill and I were still standing in the kitchen with our coats on when we heard the key turning in the front door. As it opened, we looked over to see Dad, Deirdre and one of the nieces standing behind them. Dad looked okay, relatively speaking. Deirdre looked exasperated, like she was at the end of her rope.

The first thing Dad said was, "Where's Teresa?"

"Teresa is here. She's okay," I said.

Dad asked, "What happened?"

"Those guys had some kind of suicide watch," Bill said. "But apparently, they were wrong."

"They were 100 percent wrong," I said.

"Is that what the doctor said?" Bill asked Deirdre. "That it wasn't a problem?"

"I don't have to talk to you," Deirdre snapped.

"You don't have to talk to me," Bill answered. "But I can still talk to you."

Deirdre pulled out a package. "Dad, these are your pills for tomorrow."

But Dad was not paying attention. He seemed out of it, like they had given him a sedative. He just said, "Hmmm?"

Deirdre repeated, "These are your pills for tomorrow."

Dad asked, "Tomorrow? What…"

Deirdre raised her voice, "These are your pills for tomorrow!"

Teresa watches as Deirdre gives some pills and water to Dad

"Okay, dear," Dad said, wincing. "Don't shout at me." Then he turned around, looking at Teresa's bedroom door. "Is Teresa here?" He knocked gently. Teresa opened the door. "Here's my girl!" he said with elation.

"Hi, Daddy!" she said.

"She's here!" Bill said happily.

"She should be," Dad said, and they gave each other a warm hug. It was a beautiful sight and I raised my camera to take some photos.

But Deirdre was unhappy. "I don't want my picture taken. Do you understand?" She looked at me angrily, "And I don't want myself recorded."

"Well, then don't talk to us," Bill answered. "It's our new policy. We're recording everything."

Deirdre pulled out some more medicine and gave it to Dad, watching him to make sure he swallowed it. She was playing the role of a dutiful caring daughter and it grated on me, knowing what she had just put Dad through. But I also knew there was no reasoning with her. In her own mind she was always right.

She turned to Dad, "I want to tell you something in front of these people."

Okay, I needed to document that. My audio recorder had been quietly running in my pocket but now I felt the urge to make a visual record too. I snapped a photo.

Deirdre continued her speech, "I have a letter from the doctor to say that this power of attorney that Franke had you sign today is not valid. I have it in writing. It's not valid."

Dad looked at her. "I don't know what this is all about. Are you going to work it out?"

"Yes," Deirdre answered. "A judge will work it out. But I got it in writing."

"But Deirdre," I said.

"Let's go," she said, turning to the door.

I followed her, saying, "We'll be filing a claim against you."

"You go ahead," Deirdre answered quietly.

"You should not have lied to Dad," I said.

"I did not lie to Dad," she said.

"Yes, you did," I said. "You deceived him by taking away Teresa without telling—"

Deirdre stepped out into the hallway and pulled the door shut, saying, "Lock the door, Dad."

"I don't know what she's talking about," Dad said.

"It's terrible," I said. "Just terrible." We stood there shaking our heads, and I asked Dad, "What happened with the doctor? Do you want to talk about it at all?"

Dad looked at me, "What?"

"What was it like in the hospital?" I asked.

"What are you talking about?" Dad asked, looking confused.

"Do you remember you were at Sunnybrook Hospital?"

"I did what?" he asked.

"You were at Sunnybrook Hospital."

He just looked at us.

"He's medicated or something," Bill said.

"Where was I?" Dad asked. Then he said, "I can't remember anything."

"They must have used some drugs," I said.

Teresa was looking at Dad, worried.

"He doesn't remember anything," Bill said.

"Right," Teresa said.

Dad looked at us, bewildered, "What am I supposed to have done?" He was in rough shape. But at least we had him back home. Dad walked into his bedroom. Hopefully, he would feel better the next day.

"Anyways," I said, "we got Teresa back. And that's good."

"Yes," Bill agreed. Then he turned Teresa. "Do you want to stay here? Or do you want to come to our place?"

"I want to stay with my father," she said.

"Okay," Bill said. Then he turned back to me. "Why don't I stay here with Teresa and Dad? I can sleep on the couch. And you can go home." So that was our plan, especially since Dad was so mixed up. I gave Teresa a hug goodnight, and she went into her bedroom.

"We got them back," I said and kissed Bill. We stood together, holding each other. I felt so thankful to have Bill as my partner. I had no idea when we first married how much I would lean on him. This crazy day, when he had helped me through all the twists and turns, showed me how lucky I was.

"Don't worry," he said, pulling me closer, "Teresa and Dad will be safe."

"But what if ..." He knew I was beginning to have doubts about what would happen next.

"We'll work it out."

"But Teresa is not safe here," I said.

"I know," he said, "and Dad knows it too. That's why he wants us to take her."

"But we don't have much time," I said. "Deirdre and Conrad ... They have not given up."

"That's why I am staying here tonight," Bill said. "And tomorrow, Teresa can move into our place ... if she's ready."

"Thank you," I said as I kissed him again. We stood there for a minute.

"It's 3:30 in the morning," Bill said.

"Alright," I said, "I'll get going." I gave him another hug and kiss. Then I walked the mile back home, my head filled with worries, trying to make sense about all that had happened on this day—a day like no other.

AFTER I LEFT, Bill grabbed a blanket and flopped onto Dad's couch. He was lying there, trying to sleep, when Dad came out of his bedroom.

"What did they do to me?" Dad asked.

Bill turned to see Dad standing in the bedroom doorway. He had taken off his sweater and was wearing a short-sleeved golf shirt. He held his arms out in front of himself and asked, "What did they do to me?" Bill flipped on the lights. Both of Dad's arms were covered with big red welts, tape and bandages. What happened? It looked like there was some trouble at the hospital. How many needles did they put in? And why? Dad must have been very upset. Did he struggle? He was perfectly fine when he left the condo. Bill took a few quick photos with his phone. And then Dad went back to bed.

Bill returned to the couch and tried to sleep as Dad's words echoed through his head, "What did they do to me? What did they do to me?" By that time I was back home, lying in our bed with questions circling in my head: "What will they do next? What will they do next?"

CHAPTER THIRTY-EIGHT

Make Peace, Not War

December 1, 2013

I WOKE UP ALONE. HALF-ASLEEP, HALF-AWAKE, I DID A MENTAL reality check.[1] What happened yesterday? Was my family destroyed forever? Was there anything I could do to make peace and still protect Teresa?

Bill was still at Dad's place. I rolled over, grabbed my phone and called him. "How's Dad?"

"He's awake, puttering around the kitchen, but still foggy. He can't remember much of anything from yesterday. But he's happy that Teresa is back. And, of course, Teresa is happy too."

"That's good, but I don't think we can relax. Yesterday, we told Dad we'd take Teresa when the time comes," I said. "I think that time is now. I'm very worried about her."

"Me too," Bill said. "Especially if Dad is even thinking of going to K-Wing."

I asked to speak to Dad. He quickly agreed that Teresa should move in with us. So then, all we had to do was convince Teresa. Bill put her on the line.

"Teresa," I said, "I was just talking with Dad, and he thinks it would be a good idea if you stayed at our house."

"I know," she said.

"So, do you want to come over to our house?"

"I'm eating breakfast right now," she said.

"But do you want to come over later? For dinner and a sleep-over?"

"Let me think about it."

"It would be wonderful and fun!"

"Thank you," she said. Then she handed the phone back to Bill.

"I think she'll agree," Bill said. "She just needs time to think. She's been traumatized by all this."

"Well, I need to write a letter to my siblings. I want to let everyone know that Teresa is going to move into our house today. Hopefully, they'll support us."

"Hopefully, they'll back off," Bill said with a laugh. "But it's worth a try. Anyway, Teresa wants to do something fun today. So, we're going to Sick Kids. Do you want to come?"

"No, I've got to write this letter," I said. "But let's invite Dad and Teresa to dinner tonight. It will be a good way to manage the transition."

"Okay, I'll ask Dad if he's up for it."

"And keep a close eye on Teresa. Don't let her out of your sight."

TWO HOURS LATER, I had my draft peace offering ready. I needed to bring my siblings on board so this battle didn't escalate into an all-out war. I wanted to let them know that even though we didn't see eye to eye, we could still work together. I phoned Bill and Teresa, and they gave my letter the thumbs up. I double-checked it, took a deep breath and hit send.

Dear Conrad, Deirdre, Siobhan, and Phoebe,

All of us are very concerned about Teresa and her future. Yesterday's events demonstrate this. They also show that we have differences of opinion on what is best for Teresa.

Our concern: A nursing home is not the right place for Teresa. Yesterday I spoke with the CEO of Aiker Place, and she agreed that it was an inappropriate placement for a forty-nine-year-old person with Down syndrome. She was thrilled to hear that we wanted to take Teresa and recommended that Teresa stay with us and still go out and do her programs.

Our offer: Bill and I want Teresa to live with us. We feel it would be ideal for many reasons. We have an extra bedroom. We work at home, and our schedules are flexible. She will be close to family members, and she will be in the same neighbourhood she grew up in. We feel we can help Teresa grow and develop to her full potential—as we have helped Teresa develop her ability to do walks such as the eight-kilometre Terry Fox walk. Our ultimate goal will be to have Teresa at a group home—if that is eventually what she wants and is in her best interests. But we are in no rush.

Please let us know if you support our decision. We would be honoured to have Teresa live with us.

Sincerely,

Franke and Bill

Siobhan was the first to respond: *You have exhibited extremely poor judgment, especially in the last few days.*

This felt like a slap in the face.

Then she flatly rejected my offer: *Teresa should not live with you. I do not believe it would be in Teresa's best interests to do so.* And she reprimanded me: *You have not provided a detailed financial plan.*

How could I do that when Conrad and Deirdre had refused to disclose any financial details?

She insisted: *Conrad and Deirdre, are the only ones who can make the final decision about where Teresa will live.*

That seemed so unfair. As far as I could see, there should be no question about Teresa's freedom or financial well-being. Dad wanted to provide her with financial support, and he had a legal obligation to do so. And, like all of us, Teresa has rights, including the right to decide where she lives.

Phoebe responded next: *This is absolutely wonderful. You have my full support.* That was a relief. Phoebe's husband also responded with a positive note, saying he supported the decision because he knew that we were acting in Teresa's best interests.

Good. We had two yes votes.

Of course, Siobhan's husband would vote no. So really, it was two yes votes (Phoebe and Spencer) and two no votes (Siobhan and Jared). But as far as family votes go, Deirdre would probably dismiss all of them. As she told me the previous week, "You don't get a vote."

Deirdre and Conrad had not responded yet. Based on their behaviour in the last few weeks, they probably wouldn't. And if so, I would have to assume we were in for a battle.

To protect Teresa, I would need to get more eyes on what was happening. The day before, the Aiker Place CEO was supportive. Maybe she could help? At the very least, I could tell her what was going on. I forwarded my family letter to her so she could see exactly what we offered. "I wanted to keep you in the loop as I am worried that my sister, Deirdre, and brother, Conrad, will want to have Teresa return to Aiker Place. I want you to know why we do not support that decision."

I also told her that Teresa had revoked the old power of attorney and signed a new one naming Dad and me as her attorneys. I closed off by providing my phone number and said, "I would be very grateful for any advice or insights you can offer."

BILL CALLED ME from a taxi on the way back from Sick Kids with Teresa. He said that they had a great time. He bought her a new book, they had lunch in the food court, and he took a photo of Teresa dancing in the rain. "The big news is," he said, "Teresa does not want to go back to the condo."

"Really! Why?"

"She's kind of afraid," Bill answered. "She wants to come straight to our house."

"That's good she's coming back here but sad too," I said. "I'm glad she understands she will be safer here."

When Bill and Teresa arrived home, I took a photo of the big moment. She smiled with a bag over her shoulder, flashing a V for victory. I gave her a big hug, and we went upstairs to Trevor's old bedroom. It was cozy with a sloped ceiling and a large window facing the street. The walls were off-white with a patterned area rug on the hardwood floor. There was a single bed with a duvet, a low chest of drawers, a desk, and a wooden chair. I handed Teresa a stack of fresh white towels and told her that this was her new bedroom in our home. It made me feel happy to help her settle in. She put her plastic bag on the desk, hung up her jacket and put her shoes under the bed, just like I did when I was a kid. Teresa decided to take a nap and Bill headed out to the grocery store.

Teresa visits her favourite place, Sick Kids Hospital, the day after her rescue

I had been planning to call the police to file a complaint about our treatment the night before. While it might not make any difference, I wanted to get it on the record. I was still shaken by how badly we were treated. Unfair treatment by the police was something I had read about many times in the news, but I had never personally experienced it. Eventually, after several redials, being put on hold, getting disconnected, calling back, and getting shuffled from one cop to another, they finally told me to call back on Monday. So that was still on my to-do list.

Teresa came back downstairs, and dinner was almost ready. She helped set the table and I hugged her again, telling her how nice it was to have her around. Not even a week had passed since Dad and Teresa had come over for a roast chicken dinner and now everything had been turned upside down. This dinner was a way to help us feel safe again.

———

REMARKABLY, WHEN DAD ARRIVED, he looked great and radiated positive energy. The four of us sat together in the living room for pre-dinner drinks. Teresa was looking at her new book about allergies and asthma, and Dad was flipping through my book, *Banned on the Hill*.

To capture the moment, I picked up my iPad and started taking another video. "So, Teresa," I asked, "what did you do at Sick Kids today?"

"We had fun!"

"And you bought that book?"

"Yes. I did. It's beautiful. And we had lunch at Sick Kids."

"That was a first," Bill said. "It was the first time we ever had lunch there."

"Right," Teresa said. "A Subway sandwich!"

"And a cappuccino," Bill added.

"And a Diet Coke," Teresa said.

"And a cookie. Ha!" Bill laughed. "We went a bit overboard. Oh, well."

"We went overboard," Teresa laughed.

"A little bit," Bill said. "Mostly, we just hung around." "That's great," I said as Teresa and Dad turned back to reading their books. "Teresa is quite a reader."

"Yes, I am," Teresa agreed.

"Teresa likes the kind of books I like—medical and science books," Bill said.

"Right," Teresa said, studying her book closely.

Dad looked up from my book, *Banned on the Hill*, and asked, "Has the government made any comments?"

"No," I said. "In fact, they said they cannot comment."

Dad and Teresa read their books as they sit on the living room couch

"This is really something!" Dad chortled.

"Thank you, I'm glad you're enjoying it," I said. "It's nice to have you over to dinner tonight."

"It's nice for us too," Dad said.

The roast chicken was ready, so we moved to the table. Everything was so normal, so relaxed, that I could hardly believe all the trouble we'd been through over the last few days. Here we were, sitting together, enjoying a home-cooked meal.

"This is delicious," Dad said. Teresa asked for more cranberry sauce and as I reached over to serve her, Dad suddenly coughed and dropped his fork.

"Dad?" I asked.

He reeled back and then, leaning forward, coughed again, harder this time.

Bill stood up. "Dad, are you okay?"

Dad waved his hand, signalling that he was fine. He put his hand on his chest as he bent forward and hacked again.

"Dad?" Teresa asked.

Dad stood up, gagging.

I jumped up. "Are you okay?"

Bill held his shoulders as Dad bent forward, coughing. I was at his side as he straightened up and tipped towards me. "Can you breathe?" I asked.

He shook his head and doubled over again. Bill thumped him firmly on the back. "Does that help? Does that help?"

Dad straightened, shook his head, then bent over again, hacking and coughing.

"What should we do?" Bill asked.

"The Heimlich manoeuvre?" We were standing on either side of Dad, holding him. Dad doubled over. Bill gave him another couple of thumps on the back.

Suddenly, Dad straightened with his mouth open, gasping for air. "Aahhh!"

"He's breathing," I said with relief. After all we'd been through…

"Yes," Bill sighed.

"Thank goodness, I could hardly breathe," Dad said. He turned and looked at me, then slumped back down into his chair, with his hand on his chest.

"Are you okay, Daddy?" Teresa asked. Dad was still catching his breath.

"Would you like a drink?" I asked.

"Yes," he said, reaching for his water glass and taking a sip.

"Are you okay?" Teresa asked.

"Something I ate," he said. "Must have gone down the wrong way."

"Don't do that," Teresa advised.

Then Dad said, "I need to lie down."

Bill and I helped him over to the couch. He lay down, and I covered him with a soft fleece blanket.

"Thank you," he said, "It's all been a bit much. I need to rest for a few minutes." Then, lying flat on his back, he folded his arms over his chest like an ancient mummy and closed his eyes.

We stood there looking at him. "What should we do?" Bill asked. "Call someone?"

"Who?" I shrugged.

"Phoebe?" Bill suggested. "She's the only one who will even talk to us."

I called Phoebe. She suggested we call Siobhan or Deirdre as they had handled all of Dad's health issues in the past, or we could go to the hospital.

I said no thank you to both options.

Bill and I decided to wait and see how Dad felt. Luckily, thirty minutes later, Dad was feeling better. I sighed with relief. We didn't need any more bad news. My mother always talked to me about the power of positive thinking. And although many things had gone wrong, miraculously, many things had gone well.

I was beginning to understand why Dad wanted one of us to live with Teresa. I knew I could never take Dad's place, but I hoped that as her sister I could open up new opportunities for Teresa. That hope kept me going. The past week had been strenuous for all of us, but especially for Dad. I offered him dessert, but he said he was exhausted. "I just want to go home and crawl into bed."

We called a taxi, and Bill and Dad were ready to go. This was the big moment. Dad was going back to the condo, and Teresa was staying.

Dad bent down and gave Teresa a kiss. "You be a good girl," he said.

"I will," she said.

"Remember, Daddy always loves you!"

"I know."

Dad turned and gave me a hug and a kiss on the cheek. "You're a sweetie. Thank you for taking care of Teresa. She means the world to me." Then he put on his grey fedora and walked out the front door.

It was the first of December, a chilly night. Teresa and I stood in the doorway, watching as Bill helped Dad get in the cab. As it pulled away from the curb, Dad lowered the window and waved goodbye. Teresa and I waved back as the car drove away and disappeared into the darkness.

We stepped back into the warmth of the house. "Let's go upstairs," I said, "and we'll make sure you have everything you need." Trevor's old room would suit Teresa beautifully. The fluffy white duvet on her bed looked cozy and inviting. "Do you want to get ready for bed?"

"But I don't have my toothbrush!" Teresa exclaimed.

"Oh! I'm sure we have an extra. I'll find you one." And then I twigged, "You don't have any pajamas, do you?"

"They're at the condo. I'll wear my T-shirt and pants."

"No, you can't sleep in your clothes!"

"I'm fine. Don't worry."

"Okay, whatever you want. We'll get your things tomorrow. And you can put them right here." I opened the top drawer of the low pine dresser to show her it was empty—just waiting for her stuff.

"Yes," she smiled. "Right here."

I sighed. Happy and relieved that Teresa was settling in.

While she was brushing her teeth, I found some grey sweatpants and a T-shirt and laid them on the bed. Then I looked out the window. Dad would be home by now, and Bill would be returning. But my heart sank as I thought about my other siblings. I couldn't make sense of what was driving them. I never could have predicted their actions. And I had no idea what they'd do next. But I stopped that train of thought.

We had done it. We were victorious! It had been a huge battle, but now Teresa was free. It felt so right to have her living with us and I wondered why I didn't know this from the very start. This is what Dad had always envisioned for Teresa, and I'm sure Mom would have been thrilled.

I started making to-do lists in my head. Anything seemed possible. I let myself paint a picture of Teresa's future: going with her to new places, discovering new things, and making new friends. This was a new beginning.

Teresa came back into the room. "Thank you for the toothbrush."

"You're welcome." She gave me a hug and I hugged her back. "Oh, that's so nice."

"You're my sister," she said.

"That's right."

"We're sisters."

BE FIERCE

A SELF-TALK POEM BY TERESA HEARTCHILD[1]

Don't be afraid.

No, there's a monster out there.

Just calm down, my daughter.

I want to warn you.

You got feelings. Relax your stomach.

I know, I know.

You'll be okay. You're fierce.

Thank you.

Epilogue

THE END OF THIS STORY is the beginning of another. Franke, Teresa and Bill's adventures continue in their next book, *Escape to Lotusland*, where Teresa speaks up to assert her rights.

Franke, Teresa and Bill in 2019

Afternote

The pseudonyms used for family members are listed in alphabetical order: Candi, Chuck, Conrad, Deirdre, Hank, Jared, Lynne, Phoebe, Siobhan, Spencer, and Tiffany. I've also used pseudonyms for my two children Trevor and Darcy. The names of the following individuals and organizations have been changed: Aiker Place, Dr. Cushmen, Hope, Mrs. Kehlmann, Dr. Mueller, Fritz Norman, Perla, Nikolas Vincente, and Wheiry Lodge.

Acknowledgements

There are many people I want to thank for making this book what it is today. To my husband Bill, and my sister Teresa, I owe the biggest debt. Teresa, of course, was the *raison d'être* for it all and has blossomed in ways I could not have imagined. And Bill gave me his unwavering support—first in the living of it, and then in the writing of it. When I struggled (for several years) to give voice to my thoughts and feelings, Bill helped me to put words to paper. In 2020, when the pandemic hit, he saw it as a perfect opportunity to get down to work. He helped me to weave my handwritten notes, and binders of documents, into a story arc that is an accurate reflection of events and meaningful to me—and I hope to readers.

My heartfelt thanks to the Terry Fox Foundation, Rare Theatre Company, Community Living Ontario, Inclusion BC, Spectrum Society for Community Living, Developmental Disabilities Association, Planned Lifetime Advocacy Network, and the Canadian Down Syndrome Association for your support in the telling of this story. My gratitude to the following individuals who have helped in multiple ways—some by appearing in the storyline itself, and some through their generous feedback: Ernie Baatz, Jim Harris, David Healy, Alanna Hendren, Isabel Mavrides-Calderon, Catherine McKercher, George Melnyk, Charles Montpetit, Rebecca Pauls, Max Power, Marty Seldman, Marjorie Simmins, David Suzuki, and Karla Verschoor.

I also want to extend my warm appreciation to the people who worked behind the scenes. Great thanks to Ray Hsu for their "readerly feedback" on Zoom. Our weekly literary sessions made me feel I was in university once again and the deadlines kept the project moving ahead. Thanks to my editor Elizabeth Eve who saw in an early draft a compelling family saga. Thanks to Justin Safayeni and Warren Sheffer for their guidance in how to tell this difficult story. Thanks to our long-time friends at Moveable Inc. for proofreading this book so meticulously. (Any remaining typographical errors are, no doubt, ones I've added with further tinkering.) Sincere thanks to sensitivity/disability readers Dustin Galer, Gabrielle Peters, and Sue Robins for their thoughtful suggestions that challenged me to remember history and think in new ways. And a warm round of applause to the cast of more than a dozen talented actors who brought *Freeing Teresa* to life as an audiobook. Hearing Jackie Blackmore, Bill Mackie, Dayleigh Nelson, Lauren Potter, and others read aloud was magical and helped us to make the print book better.

And finally thanks to you for reading my story! Your comments on the book, and what it meant to you, are most welcome. A brief review on Amazon, Goodreads, or others would be appreciated. I am happy to drop in (virtually) to book clubs and talk about *Freeing Teresa*. To reach me directly, please write to franke@frankejames.com.

List of Photos
and Illustrations

General notes on images and photos:

- The images of Dad's face have been blurred since none of my siblings (except for Teresa) support the telling of this story.

- The images of some family members appear as silhouettes. They have been blanked out echoing their absence in my life.

- The faces of the police officers have been redacted from photos.

- Dad and Teresa's family name has been redacted with black bars in any photos where it appeared in order to help protect the identities of other family members referenced in this book.

- Faces of unknown third parties who appear in some photos have been blurred or anonymized with licenced stock photos.

- The backgrounds of photos taken in medical institutions, like Aiker Place and Sunnybrook Hospital, have been recreated as grey and white sketches.

- The background of photos taken inside Franke's siblings' homes have been sketched and colourized in order to remove identifying details.

Front Matter

Those Monsters.
Illustration by Teresa Heartchild from her book, *Pretty Amazing: How I Found Myself in the Downtown Eastside*, 2016.

Who are you going to be?
Illustration by Franke James, 2009.

Chapter 1. The Silver Recorder

Dad, washing the dishes: "My goodness, you guys are real pushers."
Film still from video by Franke James, November 30, 2013.

Bill and Teresa with her calendar and trophies.
Film still from video by Franke James, November 30, 2013.

The police arrive at Dad's condo.
Film still from video by Franke James, November 30, 2013.

Franke with her camera earlier that day at Aiker Place.
Film still from video by Billiam James, November 30, 2013.

Chapter 2. Eyes Fly Open

At the subway, Teresa sticks out her tongue and Franke laughs.
Photo by Billiam James, February 23, 2013.

Bill makes a funny face as he sits with Teresa outside the theatre.
Photo by Franke James, February 23, 2013.

After the play, Rare *actor Dylan Livaja with Teresa.*
Photo by Franke James, February 23, 2013.

Chapter 3. The Blacklisting Party

The unnamed official reacts to the news of Franke's art show.
Illustration by Franke James, from *Banned on the Hill*, 2013.

Franke stands by her poster, "Dear Prime Minister, Please Stop Blacklisting."
Photo by Billiam James, September 14, 2011.

If we don't tax polluters who will pay to clean up the mess?
Illustration by Franke James, from "Dear Prime Minister," 2008.

Siobhan, Jared, and two guests join the party.
Photo by James Coburn, Central Image Agency, September 23, 2011.

Fellow disrupter Colin Mutchler joins the party from San Francisco.
Photo by Franke James, September 23, 2011.

Chapter 4. Exploding the Myth

Close up from Exploding the Myth *showing thirteen-year-old Teresa.*
Film still from the 1979 TV documentary *Exploding the Myth*,
produced by OAMR (Community Living Ontario) and the Ontario
Ministry of Community and Social Services. Image and text used with
permission from Community Living Ontario.

Teresa is featured in a newspaper ad for Exploding the Myth, *1979.*
Image and text used with permission from Community Living Ontario.

Siobhan, Dad, Mom, and Conrad during the Exploding the Myth
interview.
Film still from *Exploding the Myth*, 1979. Images and text used with
permission from Community Living Ontario.

Teresa pours coffee and irons a shirt.
Film stills from *Exploding the Myth*, 1979. Images and text used with
permission from Community Living Ontario.

Bill, Teresa, and Franke in 1979.
Photo from the James' family collection, 1979.

Chapter 5. The Dinner Party

The "Do Not Talk About Climate Change" poster on display in Ottawa.
Photo by Fred Chartrand, 2013.

Yellow roses, blue thistle, and sprigs of berries for the summer dinner party.
Photo by Franke James, July 2013.

Phoebe smiles beside Spencer as he reads Banned on the Hill.
Photo by Franke James, July 6, 2013.

Siobhan and Jared relax on the couch amidst Franke's collection of art books.
Photo by Franke James, July 6, 2013.

Bill lights the candles for dinner with Jared, Phoebe, Siobhan, and Spencer.
Photo by Franke James, July 6, 2013.

Franke's waterlogged studio after the flood.
Photo by Franke James, July 8, 2013.

Chapter 6. What's Wrong with Teresa?
Bill cheers Teresa's progress as they walk along a leafy trail.
Photo by Franke James, 2011.

Chapter 7. The Elephant on the Whiteboard
The writing on the wall by Teresa's whiteboard and nightstand.
Photos by Franke James, November 28, 2013.

Chapter 8. Teresa and Terry
Teresa with Franke and Bill on the Terry Fox Run.
Photos © Billiam James and Franke James, 2012.

Teresa dancing at the Terry Fox Run in Toronto.
Photo by Franke James, 2012.

Teresa raises her hands at the Terry Fox Run.
Photo by Franke James, 2012.

Teresa enjoys brunch with Bill and Franke.
Photo by Franke James, 2012.

Chapter 9. Arm-Twisted in Perpetuity
Conrad after the fire.
Photo-realist painting by Franke James, circa 1974

Chapter 10. Dad's Power
Dad and Teresa dressed in matching powder blue on Labour Day.
Photos by Franke James, September 2, 2013.

Chapter 11: My Troublesome Conscience

Because I was always taught to speak up!
Illustration by Franke James, *Banned on the Hill*, 2013.

"The Troublesome Artist" in Halifax.
Photo by Nick Pearce, *Dalhousie News*, September 12, 2013.

Silver Donald Cameron introducing Franke for The Green Interview.
Film still from *The Green Interview: Franke James, the Art of Activism*, recorded on September 18, 2013. Images and text used with permission from the producer's estate. *The Green Interview* was the creation of the late Silver Donald Cameron (1937-2020) with his business partner and director, Chris Beckett. *The Green Interview* is permanently housed at Library & Archives Canada which has called it a "national treasure."

Franke is animated as she tells her story.
Film still from *The Green Interview: Franke James, the Art of Activism*.

Chapter 14. Do Not Talk About That

"Franke James Goes to Washington" as it appeared in the Toronto Star.
Jane Gerster, *Toronto Star*, October 7, 2013. From Toronto Star. © 2013 Toronto Star Newspapers Limited. All rights reserved. Used under license.

At the National Press Club in Washington: Bill Burton, David Suzuki, Franke James, Tzeporah Berman, Tim Gray, and Danny Harvey.

Photo by Billiam James October 11, 2013.

"Canada is the Dirty Old Man" poster in Washington.
Photo by Logan Mock-Bunting, Washington DC, November 1, 2013.

The "Do Not Talk About Climate Change" poster appears in Washington.
Photo by Logan Mock-Bunting, Washington DC, November 1, 2013.

Chapter 23. A Crack in Everything

Teresa and Dad enjoying dinner at Franke's home, six months earlier.
Photo by Franke James, June 9, 2013.

Chapter 24. The Kindness of Their Hearts

Teresa wearing her finisher's medal after doing a five-kilometre walk with Bill.

Photo taken with Bill's camera by a friend, September 22, 2013.

Chapter 25 Stay with My Father

Dad, Teresa and Franke at dinner.

Photos by Teresa Heartchild, Franke James and Billiam James, November 25, 2013.

Chapter 30. Heartbreak Place

Teresa sits on her single bed at Aiker Place.

Photo by Franke James, November 28, 2013.

In the rush to put Teresa in the nursing home, her framed school photo and her Sick Kids bottle with her finisher medals in it were left behind.

Photo by Franke James, November 30, 2013.

Teresa and Franke sitting on Teresa's single bed at Aiker Place.

Photo by Billiam James, November 28, 2013.

Chapter 31. Kidnapped

Teresa and Dad, relaxing at his ninetieth birthday party hosted by Siobhan.

Photo by Franke James, 2012.

Chapter 32. Against Medical Advice

Dad is resolute as he leaves the condo to catch the cab to Aiker Place.

Photo by Franke James, November 30, 2013.

Where Is My Daughter? Dad asks as he gestures to her empty bed.

Photo by Franke James, November 30, 2013.

Dad leans over to kiss Teresa, then talks to her about going back home.

Photo by Franke James, November 30, 2013.

Teresa gets ready to blow her emergency whistle.

Photo by Franke James, November 30, 2013.

Dad hugs Teresa hoping that he can bring her home.
Photo by Franke James, November 30, 2013.

Franke tells the story about Teresa's personal trainer Mrs. Kehlmann.
Film still from video by Billiam James, November 30, 2013.

Franke and Dad on the phone pleading with Aiker officials.
Film stills from video by Billiam James, November 30, 2013.

Chapter 33. The Celebration

Teresa, happy to be back in her own bedroom at the condo.
Film still from video by Franke James, November 30, 2013.

Teresa raises her coffee cup to cheer her return home.
Photo by Franke James, November 30, 2013.

Teresa and Dad together, happy to be home.
Photo by Franke James, November 30, 2013.

Chapter 34. Return Teresa (or Else)

Dad on the phone, "I'll tell you—you won't get away with this!"
Photo by Franke James, November 30, 2013.

Dad fills out the power of attorney forms, reading the instructions online.
Photos by Franke James, November 30, 2013.

Teresa signs her power of attorney for personal care.
Photo by Franke James, November 30, 2013.

Bill serves pizza at Dad's condo while we wait for the Toronto police.
Photo by Franke James, November 30, 2013.

Chapter 35. Apprehension

Teresa holds up her book while Bill holds out Teresa's Terry Fox Run photo.
Film still from video by Franke James, November 30, 2013.

The Toronto police officer orders Franke to leave Dad's condo.
Film still from video by Franke James, November 30, 2013.

Chapter 36. My Manifesto

Teresa and Franke power walking on a summer day.
Photo by Billiam James, 2011.

Eleven months earlier, Franke visits Siobhan to wish her a Merry Christmas.
Photo by Billiam James, 2012.

Chapter 37. Nightmare at Sunnybrook

For the emergency room wait: Bill carries drinks, and Teresa carries extra clothes.
Photo by Franke James, November 30, 2013.

Teresa watches as Deirdre gives some pills and water to Dad.
Photo by Franke James, December 1, 2013.

Chapter 38. Make Peace, Not War

Teresa visits her favourite place, Sick Kids Hospital, the day after her rescue. Photo by Billiam James, December 1, 2013.

Dad and Teresa read their books as they sit on the living room couch.
Film still from video by Franke James, December 1, 2013.

Epilogue and Extra Photos

Franke, Teresa and Bill in 2019.
Photo by Melissa Newberry, July 22, 2019.

Franke as a teen, falling in love with BC.
Photo by friend, 1974.

Teresa at eight with her favourite doll.
Photo by Franke James, 1972.

Photo Collage.
Photos by Franke James and Billiam James 2010-2014

Teresa Heartchild is free.
Photo by Billiam James, August 19, 2021.

Franke as a teen, falling in love with BC

Endnotes

STRANGER THAN FICTION: Much of the source material for this book was previously submitted as evidence to the Ontario Superior Court in 2014. This court case was initiated by Deirdre, Conrad and Siobhan, who filed an application against Dad and Franke. The court records in these endnotes are marked with an asterisk(*) and include audio recordings, telephone recordings, emails, videos, photos, police records, and medical records.

Epigraph. The Monsters

1. Teresa Heartchild, "The Monsters," a self-talk poem adapted from *Pretty Amazing: How I Found Myself in the Downtown Eastside*, 2016. Teresa's poems are based on her self-talk and her writing. Her poems often feature dialogue where Teresa role plays different characters. In "The Monsters," she is having a conversation with herself and her father who says, "Protect my daughter." Teresa's self-talk poetry helps her to express her innermost thoughts and feelings.

Chapter 1. The Silver Recorder

1. Source material: audio recordings,* emails, videos, photos, author's journals, police records,* and medical records.* Event date: November 30, 2013, 8:00 pm

Chapter 2. Eyes Fly Open

1. Source material: photos, emails, author's journals, the play *Rare*, and research. Event date: February 23, 2013.

2. *Rare* Cast Members: Nicholas Herd, Suzanne Love, Krystal Nausbaum, Sarah Carney, Nada Marie Christiane Mayla, James Hazlett, Dylan Harman Livaja, Andreas Prinz, and Michael Liu.

3. Used by permission of Judith Thompson, Krystal Nausbaum, Dylan Livaja, and *Rare* Theatre Company. © Judith Thompson, 2013.

4. The Euthanasia Program, United States Holocaust Memorial Museum, ushmm.org.

5. Julian Quinones and Arijeta Lajka, "What kind of society do you want to live in?" *CBS News*, August 14, 2017. CBSNews.com

Chapter 3. The Blacklisting Party

1. Source material: audio recordings, videos, photos, author's journals, the book *Banned on the Hill*, and news reports. Event date: September 14, 2011

2. Tonda MacCharles, "Artist sees red over government 'blacklisting'," *Toronto Star*, July 28, 2011. thestar.com

3. Tonda MacCharles, "Artist sees red over government 'blacklisting'," *Toronto Star*, July 28, 2011. thestar.com

4. Douglas Smith, as quoted in "Guess Who Came To The Blacklisting Party?", Franke James, 2011. frankejames.com

5. Toby Heaps, as quoted in "Guess Who Came To The Blacklisting Party?", Franke James, 2011. frankejames.com

Chapter 4. Exploding the Myth

1. Source material: emails, photos, the documentary "Exploding the Myth," news reports, and research. Event dates: 1977–1979.

2. "Exploding the Myth" a documentary produced by OAMR (Community Living Ontario) and the Ontario Ministry of Community and Social Services, 1979. Images and text used with permission from Community Living Ontario.

3. Print ad for "Exploding the Myth." Used with permission from Community Living Ontario.

4. Dustin Galer, *Working Towards Equity*, University of Toronto Press 2018. Used with permission from the author.

5. "Huronia Regional Centre," Wikipedia. wikipedia.org

6. Harvey G. Simmons, *From Asylum to Welfare*, National Institute on Mental Retardation, 1982.

7. Pierre Berton, "Huronia: Pierre Berton warned us 50 years ago," *Toronto Star*, September 20, 2013. thestar.com

8. Ivor Brown and John Radford, "The Growth and Decline of Institutions for People with Developmental Disabilities in Ontario: 1876–2009," in *Journal on Developmental Disabilities*, Volume 21(2), 2015.

9. Mary Johnson, *Make Them Go Away: Clint Eastwood, Christopher Reeve & The Case Against Disability Rights*, Advocado Press, 2003. Used with permission from the Center for Accessible Living, the Advocado Press Board, and by the author.

10. Doug Firby, "Retarded hampered by myths, meet told," *Windsor Star*, June 20, 1979.

11. Rick Belanger, "CBC has fine look at mental retardation," *Ottawa Citizen*, March 7, 1979.

12. "Doug Ford draws criticism for saying group home 'ruined community'," *The Globe and Mail*, May 17, 2014. theglobeandmail.com

13. Two major declarations on persons with disabilities were adopted by the UN General Assembly: the *Declaration on the Rights of Mentally Retarded Persons* in 1971 (ohcr.org), and the *Declaration on the Rights of Disabled Persons* in 1975 (ohcr.org).

14. Article 15(1) in the Canadian Charter of Rights and Freedoms, 1982

Chapter 5. The Dinner Party

1. Source material: emails, photos, author's journals, and news reports. Event date: July 6, 2013.

2. Suzanne Goldenberg, "Artist finds inspiration in Canadian government's attempt to silence her," *The Guardian*, May 17, 2013.

3. Don Martin, *Power Play*, CTV, May 30, 2013.

4. Franke James, "My SUV and Me Say Goodbye," 2007; also *Bothered by My Green Conscience*, New Society Publishers, 2009.

5. Carys Mills, "Toronto's July flood listed as Ontario's most costly natural disaster," *Toronto Star* Aug 14, 2013, thestar.com

Chapter 6. What's Wrong with Teresa?
1. Source material: emails, photos, journals and observations. Event date: August 13-18, 2013.

Chapter 7. The Elephant and the Whiteboard
1. Source material: emails, photos, author's journals, and research. Event date: August 18–26, 2013.

2. "Alzheimer's Disease in People with Down Syndrome," National Institute on Aging. nia.nih.gov

Chapter 8. Teresa and Terry
1. Source material: emails, photos, author's journals, Terry Fox Foundation, news reports, and research. Event date: September 16, 2012.

2. Terry Fox, Terry Fox Foundation, 1980. Used with permission.

3. Terry Fox, Terry Fox Foundation, 1980. Used with permission.

4. Terry Fox, Terry Fox Foundation, 1980. Used with permission.

5. Terry Fox, "As it Happens: The Marathon Episode," CBC, 1980.

6. Pierre Trudeau, addressing the House of Commons, 1981. wikipedia.org

7. Terry Fox, as quoted by Leslie Scrivener, *The Terry Fox Story*, revised edition, McClelland & Stewart, 2010.

8. As of 2021, the Terry Fox Run has raised $850 million.

Chapter 9. Arm-Twisted in Perpetuity
1. Source material: emails,* author's journals, news reports, medical records,* and research. Event date: August 29, 2013.

2. Moira Welsh, "Abuse, rape uncovered in Ontario nursing homes," *Toronto Star*, November 17, 2011. thestar.com

3. Samuel Gregg, "A Father's Love: The Story of Charles and Anne," *Catholic World Report*, 2017. catholicworldreport.com

4. "Kupferberg Holocaust Center Exhibition," Queensborough Community College. qcc.libguides.com

5. Kelly Fritsch and Fady Shanouda, "Warehousing disabled people in long-term care homes needs to stop. Instead, nationalize home care." *The Conversation*, January 12, 2022. theconversation.com

Chapter 10. Dad's Power

1. Source material: emails,* author's journals, news reports, medical records,* and research. Event dates: August 31–September 6, 2013.

2. Paul R. Henry, "Do it yourself is big business," *National Post*, September 11, 1971.

3. "Group Home Residents with Developmental Disabilities More Likely To Die From COVID-19," *Disability Scoop, 2020.* disabilityscoop.com

Chapter 11. My Troublesome Conscience

1. Source material: emails, author's journals, the book *Banned on the Hill*, news reports, and research. Event date: September 12, 2013.

2. Suzanne Goldenberg, "Artist finds inspiration in Canadian government's attempt to silence her," *The Guardian*, May 5, 2013. theguardian.com

3. Steve Manelle, as cited by Marie Visca, "Painting a Picture of Dissent," *Dal News*, Dalhousie University, 2013. dal.ca

4. "The Green Interview," produced by Silver Donald Cameron. Excerpts and quotes used with permission of the producer's estate. *The Green Interview* was the creation of the late Silver Donald Cameron (1937-2020) with his business partner and director, Chris Beckett. *The Green Interview* is permanently housed at Library & Archives Canada which has called it a "national treasure." thegreeninterview.com

Chapter 12. The Set-Up

1. Source material: emails and attachments,* author's journals, medical records,* and research. Event dates: September 16–October 1, 2013.

2. Franke James, "A Green Winter: Will Global Warming be Good for Canada?" and "Six Tools for Climate Change Art," McMichael Gallery, 2007. frankejames.com

3. "Anticoagulants the Leading Reported Drug Risk in 2011," Institute for Safe Medication Practices, 2012. ismp.org

Chapter 13. Behind My Back

1. Source material: emails*, author's journals. Event Date: October 1, 2013.

Chapter 14. Do Not Talk About That

1. Source material: news reports, emails, photos, author's journals, and research. Event dates: October 7–10, 2013.

2. Jane Gerster, "Franke James Goes to Washington" (Online: "Toronto activist Franke James takes protest art to Capitol Hill"), *Toronto Star,* October 7, 2013. thestar.com

3. "Franke James Goes to Washington" print edition. *Toronto Star,* © 2013 Toronto Star Newspapers Limited. All rights reserved. Used under license.

4. David Suzuki, "What Happened to Canada?" NRDC (Natural Resources Defense Council), October 11, 2013. nrdc.org

5. David Adam and James Randerson, "Copenhagen conference: The countries to watch," *The Guardian*, November 30, 2009. theguardian.com

6. Nicolas Kristoff, "To Beat Trump, Mock Him," *The New York Times*, September 26, 2020. nytimes.com

7. Paul Koring, "David Suzuki slams Harper science policy in Washington speech," *The Globe and Mail*, October 11, 2013. theglobeandmail.com

8. Franke James as cited in "Canadian Scientists Expose Their Government's Tar Sands Obsession at DC Briefing," *EcoWatch*, October 11, 2013. frankejames.com

9. Jason Fekete, "Federal government prepares $24-million oil sands advertising blitz," *Financial Post,* October 11, 2013. financialpost.com

10. Paul Koring, "David Suzuki slams Harper," *The Globe and Mail,* October 11, 2013. theglobeandmail.com

11. Franke James as cited by Laura Barron-Lopez, "Anti-Keystone XL poster campaign hits Washington, D.C." *The Hill,* October 23, 2013. thehill.com

Chapter 15. What If Dad Dies?

1. Source material: email, medical records,* author's journals. Event date: October 23, 2013.

2. "Nothing about us, without us: Human Rights and Disability," Wikipedia. wikipedia.org

3. Eli A. Wolff and Dr. Mary Hums, "Nothing about us without us: Mantra for a Movement," *Huffpost,* September 5, 2017. huffpost.com

Chapter 16. See the Liability

1. Source material: emails,* author's journal, medical records,* and court records. Event dates: November 3–6, 2013.

2. Jean, "Day 3: Mary Frances and Jean," Down Syndrome Awareness Week, Canadian Down Syndrome Society, November 3, 2013. Used with permission.

Chapter 17. Mount Everest

1. Source material: telephone recordings,* emails, author's journals, and research. Date: November 4, 2013.

2. "What is Down Syndrome?" Canadian Down Syndrome Society. cdss.ca

3. Theresa Vargas, "Virginia woman with Down syndrome becomes hero to the disabled," *Washington Post,* August 17, 2013. washingtonpost.com. Daily Mail Reporter, "Woman with Down syndrome seeks to overturn her parents' decision," *Daily Mail,* July 21, 2013. dailymail.co.uk. The Jenny Hatch Justice Project. jennyhatchjusticeproject.org

4. Moira Welsh, *Happily Ever Older,* ECW Press, 2021.

Chapter 18. They Can't Send her Back

1. Source material: telephone recordings,* emails, author's journals, and research. Event date: November 11, 2013.

2. "Rights of people with disabilities," Government of Canada, <u>canada.ca</u>

3. Article 19, "United Nations Convention on the Rights of Persons with Disabilities," United Nations, <u>un.org</u>

Chapter 19. Are You in My Corner?

1. Source material: telephone recordings, emails, author's journals, news reports, medical records,* and research. Event date: November 12, 2013.

2. Moira Welsh, "Nursing home abuse and neglect targeted by task force," *Toronto Star,* May 15, 2012. <u>thestar.com</u>

Chapter 20. A Bulletproof Plan

1. Source material: telephone recordings,* emails, author's journals, news reports, medical records,* and research. Event date: November 13, 2013.

2. Ivanova Smith, "Mental Age Theory Hurts," *Spectrum Life,* 2021. <u>spectrumlife.org</u>

3. Tim Alamenciak, "Senior accused in retirement-home killing appears in court," *Toronto Star,* November 13, 2013. Alyshah Hasham, "Senior with dementia guilty in death of nursing home resident," *Toronto Star,* December 1, 2016. <u>thestar.com</u>

Chapter 21. Crisis at the Condo

1. Source material: telephone recordings, emails, author's journals, medical records.* Event date: November 21, 2013, 6:30 p.m.–7:00 p.m.

Chapter 22. You Don't Get a Vote

1. Source material: telephone recordings,* emails, author's journals, news reports, medical records,* and research. Event date: November 21, 2013, 7:00 p.m.–7:30 p.m.

Chapter 23. A Crack in Everything

1. Source material: emails,* author's journals. Event date: November 21, 2013, 7:30 p.m.– 9:00 p.m.

2. "Day 3: Mary Frances and Jean," Down Syndrome Awareness Week, Canadian Down Syndrome Society, November 3, 2013.

Chapter 24. The Kindness of Their Hearts

1. Source material: emails,* author's journals, court records, and news reports. Event date: November 22, 2013.

2. Dale Brazao, "Retirement home that neglected residents loses its licence," *Toronto Star*, November 22, 2013. thestar.com

3. Dale Brazao "Reporter's diary reveals substandard conditions at retirement home," *Toronto Star*, October 1, 2010. thestar.com

Chapter 25. Stay with My Father

1. Source material: audio recordings,* emails and attachments,* author's journals. Event dates: November 25-26, 2013.

Chapter 26. Teresa and Dad Update

1. Source material: emails,* author's journals, medical records,* and court documents. Event date: November 27, 2013, 5:00 p.m.–6:00 p.m.

2. President Obama, "Remarks by the President on Climate Change," June 25, 2013.

Chapter 27. All Hell's Breaking Loose

1. Source material: telephone recordings,* emails, author's journals. Event date: November 27, 2013, 8:00 p.m.

Chapter 28. The Morning After

1. Source material: telephone recordings, emails,* author's journal. Event date: November 28, 2013, 8:00 a.m.

Chapter 29. Summer Camp

1. Source material: telephone recordings, emails,* author's journal, medical records,* legal documents,* and court records. Event date: November 28, 2013, 8:00 a.m.–6:00 p.m.

Chapter 30. Heartbreak Place

1. Source material: audio recordings, emails, photos, author's journals, news reports, medical records,* and research. Event date: November 28, 2013, 7:30 p.m.

2. Johnathan Marchand as quoted in interview with Archy Mann, "Burn It Down," Canadaland Podcast, July 2020. canadaland.com

3. "Huronia survivors reach $35-million settlement with Ontario government," *The Globe and Mail,* September 17, 2013. theglobeandmail.com

4. Pierre Berton, "Huronia: Pierre Berton warned us 50 years ago," *Toronto Star,* September 20, 2013. thestar.com

1. Source material: telephone recordings, emails,* author's journals. Event date: November 29, 2013.

Chapter 31. Kidnapped

2. Dr. Elia Abi-Jaoude, "Re: Franke's sister, Teresa, is in crisis," email, November 28, 2013. Used with permission.

3. Lois Sampson, "Re: Franke's sister, Teresa, is in crisis," email, November 29, 2013. Used with permission.

Chapter 32. Against Medical Advice

1. Source material: audio recordings, video, emails, photos, author's journals, medical records,* legal documents,* and court records.* Event date: November 30, 2013, 11:00 a.m.–3:00 p.m.

Chapter 33. The Celebration

1. Source material: audio and telephone recordings,* video, emails, photos, author's journals, medical records,* legal documents,* and court records.* Event date: November 30, 2013, 3:30 p.m.–4:00 p.m.

Chapter 34. Return Teresa (Or Else)

1. Source material: audio and telephone recordings,* videos,* emails, photos, author's journals, police records,* legal documents,* and court records.* Event date: November 30, 2013, 4:00 p.m.–7:30 p.m.

Chapter 35. Apprehension

1. Source material: audio recordings,* video, emails, author's journals, medical records,* police records,* legal documents,* and court records.* Event date: November 30, 2013, 8:00 p.m.–8:30 p.m.

Chapter 36. My Manifesto

1. Source material: audio recordings,* emails, photos, and author's journals. Event date: November 30, 2013, 8:30 p.m.–8:45 p.m.

Chapter 37. Nightmare at Sunnybrook

1. Source material: audio recordings, emails, photos,* author's journals, medical records,* police records,* legal documents,* and court records.* Event date: November 30, 2013, 9:00 p.m.–December 1, 2013, 3:00 a.m.

Chapter 38. Make Peace Not War

1. Source material: audio recordings, videos, emails,* photos, author's journals. Event date: December 1, 2013.

Epigraph. Be Fierce

1. Teresa Heartchild, "Be Fierce," adapted from a self-talk poem in *Pretty Amazing*, 2016. Her poems often feature dialogue where Teresa role plays for example, using her father's voice she says, "Just calm down, my daughter." Teresa's self-talk poetry helps her to express her fears and courage.

Franke's photo of Teresa at eight with her favourite doll

Authors and Contributors

FRANKE JAMES
Author

Franke James is an activist, artist, and the author of four books on climate change, free expression, ethics, and now disability rights. For Franke, the diverse issues in *Freeing Teresa, Banned on the Hill, Bothered by My Green Conscience*, and *Dear Office-Politics* are all connected by the need to speak up and take action. The spark for *Freeing Teresa* was lit in 2013. Franke and her husband Billiam James helped her younger sister Teresa get out of a nursing home, regain her decision-making rights, and get a public apology from the Ontario government.

In 2014, Franke won the BC Civil Liberties Association's "Award for Excellence in the Arts" for her national campaign on the importance of free expression. Her poster campaign, "Do Not Talk About Climate Change," appeared in three Canadian cities and Washington DC. In 2015, Franke was awarded PEN Canada's Ken Filkow Prize for her "tenacity in uncovering an abuse of power and her commitment to fostering a national conversation in the face of censorship." She lives in Vancouver, BC, with her husband Bill and her sister Teresa.

BILLIAM JAMES
Co-author

Billiam James is an artist, designer and writer. In 2013, he helped his wife, Franke, get her younger sister, Teresa, out of a nursing home and brought her to live with them. Together, they helped Teresa ask for an apology for the wrongful institutionalization. After two years of campaigning, the Ontario Minister of Health publicly apologized to Teresa.

Billiam's creative work is focused on disability rights, mental health, climate change, and free speech. He combines storytelling, visual art and music with social activism to help people see things from different perspectives. He lives in Vancouver, BC, with Franke and Teresa.

TERESA HEARTCHILD
Contributor

Teresa Heartchild is an artist, poet, author, and self-advocate who has Down syndrome. Teresa has shown remarkable resilience and courage. In 2013, an Ontario government social worker determined that she was "not capable," and immediately, she lost her right to decide where she would live. Teresa was put into a nursing home by two of her older siblings. However, Teresa did not have any medical need to be in long-term care. Within days, her father, sister Franke James, and brother-in-law, Bill James, helped her get discharged.

Then Teresa had a new capacity test done that determined she could decide where she lived, and who would take care of her. In March 2014, Teresa moved across the country with the Jameses to British Columbia, where she started an online petition asking for an apology. In the Change.org video, Teresa said it was wrong to put her in a nursing home. On behalf of Teresa, the BC Civil Liberties Association wrote to the Ontario Minister of Health, saying, "We are gravely concerned that the government, through its actions, appears to condone the forced placement and mistreatment of developmentally disabled adults." With further publicity and after two years of campaigning, the Ontario Minister of Health publicly apologized to Teresa.

In 2016, Teresa published an illustrated poetry book, *Pretty Amazing: How I Found Myself in the Downtown Eastside.* In 2018, she followed up with her second book, *Totally Amazing: Free to Be Me.* She has had solo and group art shows and won arts awards including two Canada Council grants to travel to art events in Boston, MA and Merida, Mexico. Teresa's successful activism for disability rights was honoured by the British Columbia Human Rights Commissioner, who named Teresa as a "Champion for Change" in 2019. In 2023, Teresa is celebrating the 10-year anniversary of her rescue with the publication of *Freeing Teresa.* She lives with Franke and Bill in Vancouver, BC.

Teresa Heartchild is free

Printed in the USA
CPSIA information can be obtained
at www.ICGtesting.com
JSHW041223080224
R13319100001B/R133191PG56575JSX00001B/1/J